BLYTHE CAMENSON
& MARSHALL J. COOK

Give 'Em What They Want

The Right Way to Pitch Your Novel
to Editors and Agents

WRITER'S DIGEST BOOKS
Cincinnati, Ohio
www.writersdigest.com

Give 'Em What They Want

BLYTHE CAMENSON
& MARSHALL J. COOK

The Right Way to Pitch Your Novel
to Editors and Agents

A Novelist's
Complete Guide to:

- **Query Letters**
- **Synopses**
- **Outlines**

Visit our Web site at www.writersdigest.com for information on more resources for writers.

To receive a free weekly e-mail newsletter delivering tips and updates about writing and about Writer's Digest products, register directly at our Web site at http://newsletters.fw publications.com.

09   08   07   06 05   5 4 3 2 1

Distributed in Canada by Fraser Direct
100 Armstrong Avenue
Georgetown, ON, Canada L7G 5S4
Tel: (905) 877-4411

Distributed in the U.K. and Europe by David & Charles
Brunel House, Newton Abbot, Devon, TQ12 4PU, England
Tel: (+44) 1626 323200, Fax: (+44) 1626 323319
E-mail: mail@davidandcharles.co.uk

Distributed in Australia by Capricorn Link
P.O. Box 704, Windsor, NSW 2756 Australia
Tel: (02) 4577-3555

Library of Congress Cataloging-in-Publication Data

Camenson, Blythe.
  Give 'em what they want : the right way to pitch your novel to editors and agents / by Blythe Camenson and Marshall J. Cook.-- 1st edition.
    p. cm.
  Includes index.
  ISBN 1-58297-330-X (pbk. : alk. paper)
  1. Fiction--Marketing. I. Cook, Marshall, 1944- II. Title.
  PN3365.C36 2005
  070.5'2--dc22
                        2005011801

Edited by Michelle Ruberg
Designed by Claudean Wheeler
Production coordinated by Robin Richie

Dedication

BLYTHE CAMENSON

To all the writers and students who have shared a bit of themselves
with me on their path toward publication.

MARSHALL J. COOK

To Ellen, who has stuck with me through all the rejections
and shared in the joy over the acceptances.

Acknowledgments

Blythe Camenson and Marshall J. Cook would like to thank the following authors, agents, and editors for their helpful guidance for negotiating the realm of writing and getting published.

A special note of thanks to those who worked with us, building query letters and synopses, and contributing samples of their work.

AUTHORS: Eva Augustin Rumpf, Jessica Barkley, James Scott Bell, Marilyn Campbell, Robyn Carr, Tom Clancy, Michelle Collier-Johns, Tracy Cooper-Posey, Cyndia Depre, Kelly Fitzpatrick, Dick Francis, John Grisham, Lucy Harmon, Peggy Hoffmann, Mary Holmes, Kelly James-Enger, David Kaufelt, Anne Kinsman Fisher, Stephen King, Gus Lee, Dean Koontz, Elmore Leonard, Gail Gaymer Martin, Ed Mattingly, Jr., Barbara Parker, Alexs Pate, James A. Ritchie, Todd Sanders, Kiel Stuart, John Tigges, Denise Tiller, Robert W. Walker, Jeanne Wallin, Mary Ellen Whitaker, Karen Wiesner

AGENTS: Kathleen Anderson, Julie Castiglia, Jane Chelius, Rob Cohen, Kate Duffy, Danielle Egan-Miller, Russell Galen, Michele Grajkowski, Anne Hawkins, Richard Henshaw, Susan Isaacs, Jeff Kleinman, Frances Kuffel, Nancy Love, Evan Marshall, George Nicholson, Lori Perkins, Pesha Rubenstein, Peter Rubie, Elizabeth Wales, Cherry Weiner, Nancy Yost, Susan Zeckendorf

EDITORS: Nancy Bereano, Marjorie Braman, Jennifer Brehl, Kent Brown, Ginjer Buchanan, Kent Carroll, Kate Duffy, Paula Eykelhof, Laura Anne Gilman, Wendy McCurdy, Robert Olmsted, Anne Savarese, John Scognamiglio, Michael Seidman, Karen Taylor Richman, Elisa Wares

Table of Contents

DEDICATION v

ACKNOWLEDGMENTS...vii

INTRODUCTION 1

Part One: The Approach

CHAPTER ONE: CREATING A SALABLE PRODUCT 4

The Five Steps to a Salable Product 4

First-Novel Problems 13

Crafting It Compellingly..22

Before You Write 23

Final Words of Advice 24

CHAPTER TWO: YOUR PUBLISHING OPTIONS 26

What's Selling ... .27

... And for How Much 28

The Nine Paths to Publication 29

CHAPTER THREE: THE SEARCH BEGINS: FINDING AGENTS AND EDITORS...............41

Organize Your Search 41

Four Ways to Approach Publishers 43

What to Look for in Agents and Publishers............................45

The Ideal Editor 46

The Ideal Agent 46

The Truth about Agents 48

How to Spot the Scams 50
What Agents Do for You 54
What Agents Won't Do for You 57
Where to Look for Editors or Agents 58
Writers Conferences...58
Market Guides 63
Trade Journals and Newsletters 63
Other Writers' Books 64
The Internet...64

CHAPTER FOUR: THE ALL-IMPORTANT QUERY LETTER...........................66
What Agents and Editors Look for in a Query....................................66
Definition of a Query Letter 67
Just a Query Letter? 68
Who Gets the Query Letter? 68
When to Send the Query Letter 69
Query Letter Formatting 70
SASEs 72
The Elements of a Query Letter...72
Query Letter Approaches with Samples 82
Full Query Letter Sample (Hook Start Opening) 87
Building Killer Query Letters 89
Back to the Plotting Board 99
Slow and Steady or the Blitz Approach? 99
Simultaneous and Multiple Submissions 100
E-mail or Snail Mail?..102
The Newest Art: E-mail Subject Lines 103

CHAPTER FIVE: THE IN-PERSON PITCH 106
Arranging the Agent/Editor Appointment 107
Who Can Pitch? 107
Battling Nerves...108
Interviewing Agents 109
Be Prepared 109
The Anatomy of a Pitch 110
What Comes After the Pitch Line? 112
Other Uses for Your Pitch Line 112

Part Two: The Package

CHAPTER SIX: GIVE 'EM WHAT THEY WANT 115
The Submission Package..116
Presentation, Presentation, Presentation...119

Following the Rules 120

Manuscript Formatting...120

A Word on Copyright 121

Adapting to Meet the Need 123

Agent and Editor Etiquette (Yours, Not Theirs) 131

Simultaneous Submissions 136

CHAPTER SEVEN: SUCCESSFUL SYNOPSES...138

Why Writing a Synopsis Is So Difficult 140

When to Write the Synopsis 141

Synopsis Format 142

Elements of a Successful Synopsis 142

How to Structure Your Synopsis 149

Four Ways to Avoid "Synopsis Speak" 150

How Long Is Long Enough? 151

Two Short Synopses 151

Building Your One-Page Synopsis 155

The Longer Synopsis 163

Rewriting Your Synopsis to Specification 187

The Chapter Outline...188

Sample Chapter Outline 189

CHAPTER EIGHT: CRAFTING THE COVER LETTER 192

Greetings and Salutations 193

What Do You Say After You Say Hello?..193

Cover Letter Format 195

Sample Cover Letters 195

Three Items Not to Include 198

Thirty-Seven Ways to Write a Rotten Cover Letter 199

Part Three: The Result

CHAPTER NINE: HANDLING THE WAIT ... AND THE REJECTION 204

How to Analyze the Silence 205

How Long Should You Wait? 206

How to Follow Up 207

How to Handle Rejection 208

When to Revise and Resubmit 210

CHAPTER TEN: GETTING TO "YES": HOW TO WORK WITH AGENTS AND EDITORS 212

What to Expect When an Agent Says "Yes" 213

What Your Agent/Writer Contract Covers 214

What You Need to Do for Your Agent 214

What You Shouldn't Do for Your Agent 216

How Agents Work 216
When You Have to Fire Your Agent 217
How to Fire Your Agent...218
Starting the Hunt Again 220
How to Get an Offer 220
What to Do When the Contract Comes 221
How You Get Paid..224
Oh Yes, You Will Need Editing 225
After Your Novel Is Published: A New Job Begins 226
How Not to Be a One-Book Wonder 227
When You Aren't Getting to "Yes" 227

APPENDIX: RESOURCES FOR WRITERS...................................229
Market Guides 229
Additional Books to Help You Publish Your Novel 231
And for Those Who Also Write Nonfiction ... .231
Print Periodicals..232
Online Periodicals 233
Writers Associations and Organizations 233
Web Sites for Writers 234
Publishers and Agents Websites 236
Online and E-mail Writing Courses 236
Sites for Writing Conferences 237
Research Sites 238

ABOUT THE AUTHORS 240

INDEX 241

Introduction

"Writing a novel is a terrible experience, during which the hair often falls out and the teeth decay."—FLANNERY O'CONNOR

Writing a novel requires time, energy, determination, perseverance, patience, faith, and courage.

So, if it's so tough, why do we do it? Because the process teaches us, nurtures us, and brings us great joy. We don't wait to be inspired to write. We write to be inspired. Like most difficult things in life, writing brings immense rewards for those called to the journey. If you've written a novel (which you most likely have, since you're reading this book), we offer our congratulations and hope you'll take time to savor your accomplishment.

But now what? You don't want to just *write* your story. You want people to read it, and the more people the better. And you wouldn't mind if they paid you for the privilege.

You want to get your novel published.

You must now make a second commitment. Getting your novel published will take the same sort of creative problem solving, the same determination and persistence, and the same refusal to quit that you brought to writing the book. Just as you learned and are learning how to write with skill and power, you now must learn how to market your work effectively. You need to know how to write good query and cover letters, how to create an effective synopsis, how to package your proposal, and how to get it into the hands of the right people.

This book will show you how to get your novel published, step-by-step, with guidance from agents, editors, and novelists. We'll begin our journey with the novel itself, helping you to create a salable product. Then we'll survey your publishing options, stressing the wisdom of finding a good agent to represent you and sell your novel to a publisher.

Next we'll get you outfitted for the search, showing you how to find and approach agents–and which agents you should avoid.

Then we'll really get down to business–learning how to craft an effective query letter, your basic tool for gaining entrée to agents and editors. We'll provide you with good examples and take you through the construction of an effective query.

You'll want to study the chapter on queries carefully and refer to it often. It's that important.

That said, we'll also show you how it may be possible to bypass the query and pitch your novel directly to an agent or editor at a writers conference.

Operating under the theory that we should give editors and agents exactly what they want, exactly the way they want it, we'll cover the basic elements of your submission package: cover letter, synopsis, chapter outline, sample chapters, and the manuscript itself. Again, we'll give you plenty of helpful examples and tips from the professionals.

After sharing hints for handling the inevitable wait and rejection, we'll get to the good stuff–what to expect and how to act when you get your agent and that first book contract!

IT'S YOUR TURN

Now it's time for you to begin your journey toward publishing your novel and fulfilling your dream. Reading and studying this book is your first big step.

Are you ready to start the journey?

Are you willing to do the work?

Then, let's get started!

Part One:
The Approach

Chapter One: Creating a Salable Product

"There are three rules for writing the novel. Unfortunately, no one knows what they are." —W. SOMERSET MAUGHAM

Before you decide which publishing options to pursue and begin your search for editors or agents, there is one very important, often overlooked factor to attend to.

As in any industry, to sell something, you must have a quality product the public wants to buy. How you go about creating that product will, in part, determine how successful you'll be.

To create a marketable product—in this case, a salable manuscript—you need to follow these five steps. Although they may seem obvious, many new writers ignore them.

THE FIVE STEPS TO A SALABLE PRODUCT

Step 1: Read before you write. Before you even sit down to write, agents and editors advise that you read other writers. Famous writers do, too. William Faulkner said, "Read, read, read. Read everything—trash, classics, good and bad, and see how they do it. Just like a carpenter who works as an apprentice and studies the master. Read! You'll absorb it. Then write. If it is good, you'll find out. If it's not, throw it out the window."

Stephen King said, "If you don't have the time to read, you don't have the time or the tools to write."

Reading the work of other writers helps give you those tools.

"The best advice I can give," says agent Nancy Yost of Lowenstein-Yost Associates, "is read, read, and read some more. It's important to read other writers and to know what other people are reading. The best writers are avid readers."

Reading other writers will give you a more in-depth understanding of what's out there, and it can help you improve your own writing as well. Read for style, read for content, read for technique. Read to understand the marketplace and to determine if what you want to write will fit in.

But there are ways to read a book to get what you need out of it. It's too easy to get lost in a good story and forget why you're reading it. Former executive editor Kent Carroll gives a few hints:

"Take a book you like and go through it a second time. Dissect it. Take it apart to see how the thing is structured, what the convention of storytelling is. Pay particular attention to how the book is organized. I think you can learn a lot from that. But don't just imitate it. Let it come from your own heart, your own mind, your own imagination."

How you read is important. But so is what you read. Read as much as you can, but not just the established writers, such as Danielle Steel or Stephen King. Make sure to be in touch with what's new. Read the work of current authors that are being put out now. This is the kind of material that publishers are looking for. The old standbys will always be there. Be aware of what currently attracts agents and publishers.

"But remember that everything you're seeing out on the shelves now was bought a while ago, so something you are sure is a new idea or a fresh twist may not be," reminds Karen Taylor Richman, editor of the Special Edition line at Silhouette.

In addition to reading current authors, make sure you're familiar with the line of publishers you'd like to write for. Richman says, "If you want to write for Silhouette, you should be reading Silhouette books to get a feel for what we're looking for." If you're writing romances, then read the books romance publishers put out. The same goes for mysteries or books in any other genre.

Former editor Michael Seidman advises, "Read fiction, all kinds of fiction. I've found that reading best-sellers is a frustrating experience, because no one can tell you why a particular book made it in spite of everything that's wrong with it. But if nothing else, it will reaffirm for you the fact that sometimes God smiles, and why shouldn't that smile grace you?"

Marjorie Braman, publishing director at HarperCollins, sums it up nicely. "If you want to be a writer, the best thing you can do for yourself, for a number of reasons, is read a lot. There's the commercial reason of knowing what's working, and how to tailor your book for a specific audience. And also, if you read voraciously, it opens you up to a broader approach in your own writing. You can hone your skills by reading people who are good writers."

Afraid to read for fear your writing will be adversely affected? Some writers make that excuse for not reading. Don't be one of them. This mindset can sabotage new writers. Nancy Bereano, former editor at Firebrand Books, says, "When writers say to me, 'Oh, I never read anyone else because I don't want to be influenced by them,' I laugh hysterically. Give me a break."

Step 2: Write for the market. Editors and agents want you to be aware of the market and to write for it. Without a commercial product, they'd have nothing to sell. "The writing I look for should be 'relentlessly commercial,'" says Kate Duffy, an editorial director with Kensington Publishing Corporation.

If you want to have your book considered by a particular publisher, become familiar with that publisher's list. There are formulas that certain genre books follow—and it's your job to be aware of them and to create a work that fits a publisher's guidelines. Senior editor Jennifer Brehl of Avon Books agrees. "Be familiar with the clichés of your genre before submitting."

How do you write for the market? Says editor Ginjer Buchanan: "You won't have a lot of success if you are just stumbling around in a vacuum. Read *Publishers Weekly*. Read magazines on the genre you are interested in. Study the markets so you know what is happening. It's basic, but you won't get anywhere without paying attention to those types of details. Later, you can rely on your agent to keep track of markets and trends, but beginning writers really have to know what the business is doing. If you don't work hard at the business end of your writing, you're just dooming yourself to disappointment."

Agents don't really want to say "no" to writers. They make their living finding good, commercial writing they can sell. "But," says agent Peter Rubie, "the reality is that the bulk of material agents receive is just not up to a publishable standard. I love to come across great material, but people don't read enough and have no idea what's fresh and what isn't, what's been done or what hasn't. I get queries that say, 'I've written a unique book about a vampire that's called AIDS.' It seems like a great idea except that I get the same idea sent to me at least ten times a week."

Laura Anne Gilman, executive editor for Roc at Dutton, says, "Know your market! Reading is the best way to study a market. You shouldn't be writing in a genre unless you enjoy it. Watch what is selling, who the authors are, and read those books. And keep trying."

Step 3: Write for yourself. Step three sounds as if it contradicts the advice in step two, but it really doesn't. Writing for the market and writing for yourself can co-exist. Market-savvy writers understand the fine line here and know how to blend both elements.

Agent Russell Galen explains: "The writing process should be shaped internally, by the writer himself, not by me or by the marketplace. It isn't simply that this makes for better books, though, of course, it does; it actually makes for more commercial books. When the writing process is shaped externally, the result is always an obvious knockoff, an ersatz Rolex made in Hong Kong, and I can spot it."

Write what you love to read. Don't shy away from the genre you love because you fear it will be too difficult to break into. Yes, Stephen King and Dean Koontz have had the horror market sewn up for years. But that doesn't mean a fresh voice in the horror world would not be appreciated. The same holds for other genres, too.

And don't make the mistake of thinking there's an easier path to publication. Occasionally, we've run across a new writer or two who thought that romance was the way to break in. But these new writers were not lovers of the genre–in fact, they had done little reading in that arena. Writing romance requires a great depth of skill. In fact, nothing is easy or easier to write. If you don't know and love the genre you are writing in, it will show and you won't make it.

Choose your genre based on what you like. John Scognamiglio, an editorial director of Kensington Publishing Corporation, says, "I don't think a writer should decide to write a historical romance just because that's what's selling now. They need to combine what they like to read or write with what's selling."

Says Anne Savarese, former editor at St. Martin's Press (now with Oxford University Press), "It's easier to sell a first novel if it fits into some kind of genre. But often writers worry too much about tailor-making their work to what they think publishers want. Even to the point of what kind of novel they're going to write. I think it's best to be true to what you want to do. If you have a novel in mind, you should write that novel as best you can. Certainly you want to send it to a publisher who will most likely be interested in it, but sometimes, for example, new writers will say, 'Oh, these techno-thrillers are really big, why don't I write one of those?' But that's usually not a good idea. If you're not writing something you're really interested in or know well, it's going to show."

Agent Evan Marshall agrees: "Don't try to fake it. Write only the kind of books you love to read and never deviate from that. Find your niche and stay in it, and believe in yourself. Don't leave it just because you get rejected. If you're really good you will be published."

Step 4: Learn how to write. This seems like such an obvious step, you might be wondering why it's even included. But it's a step many new writers often overlook. You might have been an avid reader all your life and feel more than ready. And yes, reading other writers does help with your own writing. But it's often not enough to bring your work up to publishable standards.

Let's compare an aspiring writer with an aspiring physician. It's true that part of the training for a medical student is to observe seasoned doctors at work. But before students are even allowed in a hospital room or an operating theater, they must sit in lecture halls, read and absorb countless textbooks, and study, study, study.

Can you imagine a med student on his first day being shown an operating table with a tray of instruments next to it–and being told to begin a surgical procedure on his own? Hardly.

Admittedly, writing a novel certainly isn't brain surgery, and nobody dies if your fingers slip on the keyboard. But the point is that learning how to write is not something that happens in a day, or in a vacuum. Yes, being an avid reader is an important part of the process, but it is an ongoing process–and there are other elements to consider as well.

Here are some avenues to pursue to learn the craft of writing:

HOW-TO BOOKS. In addition to your mainstream or genre reading, don't forget the textbooks of the trade. Hundreds of how-to books are available on every aspect of writing the novel. They cover writing in general and also narrow in on specific topics. Want more insight into plot, dialogue, characterization, voice, style, viewpoint, action, or conflict? There's a book that covers it.

There are books on grammar, too. You've probably heard about this or that famous writer who couldn't spell or whose grammar would have horrified his seventh-grade English teacher. That's what editors are for, right?

Wrong. In today's market that writer would have a difficult time getting his work considered seriously, never mind published. Of course, an agent or editor might overlook the glaring mistakes. But the story and characters would have to be pretty outstanding to keep the agent or editor's attention beyond the first paragraph. Why lessen your chances?

MAGAZINES AND NEWSLETTERS. In addition to how-to books, there are very good periodicals out there that can help you. *Writer's Digest* magazine, *The Writer,* and countless newsletters put out by various writers associations are all good sources from which to glean information. Check out our appendix on page 229 for extra resources.

UNIVERSITY WRITING PROGRAMS. Many new writers enroll in university master's degree writing programs. For some this is an excellent way to hone skills, but there are authors, agents, and editors who have mixed feelings about these programs.

Former editor Michael Seidman says, "I think they can be brilliant training grounds, but too many of them are insular and wind up teaching you how to teach a master's course.

"But, they can serve to stretch your imagination and force you to look at writing from perspectives that might not be your usual ones. So, in the end, if you have the time and finances to attend, I'd go for it."

Best-selling author Susan Isaacs is glad she didn't attend a writing program. "If I had taken a writing class, I would surely have lost it [her own writing voice] and come out writing present tense fiction like everyone else in New York."

Author Flannery O'Connor wryly pointed out: "Everywhere I go I'm asked if I think the university stifles writers. My opinion is that they don't stifle enough of them. There's many a best-seller that could have been prevented by a good teacher."

ADULT EDUCATION PROGRAMS. While there might be a bit of snobbery attached–for and against–attending a university master's course in creative writing, there are many fine adult education programs out there offering workshops, seminars, and classes, taught by solid, experienced writers and teachers. Marshall Cook has coached writers through one such program at the University of Wisconsin-Madison, Division of Continuing Studies, for almost three decades.

Adult education classes, especially those focused on writing, generally attract serious people who want to improve their craft and learn how to get published. You'll meet other people with the same interests and concerns you have. Through adult education classes you can find other writers with whom you can start a critique or writers support group that continues to meet after the adult education class is over. The contacts you make and the support you receive will be invaluable.

You can find adult education classes through your local school board or nearby community colleges or universities.

WRITERS CONFERENCES. Writers conferences are another good vehicle for learning how to write. While excellent for meeting agents and editors and other new writers, (which you'll learn more about in upcoming chapters) they also afford you the opportunity to hear successful authors speak on novel-writing techniques.

Workshops can cover everything from novel openings to characterization to dialogue or conflict. You can learn how to pace your thriller or plant clues for your mystery. Some conferences also offer manuscript critiquing for an additional charge.

It's important for a new writer to invest some time, money, and energy in learning the craft, and a writers' conference is a good place to do that.

Says agent Julie Castiglia, "People sometimes think they can tackle a book without spending any money or effort on training. They expect their book to be top-notch without going to writers' conferences, taking classes, or learning the craft of writing. Even if you are very talented, you need instruction and networking in order to develop your writing to the fullest potential. If you haven't invested yourself in learning to write, you are wasting your time seeking an agent."

SUPPORT GROUPS. Many writers depend on critique or support groups. It's difficult to improve your craft writing in a vacuum. A well-chosen group with a particular focus and a set of guidelines to follow can provide valuable feedback on your work.

Editorial director John Scognamiglio says, "You should always try to get someone to read your work. A lot of times writers can't distance themselves enough and someone else might find something you might have missed. A writer shouldn't be afraid of criticism; part of writing is rejection. It's just a matter of building a tough shell and knowing what your strengths and weaknesses are."

You can find other writers through taking adult education classes, belonging to local writers organizations such as the SouthWest Writers, or by joining online groups such as Fiction Writer's Connection, which Blythe Camenson runs. Through FWC, members can contact other members and form e-mail or chat room support groups. Also try local libraries. Many provide space for writers to meet regularly for discussion and critique.

Although writers groups can be very helpful, it's also important not to become so dependent on them that you lose your own voice. Agent George Nicholson of Sterling Lord Literistic says, "It's important to be your own person. Too many novice writers are uncertain about their skills and pay too much attention to what others say. While it is important to listen to what others say, trust in your own instincts and judgment."

CRITIQUES. Paid critiquing–by a trusted professional–is also a possibility to consider. The critiquer's comments can help pinpoint your problem areas and offer suggestions on how to correct them.

Good critiquers usually provide margin notes, circling errors and noting questions that need addressing. In addition, they usually type up full reports covering any of the writing or plotting problems identified in your manuscript. The report could cover everything from how best to open your manuscript, to pacing, characterization, dialogue, and action. Through FWC, Blythe has critiqued hundreds of manuscripts over the years. She helps writers learn how to write more tightly and avoid the first-novel problems covered in the following section.

If you're open to improving your work, and need one-on-one feedback, a critique could be the way to go. Just make sure the critiquer is known and has a good reputation, and that his or her fees are reasonable. Critiques usually run between three and five dollars a page or more, depending upon the skill of the writer. Line edits, which promise comments or notations on every error, would cost more.

You can find critiquers through adult education classes and university writing programs, or online.

Step 5: Polish your product. Many new writers are so excited about the prospect of seeing their name in print that they rush too quickly to get their material out there. Typing "The End" on that last page isn't necessarily your signal to get the mailers and your self-addressed, stamped envelopes (SASEs) ready.

Yes, it is cause for celebration. Many people will tell you they have a great book in them. But only a small percentage actually sit down and write that book. You're one of a select few who applied bottom to chair and produced a finished product.

Or is it really finished? Your product might not be ready for the marketplace. In the rush to publication, many new writers inadvertently defeat their efforts for success. They send out their first draft instead of their tenth. They send out sloppily prepared manuscripts. They send out novels with grammatical errors and typos. They send out novels with technical errors, point–of–view problems, plotting mistakes, characterization inconsistencies, and loose ends galore.

"Put down everything that comes into your head and then you're a writer. But an author is one who can judge his own stuff's worth, without pity, and destroy most of it." This hard-nosed quote is attributed to author Colette.

In a similar vein, Oscar Wilde said, "I was working on the proof of one of my poems all the morning, and took out a comma. In the afternoon I put it back again."

Self-editing is an important part of the polishing process. "I really believe in writers rewriting their material," says editorial director John Scognamiglio. "When someone sends something off it should be really polished. Writers learn a lot when they go over their material. I think you can get better if you keep working at it."

Agent Elizabeth Wales agrees. "Work on your craft and polish what you are offering: Don't send out drafts!"

These five steps to a salable product really do work–if you follow the steps. Look back on our earlier example of the doctor learning his profession. Considering the investment of both time and money a doctor has to make to pursue a medical career, writers have it easy. A few how-to books, market guides, a well-chosen conference or two a year, and perhaps a manuscript critique, all add up to a small amount of money, comparatively speaking, and it is money well spent.

As agent Evan Marshall says, "Before you even approach an agent, learn your market inside out and master the techniques of your craft the best you can."

FIRST-NOVEL PROBLEMS

On the whole, agents and editors receive countless submissions. And most of those are rejected. Some submissions are inappropriate. They have been mistargeted–sent to the wrong agency or house. Others shriek of amateur writing or offer tired story lines.

Editors and agents can easily spot first-novel problems. If you learn how to spot those problems in your own work before sending it out, you'll be giving yourself an edge against the competition.

First-novel problems are mistakes that agents and editors see over and over in dozens, even hundreds, of submissions they receive. On the one hand, you can take heart that you're not the only person making mistakes. On the other hand, learn what mistakes are common to new writers ... and then learn how to avoid them.

Listen to what the experts say. Here, several agents and editors comment on what they consider to be deal-breakers–sure guarantees of a rejection letter finding its way into your SASE.

Plotting

EVAN MARSHALL, AGENT

"I get novels in which it looks as if someone just sat down and started typing without any overall plan, didn't think about who would be the best viewpoint character, for example. I've seen every possible kind of craziness. Books told completely in summary, novels all in narration, or all in dialogue.

"Not paying attention to plot is like saying you want to paint but you don't know how to open the tubes. Plot is not just a series of events worming their way around. Everything has to grow organically from what happened before it."

The Hook

MARJORIE BRAMAN, HARPERCOLLINS

"Often, new writers don't understand how important the first part of the book is. The success of the first half of the book is, in some ways, more important than the success of the second half of the book. The opening scene of a book is especially important. It's not the place to establish plot or setting. The first scene or the first chapter of a book is the place to draw the reader in and get them hooked. There are a number of different ways to do it, but too often I see too much effort going into setting up the book in the first chapter. That's not what a first chapter is for."

WENDY MCCURDY, BANTAM BOOKS

"It can't just be another formula story, no matter how well done. That's just not going to be good enough. I am looking for something with a real hook, something for which I can visualize the niche it's going to reach."

Pacing

RUSSELL GALEN, AGENT

"Timing, pacing, rhythm. Inexperienced writers often neglect to put themselves in the readers' shoes and envision for themselves what the reading experience will be like, and as a result, their books are often paced in a way that isn't as enjoyable for the reader as it should be. Most commonly, this shows itself in pacing that is too slow, scenes that drag on, revelations that take forever to come, and which finally come after it's too late and we've lost patience and interest."

ANNE SAVARESE, OXFORD UNIVERSITY PRESS

"New writers often have trouble balancing all the different elements of the story. It has to move along at a pace the reader won't lose patience with. Sometimes I get the sense that the writer is having such a good time creating the set-up, he forgets about the book as a whole."

Narrative Tension

SUSAN ZECKENDORF, AGENT

"Another problem, which is especially true of mysteries and thrillers, is that there isn't enough suspense or narrative tension. There needs to be something to make the reader want to keep turning the pages."

Storytelling

LAURA ANNE GILMAN, ROC/DUTTON

"A writer may have a good story, and may write well, but won't know how to tell the story. Sometimes the story isn't developed properly. There may be only 70–80,000 words written, but the story could be expanded to develop it better. Or the opposite can happen, that too much is being told. A writer may put everything in from the research where only enough is needed for flavor and accuracy."

MICHAEL SEIDMAN, FORMERLY OF WALKER AND COMPANY

"A good book is a combination of factors, all of which lead back to the same point–storytelling. If a writer is aware that storytelling is an extension of an oral tradition, if there's a distinctive voice, if something's happening that makes a difference in the reader's life, if there are characters you can believe in and care about who speak the way people speak, that's all that counts."

PETER RUBIE, AGENT

"A lot of people come up with good ideas but don't know how to tell it. But you could take a fairly mundane idea and if you tell it well enough, you can probably get it published."

Characters

ANNE SAVARESE, OXFORD UNIVERSITY PRESS

"Characters can make or break a novel and that's what I tend to look for. With mysteries, plot glitches can be fixed if the basic story is there, but if you have characters that seem flat, then that's more of a problem. Characters should have reactions that aren't predictable, and they should change over the course of the story, just as real people develop and grow."

MARJORIE BRAMAN, HARPERCOLLINS

"Anytime I like a character immediately or want to know more about him or her, then the author has done his job of at least attracting my attention. I'm always drawn in by character, and less by plot. As an editor, plot is something I can help with suggestions about, but character and the emotional content of a book are something I can't teach. It's something that's either natural or not, so if an author has that, he's won a big battle."

SUSAN ZECKENDORF, AGENT

"Sometimes characters are not particularly original or well developed. They should be described—not just in narrative, but through their actions and dialogue. And if too many characters are introduced up front, it's difficult to remember who they all are."

"I look for stories where the characters really come to life."

JOHN SCOGNAMIGLIO,
KENSINGTON PUBLISHING CORPORATION

NANCY LOVE, AGENT

"The thing that hooks me right off in a novel is the characters. Characters are the beginning of a book. If I don't care about the characters and the writing is not terrific, I will reject it right away."

Dialogue

EVAN MARSHALL, AGENT

"Dialogue is another trouble spot. It's stiff and unrealistic or it doesn't get us anywhere. Dialogue should pretend that it's imitating life but it doesn't really. It isn't supposed to have the incidental inconsequentials we say every day, like, 'Hi, how are you?'"

ANNE SAVARESE, OXFORD UNIVERSITY PRESS

"Characterization can come through in dialogue. A good test is to read it aloud. Does it sound like something someone would actually say, or does it sound stilted?"

MARJORIE BRAMAN, HARPERCOLLINS

"I think that dialogue can be difficult, and to write realistic dialogue, you have to have a good ear. All you really have to do, of course, is listen to people around you, to strangers, to friends, and to family. But somehow, when it gets put down on paper, especially by a first-time novelist, it tends to turn rather unrealistic. An ear for good dialogue is something I think must come with time, but it should be paid attention to."

CHERRY WEINER, AGENT

"Often I see authors who are 'aspiring toward literary.' In effect, what happens is that the dialogue is stilted and formal. It doesn't sound like natural, everyday language."

The Writing

EVAN MARSHALL, AGENT

"The texture of the writing itself is often a problem, using too many adjectives and adverbs or giving every line of dialogue a tag with an adverb attached. That's amateurish. You can tell they're either not reading the books that explain what good writing is or they're not absorbing the information. Editors are fussier than ever, and so often I get fiction that is untrained as far as the technical aspects—viewpoint, dialogue, writing style, the misuse of adjectives and adverbs, whatever constitutes good writing as opposed to bad writing."

LAURA ANNE GILMAN, ROC/DUTTON

"Good writing gets me excited. The story can be mediocre, but if you can write, I will give you the story back and tell you to send me another story. Good writing will overcome just about anything.

"Expository lumps are a turnoff! It's more than just going on and on without saying anything. It's writing for the sake of the words when there is no action. If you are reading and your eyes glaze over or you begin skipping lines, that's an expository lump."

JEFF KLEINMAN, AGENT/PUBLISHING LAW ATTORNEY

"Generally, it's pretty tough to break out new novelists; they really need a plot and a control over language that is unique, different, out-of-the-ordinary."

"A lot of the novels I see need much more tightening up. The writer sends it out too soon. The manuscript could benefit from a workshop or critique group."

NANCY LOVE, AGENT

Content

EVAN MARSHALL, AGENT

"A lot of the books I get are about things that aren't of interest anymore, or never were. This has to do with awareness of market. For example, there are really very few KGB/CIA thrillers published anymore, but I still receive tons of it. Or books about an AIDS virus that's decimating the country and some brave heroine is going to find out what laboratory is doing this. Or novels of historical fiction without a romance element set in some obscure time period in some obscure place with little interest to anyone. And no one's publishing multi-generational sagas unless you're a big name. The writer is confusing fresh ideas with out-of-the-market ideas. First, be within the market and then be fresh."

"Too many first novels often tend to be coming-of-age novels, autobiographical in nature, about that person's experiences growing up. But a coming-of-age novel is extremely difficult to sell at this time. Several years ago the coming-of-age novel was hot. It just isn't anymore."

FRANCES KUFFEL, FORMER AGENT

Voice

MARJORIE BRAMAN, HARPERCOLLINS

"If a book is written in a voice that I don't like, then that's a turnoff. For example, I'm not very fond of a humorous voice in mysteries, or one that tries too hard to be humorous.

"And an author who stands on a soapbox in his novel turns me off. Certainly, there are ways to get your point across and be entertaining at the same time, but if I feel I'm being preached to, I don't feel I'm being entertained. In fiction, the first goal is to entertain."

Viewpoint

EVAN MARSHALL, AGENT

"I advise new writers to avoid using the first person. It smacks of first novel or of gothic, and first person is difficult to sell. Some editors just don't like it. When you're just starting out you want everything going in your favor. Why turn off three out of ten editors because of the viewpoint you've chosen?

"But the place to start thinking about this is before you begin writing. You have to decide who your viewpoint characters will be, from whose point of view will the story be told.

"A lot of authors don't understand the concept. That includes everything from knowing how to keep to one viewpoint in a scene, all the way to deciding who's going to be your viewpoint character.

"A multiple-third-person point of view (telling the story from several main characters' point of view) is right for a bigger book with a more ambitious plot. You decide on four or five main viewpoint characters and you stick to them, and you do each scene using just one of those viewpoints. You don't change viewpoints in the middle of a scene; the editors shriek and grimace when they see it.

"For a smaller book, especially in certain genres, sometimes one viewpoint character is right, such as in a woman-in-jeopardy or a mystery. Use only one character's viewpoint and tell it in third person."

Backgroound Details

ANNE HAWKINS, AGENT

"I think the most common problem among new fiction authors is their compulsion to include tons of background material in the opening chapters of a novel. This is deadly to the pace and hook of the story, and will probably draw a speedy rejection. The professionals know how to get a story off the ground right away and fill in the necessary history later."

RUSSELL GALEN, AGENT

"Many books begin with long expositions of background, postponing until deep in the book any clear reason to keep reading. It's almost as common for a book to rush on too fast, not slowing down to lay in the necessary rich detail and background that enables characters to come alive."

LAURA ANNE GILMAN, ROC/DUTTON

"Slighting the backstory is another problem. Either the writer will throw in so much background material to tell what happened in the beginning, or omit so much it leaves the reader guessing. A balance has to be made, and that is difficult to do. It's not uncommon for writers to have problems with this on their second or third novels, as well."

Overwriting

PESHA RUBENSTEIN, AGENT

"A new writer often tries to present life exactly like it is, such as telling me every minute of the day, or overdoing the dialogue. Things have to be true-to-life, but it can't be verbatim. Linear writing is also a problem. It's not necessary to chronicle every minute of every day in sequence. You need to jump right into the action."

ANNE SAVARESE, OXFORD UNIVERSITY PRESS

"First of all, people tend to overwrite. They put too much into the book because they have so much they want to say, so many details they want to include. I've seen some first-person mysteries, the first in a potential series, and the writer gets so involved developing the character, he loses sight of the rest of the book. Too much wise-cracking, too much time spent in the kitchen cooking—at the expense of the plot development."

JOHN SCOGNAMIGLIO, KENSINGTON PUBLISHING CORPORATION
"Another mistake first-time novelists often make is that they'll overdo the detail, especially with historical novels. Too much narrative."

Grammar

LORI PERKINS, AGENT
"Clean up your grammar! It's not that most people can't write, but often new writers have terrible grammar, spelling, and punctuation. Study it and give me a high quality manuscript."

Word Count

LAURA ANNE GILMAN, ROC/DUTTON
"We use word count rather than page length because printers can vary so. A novel should be somewhere between 70–75,000 words to 100,000 words. Anything shorter than that isn't a novel. Longer than, say, 120,000 words is what we call a 'fat book' and becomes extremely hard to sell because the cost of printing it is so high. Mostly that length is reserved for the established or the breakout authors.

"A breakout author sells much better than the publisher had anticipated, becoming a surprise best-seller. An example would be Robert James Waller and his book *The Bridges of Madison County*. The original print run was very small."

FRANCES KUFFEL, FORMER AGENT
"Keep it short. I have a novel right now that's pretty good, but it's 600 pages long. That will never sell because of the publisher's cost for actually producing the work. People should be thinking in terms of 'How can I make this shorter, how can I make it tighter?'"

"[Writers] don't research the word length that publishers are looking for. Over the years these word lengths have changed. But when you have a publisher looking for a 100,000-word novel (the norm these days), don't do one that's 250,000 words."

CHERRY WEINER, AGENT

EVAN MARSHALL, AGENT

"When a writer tells me: 'I've written a 200,000-word novel,' that shows me he doesn't know what he's doing. Length is determined by the genre (60,000 to 120,000 words), but nothing is 200,000 words. There are books on the subject; publishers will send out their tip sheets and guidelines. It's not enough to have writing talent; some market savvy is also crucial."

CRAFTING IT COMPELLINGLY

You've read all the books in your genre; you've devoured the how-tos; you've attended conferences and picked the brains of successful writers; you've written and rewritten until you're sure you've got a salable product. But even then things can still go wrong.

Even with all the rules and all the advice, judging fiction will always be a subjective and personal process. Often editors and agents can't even put a finger on it themselves.

Editor Anne Savarese points out that often books can be very well written, but are just not compelling enough. She says, "A lot of books we see are competent, but not so good we think we have to publish them. Those are more problematic—there's no one thing that's specifically wrong. It just doesn't raise the temperature of the editor who's reading it, to make him take the next step. And it's harder to really define why that happens. It just doesn't grab you, or it grabs you a little but not enough, or it seems derivative, just like ten other novels you've read that year."

Most importantly Savarese adds, "The mark of a skillful writer is that his work stands out."

Agent Russell Galen agrees: "I can't tell you in advance what will work for me. It's different every time and the answers contradict one another. If I say, 'good writing,' that leaves out the poorly written novel that has some fresh perspective, some locale or character that speaks to me in some way that has meaning for me. If I say, 'good storytelling,' that leaves out the chaotic, plotless shamble that works for me because of the writing or a particular character to whom I relate. If I say 'freshness and originality,' that leaves out the formulaic novel, which is good of its kind and keeps me entertained."

Editor Wendy McCurdy says what impresses her: "Spectacular writing starts with the quality of the writing."

Creating a salable product is no easy task. If it were, everyone would be doing it and there would be no room left in the marketplace for yet one more writer–you.

Agent Peter Rubie sums it up nicely. "I think the best a writer can ever do is do what he wants to do, as best as he can do it. Be true to yourself and everything else will follow."

BEFORE YOU WRITE

Every writer approaches that first blank page or screen differently. Some complete a full outline and character history before they even begin to write, while others set out with only a vague plan mapped out in their minds. With the first approach, however, writers can get so bogged down with details that nothing feels fresh when they sit down to write. And everyone knows that vague maps can lead to wrong turns and you can end up in unexpected, and often, undesirable places.

Using a plot chart can put you somewhere in between the two extremes. A plot chart is simply a list of plot points, or scenes, arranged in chronological order. Think of everything you want to happen in your story. Write it all down, then go back and number what should come first, second, and so on. As you complete each scene, cross it off your list with a red pen and go on to the next. Leave spaces on your plot chart to insert new scenes as they come to you.

You can refer to your list as your work progresses, and all those bright red strikethroughs will signal how much you've accomplished.

Revise, Revise, Then Go Back and Do It Again

"What's a rewrite?" Tom Clancy quipped at a writers' conference. "I write them pretty much the way you guys read them, and I turn in a fairly clean product."

Clancy is the exception to the rule. Most of us go through many drafts before we're done. But by the time you've read and reread your work ten or twenty times, it can become too familiar to you, making it next to impossible to flush out mistakes and recognize areas that could use some reworking. Each reading seems to accomplish less than the one before. Here's a tip to help make your revision time more productive. Take a piece of paper and list the problems you hope to discover and correct. Your list could look something like this:

1. Look for the deadwood, the unnecessary bits that don't move the story forward.

2. Check the first paragraph of each chapter for hooks.

3. Check the end of each chapter for good cliffhangers.

4. Examine each page for balance between dialogue, action, introspection, and description.

5. Find places to build in character traits.

6. Look for inconsistencies.

7. Look for repetition and words repeated too often or too close to each other.

8. Find typos and grammatical errors. *

Each time you sit down to reread your manuscript, choose one point from the list to look for; ignore everything else. Every rereading needs to accomplish something specific. Have a set goal in mind each time you start. Know what it is you plan to accomplish, and your rereading time will accomplish more.

> *** Hint: Always save typo hunting for last. Rereading leads to rewriting, and rewriting leads to more typos.**

FINAL WORDS OF ADVICE

Editor Anne Savarese offers these final thoughts: "I always encourage new writers because I know trying to get published can be a very long, discouraging process. But if you have a book you really believe in, and you really worked hard on it and think it's something good, you shouldn't give up. There is a market for first novels out there, and though it is competitive, it's not impossible to get published. If writing is something you are committed to, you should keep trying, and do everything you can to hone your craft."

If you keep trying to hone your craft, and follow all of the steps in this chapter, you most likely will have a completed manuscript with market potential. The remainder of this book will show you how to tap into that market in the most professional way.

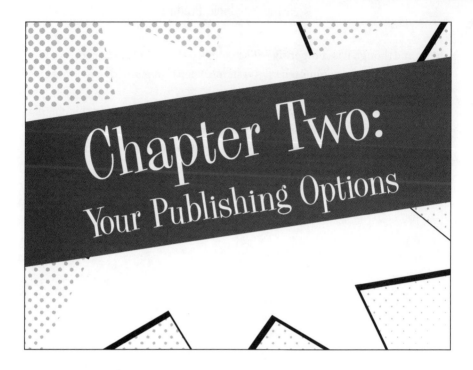

Chapter Two:
Your Publishing Options

"If you do not write for publication, there is little point in writing at all."—GEORGE BERNARD SHAW

Ready for some big numbers?

Commercial publishers will publish more than 150,000 books in the United States this year. That translates to more than four hundred books a day!

In 2002, the last year for which the Association of American Publishers offers complete statistics, book sales in the United States totaled almost $27 billion. Sales were up in almost all publishing categories, including trade paperback, hardback, and juvenile. Paperback sales were down slightly (1.3 percent).

Book publishing is big business, and it continues to get bigger.

Although popular fiction accounts for more than half of all books sold, only about 15 percent of those 150,000 published titles are fiction. (And about half of those titles are romance novels.) A few specific fiction titles accounted for a huge number of sales: fifteen to twenty novels each sold a million copies or more.

In a typical year, a handful of writers will account for two out of every three novels sold. You know the names of these titans, folks like John Grisham, Stephen King, Michael Crichton, Tom Clancy, Danielle Steel, Mary Higgins Clark, James Patterson, and Dean Koontz. As we write these words, Nora Roberts has not one, not two, but three titles on *The New York Times* best-seller list. While Dan Brown's *The Da Vinci Code* was topping the hardcover list, he also had three best-selling paperbacks out.

These folks sell a lot of books and make it profitable for publishers to keep producing novels, which gives the rest of us a chance to break in. The market uncovers new and talented writers each year. Recent examples include Carolyn Chute (who had to borrow money for postage to submit her first manuscript to a publisher), Leif Enger, and Gus Lee.

Alexander McCall Smith opened up new territory in mystery writing with the spectacular success of his gentle blockbuster, *The No. 1 Ladies' Detective Agency*, and the subsequent titles in the series.

New authors are finding niche markets. Attorney James Scott Bell is selling well in the "religious/courtroom drama" sub-genre, for example.

Talented writers are still breaking the publishing barrier, and you can too.

And when you do, the rewards will be great, starting with the feeling of elation you'll receive. "For several days after my first book was published," James M. Barrie, author of *Peter Pan*, once commented, "I carried it about in my pocket and took surreptitious peeps at it to make sure the ink had not faded."

WHAT'S SELLING ...

Children's books dominate the top categories of best-selling books. Top sellers are generally children's age 9–12 trade paperbacks, children's age 4–8 trade paperbacks, and children's age 4–8 hardcovers. Romance novels are the fourth-largest category and account for more than half of all mass-market paperbacks published each year.

After two nonfiction categories fill the fifth and sixth slots, general fiction trade paperback, general fiction hardcover, and general fiction mass-market paperback rank seventh, eighth, and ninth, with mass-market paperback mysteries tenth.

... AND FOR HOW MUCH

The prices of books vary based on the books' size and format. The average retail price (the full cover price you pay in the bookstore if there are no sales or discounts) of a hardcover novel is about $25.00. Trade paperbacks, the larger, more expensive softcover books, sell for around $16.00. The average mass-market paperback–the smaller softcover books–comes in at about $7. 50. Children's books are generally less expensive: Hardcover books are priced at about $17.00; trade paperbacks sell for about $12.00.

Who Owns All Those Publishers?

Three multi-national corporations, Pearson, Bertelsmann, and Holtzbrinck, dominate book publishing worldwide.

Started in 1937, Holtzbrinck owns some of the biggest and most influential imprints in the world, including St. Martin's Press, Farrar, Straus & Giroux, Henry Holt, and Tor Books.

Under the large umbrella of Random House, Bertelsmann owns Alfred A. Knopf, Ballantine, and Doubleday, among others.

Pearson owns the Penguin Group, which publishes under the Putnam, Dutton, Viking, and Berkley Books imprints, among others.

Multimedia groups like Viacom now challenge these three media giants. Although primarily involved in broadcasting and movies (Viacom owns Paramount Pictures and MTV), Viacom also owns Simon & Schuster, which encompasses Pocket Books, Scribner, and others.

This does not mean that the fate of your novel lies in the hands of only three or four powerful corporate moguls. Just because a single corporation owns Ballantine, Doubleday, Knopf and other publishers, for example, does not mean that a single acquisitions editor or makes all the decisions for all the houses. Editorially, the houses operate independently of one another and have different needs and requirements.

After these giants, there are another 2,200 small and mid-level publishers listed by the U.S. Department of Commerce. There are still lots of places to publish our novels!

THE NINE PATHS TO PUBLICATION

1. Commercial: National/International Publishers. These are the imprints like Avon, William Morrow, HarperCollins, Putnam, Simon & Schuster, Random House, Little, Brown and Company, Farrar, Straus & Giroux, St. Martin's, and Knopf.

If you can obtain a publishing contract with one of these folks, you're definitely running with the big dogs.

> **ADVANTAGES.** The big houses know how to market. They can get wide distribution and a spot on the shelves at Borders and Barnes & Noble. Books with big-name imprints stand a much better chance of being reviewed, especially in prestigious publications like *The New York Times Book Review*. You also have a better chance of having your novel picked up in translation by foreign publishers or even having the movie rights optioned.
>
> If you seek a large audience and perhaps even a shot at the best-seller list, your novel needs to carry one of these major imprints.
>
> Commensurate with their size and the expected sale of your book, the big corporate publishers pay relatively large advances. (That's an advance against royalties, a prepayment before you actually begin to earn royalties from sales of your book. We'll discuss this in Chapter Ten.)
>
> **DISADVANTAGES.** Because they're visible and powerful, the national and international commercial publishers get mountains of submissions. They can afford to be extremely selective about the projects they look at, let alone publish. Competition is fierce. Only commercially viable proposals, presented professionally (almost always through an agent) stand a chance. That makes it tough, but it doesn't make it impossible. Plenty of new writers get picked up by these publishers each year.
>
> Often, the larger the house, the less control you have over the editing of your book.
>
> **APPROACH.** Find a literary agent to help you break in. We'll tell you how in Chapter Three.

2. Commercial: Regional/Small Presses. America is blessed with thousands of wonderful regional and niche book publishers, most of which never see the light of *The New York Times Book Review* or the best-seller list.

For the most part, they operate in the same manner as the big boys, but on a much smaller scale.

ADVANTAGES. Small presses can afford to take chances because they can survive on considerably smaller sales than the larger, more cumbersome houses.

They are often superb at servicing specialty and special interest markets and specific regions of the country. If your novel deals with a red-haired, left-handed Virgo trying to find love in the mountains of northern Idaho, you might just find a small press specializing in books featuring red-haired, left-handed Virgos in northern Idaho.

Many small presses are founded and run by writer-editors who are disgusted with the offerings on the best-seller lists and are dedicated to publishing outstanding literary fiction. Find one of these to love your book and you'll have a passionate champion.

Unlike the big commercial publishers, regional and small presses are open to unagented submissions.

With a smaller press, you're likely to have much more input into the production and marketing of your book.

DISADVANTAGES. There's no such thing as a typical small press, but you would expect to find that a small press publishes fewer titles (as few as one per year), has a smaller pressrun for a first edition (often in the hundreds rather than thousands), and offers small or nonexistent advances.

Most small presses lack the firepower to get national distribution and the kind of push needed to generate big sales. However, a small press sometimes experiences a breakout book that finds a national market. Your book could be the one.

APPROACH. Most small presses prefer to be contacted by the author directly rather than through an agent. Find the name (and correct spelling) of the appropriate editor (who is often also the publisher), and send your proposal directly.

CAUTION. Don't think for a minute that the small press is a place to try to peddle second-rate material. They may be smaller, but they are no less discriminating (and in many cases are more) than the big guys.

A Few Good Small Presses

You may have never heard of these small, independent presses, but one of them might be the perfect publisher for your novel. Here's a brief sampling of the best.

BLACK HERON PRESS

Jerry Gold; P.O. Box 95676, Seattle, WA 98145; Web site: www.mav.net/blackheron/

They publish four to six titles per year and specialize in literary fiction. Established in 1984, this veteran press has an extensive backlist of fine novels. Authors should query with a cover letter and the first 30–40 pages of the novel. They don't accept e-mail queries.

BLEAK HOUSE BOOKS

Benjamin LeRoy and Blake Steward; P.O. Box 8573, Madison, WI 53708; Web site: www.bleakhousebooks.com

They specialize in mysteries but have also created children's books under the James Street Press imprint. Still relatively new, they are gaining momentum fast and recently signed with a big international distributor. They are the publishers of Marshall Cook's Monona Quinn Mystery series, and he sings their praises.

CROSS + ROADS PRESS

Norbert Blei; P.O. Box 33, Ellison Bay, WI 54210

A relatively new press with a veteran author/publisher at the helm, Cross + Roads specializes in discovering new writers of mainstream or literary fiction. They want to be the first publisher that gets you started on your publishing career.

PUSHCART PRESS

Bill Henderson; P.O. Box 380, Wainscott, NY 11975

You don't know small presses unless you know Henderson and his Pushcart Press. Established in 1972, they publish the anthology *The Pushcart Prize: Best of the Small Presses* and sponsor an annual editors' book award for manuscripts overlooked by commercial publishers.

SAVAGE PRESS

Mike Savage; P.O. Box 115, Superior, WI 54880; Web site: www.savpress.com

Savage Press published Marshall's two baseball novels, *The Year of the Buffalo* and *Off*

Season, and here again, he recommends them highly. They've developed a fine track record and an extensive backlist of titles.

THE SPIRIT THAT MOVES US PRESS

Morty Sklar; P.O. Box 720820, Jackson Heights, NY 11372-0820

Established in 1975, Spirit provides, in the words of its founder, "a place for fiction where the main criteria are quality, originality, and work that communicates on a human level."

STEERFORTH PRESS

25 Lebanon Street, Hanover, NH 03755; Web site: www.steerforth.com

Established in 1993, Steerforth publishes eight to ten titles a year, with an average press run of five thousand, and specializes in literary fiction. Like many of the larger presses, Steerforth does not accept unsolicited proposals or manuscripts. You'll need an agent to pitch to them.

AND THE FOLKS WHO KEEP TRACK OF IT ALL . . .

DUSTBOOKS

Len Fulton; P.O. Box 100, Paradise, CA 95967; Web site: www.dustbooks.com

Len Fulton is godfather and midwife to the small press movement in America. He self-published his novel, *Dark Other Adam Dreaming*, and applied what he learned about production and marketing to become the foremost small press publisher in America. Dustbooks publishes a monthly magazine reviewing small press publishers and for almost four decades has produced the yearly *International Directory of Little Magazines & Small Presses*. If you want to know small presses, you've got to know Dustbooks.

3. University Presses. University presses generally serve a well-educated and discriminating audience. Most university presses specialize in particular subjects, but many also publish mainstream books.

> **ADVANTAGES.** University presses have better access to certain specialized and niche markets. Most enjoy fine reputations. Your project will get professional care.

> **DISADVANTAGES.** Most university presses publish little or no fiction, though there are exceptions. Few university press books break through to a large, national audience. Advances range from nonexistent to small.

APPROACH. As with the small and regional presses, most university presses will accept proposals directly from the author, and many avoid agents, who don't have much knowledge of or interest in university presses anyway.

4. Organizational/Sponsored Presses. Many organizations have their own publishing imprints, and some sponsor or subsidize projects of special merit and interest to their constituents. For example, the Adoption Awareness Press, a division of the Musser Foundation, Cape Coral, Florida, published *Chasing Rainbows: A Search for Family Ties*, about a woman who finds her birth mother at about the time the daughter she had given up for adoption finds her.

ADVANTAGES. You've got a novel that would really appeal to folks who build their own airplanes for fun? Try the Experimental Aircraft Association (EAA) in Oshkosh, Wisconsin. They can reach those folks better than anybody.

Every once in a while, a novel issued by an organizational or specialty press breaks through and finds a national market. Can you name Tom Clancy's first publisher for *The Hunt for Red October*? It's Naval Institute Press, which nearly sank trying to keep up with the demand before selling the rights to a major publishing house.

DISADVANTAGES. The smaller press is less likely to find a huge audience. If you think your book might have a real shot at best-seller status, you should first try to get an agent and publish with a large commercial publisher.

APPROACH. Find the appropriate name on the organization chart and make an initial inquiry by letter or phone before launching a proposal.

5. Subsidy Publishers. You've no doubt seen the ads that announce "Publisher Seeks Manuscripts." Next time you see one, turn the page.

Subsidy publishers (also known as "vanity presses") prey on writers frustrated by their failure to find a publisher and on folks who just don't know any better. They act like commercial publishers, "evaluating" your project and offering a publishing contract. But when it comes time for money to change hands, it's your money, a lot of your money, going to the publisher, instead of the other way around.

ADVANTAGES. You do get a book published. Some subsidy houses offer minimal help with marketing.

DISADVANTAGES. You pay and pay and pay. Editing is often minimal or inept. Production is often shoddy. Libraries won't buy your book. Reviewers won't touch it. Often all advertising and publicity are left to you. And you don't even own the books you paid to have published!

APPROACH. Never.

6. Cooperative Publishers and Book Producers. Cooperative publishers ask the author to participate in the costs of producing the book. That means you put up part of the cost of printing and binding, and thus share the risk with the publisher. (In subsidy publishing, you pay the entire expense, plus a hefty markup for the publisher's overhead and profit.) Or the publisher may ask you to supply camera-ready copy, meaning you're responsible for editing and typesetting your manuscript or having that work done.

Many small publishers work in all three categories, publishing some books on a commercial basis, some with a co-op deal, and still others on full author subsidy. You'll need to evaluate any contract you receive from a publisher carefully to make sure you understand the terms before you sign.

A book producer will take your book from manuscript to finished product, often helping you with promotion and distribution, all for a fee. The major difference between these presses and subsidy houses are: (1) You won't pay nearly as much, and (2) You'll own all the books.

Contracting with a book producer is essentially like hiring a contractor to help you build your own house. It's your project, but you pay for expert help. Publishing a novel this way carries many of the same advantages and disadvantages of self-publishing, which we'll discuss in a moment.

ADVANTAGES. A lot of these folks do a fine job for a reasonable charge. Many can help you with publicity and distribution. Their imprint on your book and a place in their catalog can help, not hurt.

DISADVANTAGES. You're still paying someone else to publish your book, and the stigma of vanity publishing is attached to some cooperative publishers, especially the ones who also issue books on a subsidy basis.

APPROACH. Try to get a commercial publisher first. If that doesn't work and you decide to go this route, then proceed with caution. Get some help in evaluating any contract you're offered.

7) Book Packagers. A book packager acts as an intermediary, selling a concept to a publisher and then contracting with the author to create the book. Often the author works for a set fee rather than receiving royalties.

Most book packagers deal with nonfiction projects, generally as part of an established series of books. For example, Marshall has published several books with CWL Publishing Enterprises. One of them, a book on management techniques called *Effective Coaching*, has become a big seller for the McGraw-Hill Briefcase Books series and has been translated into four languages.

> **ADVANTAGES.** The author is assured of publication and a prearranged payday. The author gets a byline and national/international exposure.

> **DISADVANTAGES.** No chance to cash in if the book sells big because you contracted for a set fee, and the packager generally retains the copyright. Also, the opportunities for fiction are scarce.

> **APPROACH.** Once you've had a few things published in magazines, a book packager may seek you out to do a nonfiction book. Aggressive and smart packagers attend writers meetings, read the acknowledgments from books in fields that interest them, and call universities and colleges to find out who the experts are in various fields.

> If a packager hears of your work and makes you an offer, consider it. But the likelihood of a packager (or anyone else) approaching you to write a novel is next to zero.

> If you have a good nonfiction idea, especially one that would fit into a publisher's existing series of books, you could send a proposal to a book packager, just as you would to the publisher.

Who's Publishing All These Books?

Books in Print, published by RR Bowker, LLC and the industry's accepted guide, lists books produced by some 73,000 publishers in the United States, including about 10,300 new publishers. That said, a handful of multinational media conglomerates, along with perhaps a dozen of the largest independent publishers, produce between 75 and 85 percent of all books published in North America today.

Regardless of size, we can categorize book publishers as:

- commercial: national/international publishers
- commercial: regional small presses
- commercial: university presses
- organizational/sponsored presses
- subsidy publishers
- cooperative publishers and book producers
- book packagers
- self-publishers
- electronic publishers

Which route should you take to publish your book? Look at your options, and evaluate the advantages and disadvantages of each, and the circumstances under which you should consider them.

8) Self-Publishers. Edgar Rice Burroughs did it. So did Zane Grey, Mark Twain, Stephen Crane, Virginia Woolf, Walt Whitman, Edgar Allan Poe, and James Joyce. They and thousands of other writers have taken their work directly to a printer and come home with boxes full of books. You have total control over the project, and you own the result outright. But you're risking your own money, and some will consider your work to be in the same category with subsidy publishing.

One of our favorite self-publishing success stories is The Dunery Press, founded by Charles and Natalie McKelvy. They're successful freelance writers who became disgruntled with the world of commercial fiction and started publishing and marketing their own fiction, one novel from each per year. They've found a small but loyal market for titles such as *Holy Orders* and *Clarke Street* (by Charles) and *The Golden Book of Child Abuse and Other Works* and *Party Chicks & Other Works* (by Natalie).

ADVANTAGES. You're in total control of the project, from idea to finished book. Every buck that comes in goes into your pocket. You own the books. You might just sell a lot of them. Occasionally a self-published novel breaks out in a big way. *The Celestine Prophecy* by James Redfield and *The Christmas Box* by Richard Paul Evans both began as self-published projects.

Nonfiction books stand a much better chance of self-publishing success, however, especially when the author has extensive knowledge of the subject (or access to the people who do) and a direct line to potential book buyers.

Tom Klein thrilled packed houses with his illustrated lectures on the loons of northern Wisconsin. When he self-published *Loon Magic*, he had himself a best-seller and the beginning of a career in publishing.

Successful or not, you'll also learn a lot about publishing in the process.

DISADVANTAGES. You have total responsibility for the project, from idea to finished book. The books sit in your basement, garage, or family room until or unless you do something to get them sold.

Every dollar comes from your pocket, and almost all of the money flows out before any starts coming in. You have to be willing to invest a lot of money and possibly lose it.

Most of the self-published books that do find a wide audience are nonfiction. Examples include *The Joy of Sex* by Alex Comfort and *What Color Is Your Parachute?* by Richard Bolles. It's much, much tougher to market a novel on your own. You'll *have* to learn a lot about publishing–and publicity and marketing and distribution–in the process.

Does self-publishing hurt your chances of getting an agent for your novel later? It depends.

"I receive queries about these all the time," agent Richard Henshaw tells us, "and unless there are some unusual circumstances, like major reviews or extraordinary sales, I try to treat them like any other query."

But now comes the bad news. "I say 'try,'" Henshaw continues, "because often these are poorly edited or packaged in an amateurish way, and sometimes that hurts a writer's chances more than a raw manuscript would. And really, even if the book is great, it's hard not to look at a self-published, subsidy, or vanity press book and not associate it with all the bad stuff out there. It's largely a matter of what makes the best first impression, and often these formats just don't do the job."

Agent Anne Hawkins is even more emphatic on the subject. "I am much less likely to pursue such a project than I am to pursue an unpublished one," she says. "Unless an author can point to impressive sales–and we're talking in the thousands here–or significant media attention beyond his or her local area, the chances of getting an agent or a traditional publisher for a self-published book are slim."

In an article called "Literary Agents and Self-Published Books," Hawkins writes, "Most agents are far, far more likely to accept an unpublished manuscript than a previously self-published book." She'll take on a self-published book that has demonstrated really good buzz and significant sales.

"If your ultimate goal is publication by a major press," Hawkins says, "think about biting the bullet and embarking on the traditional query process at the outset. If you do not find an agent or publisher, or if the process becomes too painful, self-publishing is always a viable option."

APPROACH. Approach this option with extreme caution. Prepare a proposal for yourself and evaluate potential markets, just as you would if approaching an agent or editor. If commercial publishers have turned you down, figure out why before you take the risk.

Portrait of a Small Press Publisher

ROBERT OLMSTED AND THE CONSERVATORY OF AMERICAN LETTERS

Under its Dan River Press imprint, the Conservatory of American Letters (CAL) strives to produce "literary works of exceptional merit without regard to commercial potential, to encourage and develop literary talent, [and] offer the reading public an alternative to mass marketing mediocrity," according to publisher Robert Olmsted.

Olmsted has been small press publishing since 1972 and has produced over 275 titles. He figures between books and fiction anthologies he's published close to 10,000 writers.

Recent Dan River Press titles include *The Rat Catcher* by Andrew Laszlo, *The Lutheran* by Jack Britton Sullivan, and *Blackbeard's Gift* by Jamie Clifford.

Olmsted also publishes poetry as Northwoods Press and produces books for authors through his Personal Publishing Program.

9) Electronic Publishers. There's a lot of publishing activity on the Internet these days. Some writers offer everything from poetry and journal entries to sample chapters or complete manuscripts of novels online. Some try to sell their material, while others simply give it away to anyone who visits their Web sites.

Cyberpublishing and the e-book have emerged as an alternative delivery system for novels. Folks buy and download novels, then either read them on the screen or print out their own copies of the work. Many e-book publishers also offer hard and softcover versions of the book, which they publish on a Print On Demand (POD) basis. Some of these publishers, such as Hard Shell Word Factory, are developing strong markets for their authors' work.

Will such cyberbooks replace books printed on paper and bound between covers? We doubt it. Each new delivery system supplements existing media rather than supplanting them. Remember, for decades radio was America's electronic storyteller. When television swept the country after World War II, the experts predicted radio's demise. Instead, radio adapted, offering music, sports, and talk.

ADVANTAGES. Cyberpublishing offers a new and potentially exciting way to publish your novel and find your audience. Some folks love the snappy links and instant searches of cyberspace and are happy to read book-length material from a computer screen.

Legitimate e-publishers pay generous royalties to their authors, and the good ones work hard to help publicize their books.

This area of publishing has grown rapidly and will probably continue to grow.

DISADVANTAGES. Although many readers are adapting to cyberspace, others still want to hold a book in their hands and take it to bed or the beach with them. Some novel readers will never adapt to online publishing.

For this and other reasons, few cyberpublishers have become firmly established economically.

There are scammers in every field, of course, but so far, they're even harder to catch online. Some fly-by-night online publishers promise payment, fail to deliver, and then vanish. Many new companies offer to post your book for free and pay you royalties, but when you get to the fine print, you learn that there are many hidden charges, such as uploading fees, and no guarantee that anyone will ever pay to download your book or that you'll ever see a royalty if they do.

Additionally, while the copyright laws apply to material published online just as they do to any other kind of publication, they're harder to enforce in cyberspace. Once your material is out there, you may have lost control over it.

And finally, it's a struggle for any first-time novelist to get attention for his or her novel, and it's even tougher in the crowded and chaotic world of e-publishing. It's easy to get lost in the vast reaches of cyberspace.

APPROACH. You approach legitimate e-book publishers with the same sort of proposal you'd use for other publishers or agents. You'll probably do so online.

Here again, use caution. If the deal sounds too good to be true, it no doubt is. But keep your eye on this growing field of publishing. Many authors have found success and satisfaction as cyber-novelists.

E-Publishing Has Its Advantages

BY TRACY COOPER-POSEY

My eleventh novel comes out some time in 2005. Eight of those novels are e-books, also published in POD paperback. Two of the eleven books were trade paperbacks published by small presses. Only one of my novels to date was a mass-market paperback.

I got into e-publishing in 1999, when it was very, very new, and most of my promotion work was educating people about e-books and battling the huge bias against them. Since then, all that has utterly changed. I've recently begun to believe that I'd *rather* be published by e-book/POD publishers and not New York. There's a huge advantage to being perpetually in print.

I like having so much control over my career and the promotion of my books. There wasn't a lot of money in it way back then, and I'm still not making enough to quit my day job, but my monthly (yes, monthly) checks have recently made a sharp spike upward: a combination of public awareness of e-books, one of my e-publishers getting titles stocked on the shelves of Borders and Barnes & Noble, and my own steady promotional efforts.

It took me a while to realize that promotion must be consistent and relentless, and also that I need to build my readership with each new book. But it's entirely possible that, with consistent effort, I can grow those monthly checks so that they start arriving in amounts high enough to quit the day job. Then I can start producing even more books and promoting more. That would be bliss indeed.

Authors' note: And speaking of promotion, check out Tracy's fine Web site at www.sashaproductions.com. Her recent books include *Heart of Vengeance*, *Forbidden*, and *Silent Knight*. Her query for her first traditionally published book is used as a sample in chapter four.

For the remainder of this book, we'll concentrate on helping you get a commercial publishing contract for your novel. If you believe in your book, you want someone to pay you to publish it. Read on to learn how.

Chapter Three:
The Search Begins: Finding Agents and Editors

"The 15 percent you pay an agent is light freight."

—GUS LEE, AUTHOR OF *CHINA BOY*

If you want one of the major commercial presses to publish your novel, you're going to need a good literary agent. If you hope to be published by a good small press, you'll probably approach the editors directly. We'll show you how to do both.

The majority of agents and major publishers are nestled within a few square miles of downtown New York City, but you don't need to go to Manhattan to contact them. You'll approach them with a well-crafted, targeted proposal, usually by mail, sometimes by e-mail.

Or, you may find the perfect agent or publisher far from New York City.

ORGANIZE YOUR SEARCH

Be prepared to be in this for the long haul. Finding an agent and getting published is not a speedy process. It could take a year, often longer. During that time, you might make dozens of contacts by sending out query letters, synopses, and full and partial manuscripts.

To make it easier on yourself (and the agents and editors), you need to have an organized, systematic approach. You'll often have several proposals circulating at the same time; you must keep accurate track of them.

Create a chart of the agents and editors you plan to contact. (More on how to select those prospects later.) Note where you found the agent or editor—for example, the page number in *Writer's Market*, or at a writers conference, or from an author's referral.

As you send your material out, note what you sent to each—query letter, sample chapters, synopsis, chapter outline—and the date you sent it. As you begin receiving requests for more material and rejection letters (yes, rejections are nearly inevitable), note the response and when you received it. And stay on top of your system. If you get too far behind in keeping track, you'll get overwhelmed.

With your tracking system set up, you're ready to start your publishing campaign.

The Long Struggle to Become an Overnight Success

"You have to work awfully hard to get lucky in this business."
—ALEXS PATE, AUTHOR OF *AMISTAD*

Alexs Pate wasn't satisfied with being a business executive by day and a writer by night. Without preamble, he quit a successful career in public relations "and became poor overnight."

He pronounced himself a novelist; his former colleagues called him crazy. He wrote relentlessly, in a fever, out of fear. "I wagered that I could produce a book that could rescue me," he says. "I had a blind, crazy, out-of-touch with reality belief that I would be what I intended to be—or die trying."

He was working on a novel that would come to be called *Finding Makeba* when his father died. "I knew I would never see him again if I didn't write about him," Pate recalls, so he started a second novel, *Losing Absalom*. When he finished it, he started knocking on agents' doors.

"I was ready to take it to Kinko's, make copies, and drop them out of an airplane," he says. "My girlfriend said I was starting to sound pathetic."

He finally landed an agent appropriately named Faith and, five years after he started the search, Coffee House Press published the novel.

Meanwhile, he finished *Finding Makeba* and also got it published by a small press. Critics liked both novels, but neither found much of an audience.

However, one very important person read Pate's work and apparently liked it—a lot. Steven Spielberg was producing a movie called *Amistad*. He called Pate to ask if he'd be interested in writing a novel based on the screenplay.

"Where do I sign?" Pate remembers saying.

Pate immersed himself in the project, writing and researching fourteen hours a day, turning down other writing jobs and thinking of little else as he found himself down in the hold of a slave ship with people who had become vividly real to him.

The novel was a huge success, vaulting onto *The New York Times* best-seller list and translated into twenty-five languages.

Now everybody knew what Pate had believed all along: He is a writer. Pate's first two novels have since been re-released, and he has had two more novels published, *West of Rehoboth* and *The Multicultiboho Sideshow*.

And still, Pate says he writes out of fear. "If I don't write, I don't get paid," he says. "If I don't write, I'm going down. And I am not going down if I can help it."

His advice for the rest of us: "Do the work. Believe in yourself. Pray."

FOUR WAYS TO APPROACH PUBLISHERS

1. "Over the Transom." Publishers still refer to an unsolicited manuscript (something they didn't ask for and didn't know was coming) as an "over-the-transom submission," even though few doors have transoms anymore. (Those are the little windows over doors that supplied ventilation before the days of air conditioning. The image is of the author literally tossing a manuscript through the transom to get it to the editor.)

Big publishers get hundreds of over-the-transom manuscripts every week. They don't have the time or patience to wade through them. They might not even have desk or shelf space for them. They usually stuff the manuscript into the SASE with a form rejection letter and send it back unread. If there's no SASE, the manuscript will probably hit the recycle bin.

That's your precious novel, the one you spent months, even years laboring over. Not a pretty picture.

At best, your unsolicited novel might land on the "slush pile" of an overworked, underpaid editorial assistant, who must screen out all but the rare project that might be worth the boss's attention.

We hear about the occasional success story, of course, but we hear about them because they're so rare, not because they're the norm. A few years back, *The New York Times* estimated the odds against publication of an unsolicited manuscript at fifteen thousand to one, which would mean that two or three unsolicited manuscripts would actually make it to publication in a given year.

We recommend that you don't make over-the-transom submissions. There's a better way, a query process that can actually get the agent or editor to *ask* for your manuscript. You'll learn about that in Chapter Four.

2. Direct Referral. Sure, a nice introductory letter from your pal Stephen King wouldn't hurt your chances of getting your manuscript read one bit. An endorsement from an author you met at a writers conference or took a workshop from might help get your project onto the editor's desk, especially if the editor knows and respects that writer's work. While we attend conferences and workshops to learn our craft and become better marketers, we also go to meet the right people.

However, solid endorsements are hard to come by, and many published authors have stopped reading beginners' manuscripts altogether.

3. Approaching an Editor. Instead of sending a manuscript, market-savvy writers send a query letter first. In later chapters we'll lay out the elements of a successful approach—query letter, synopsis, chapter outline, sample chapters, and cover letters—and teach you how to create a winning submission.

The purpose of the query letter—your initial approach—is to get the editor to ask for the rest of the manuscript. That way, the manuscript bypasses the deadly slush pile and goes directly to the editor for evaluation.

4. Approaching an Agent. Best-selling author John Grisham says, "Having an agent is the difference between being published and not being published."

If you want to have a chance with a major publisher, you need to get an agent to represent you and your work. You'll need to send them the same sort of submission package you'd send to an editor. We cover this in full in the chapters in Part Two.

Find Somebody to Love Your Novel

"I'm the poster boy for your hope."
—GUS LEE, AUTHOR OF *CHINA BOY*

He graduated from West Point, went to law school, served as a paratrooper and a JAG officer, and became a district attorney.

Then Gus Lee became a best-selling author.

When his daughter was seven, Lee tried to write a memoir of his childhood for her. His mother had died when he was five years old, leaving Lee to cope with an abusive stepmother, an angry father, and a tough minority neighborhood in San Francisco.

The story poured out of him. "I couldn't violate the truth," he says, even if it meant exposing the family's weaknesses.

Worrying that he would bring shame to his family, he changed the names and some of the details and called his book a novel. His friend Bill Wood urged him to try to get the book published, so he sent it to a top literary agent, Jane Dystel, who gave it to an intern named Marian Goderich, along with a lot of other "slush."

Goderich knew she was expected to reject Lee, along with the other unknowns, but twice she insisted that her boss read the manuscript, risking her job in the process. Dystel finally read it, loved it, and submitted it to three top publishing houses, provoking a bidding war.

Goderich became a vice president at the agency, and *China Boy* became a best-seller.

WHAT TO LOOK FOR IN AGENTS AND PUBLISHERS

To begin with, focus on agents or publishers who handle the kind of book you've written. It sounds obvious, but many new writers overlook this. Mistargeting your submissions is a waste of everyone's time and your postage. Sending fiction to a house that publishes only nonfiction or submitting your historical romance to an agent who handles only contemporary mainstream won't bring you any closer to publication.

Agent George Nicholson of Sterling Lord Literistic says, "I'm bothered by writers who don't do their homework and writers who don't really know what an agent can and cannot do for them. I have to do a lot of homework to know where to submit manuscripts for the writer. Knowing the reputation of the agent or agency and what they require in the way of submissions is part of the homework a writer must do before even submitting to an agent. Too often the writer doesn't research who to submit to and very often sends material to the wrong people."

THE IDEAL EDITOR

John Cheever once said, "My definition of a good editor is a man I think charming who sends me large checks; praises my work, my physical beauty, and my sexual prowess; and who has a stranglehold on the publisher and the bank."

So much for wish lists. But there is one item on Cheever's list that merits serious consideration. Your editor (as well as your agent) should definitely believe in your book. While lavish praise might not always be forthcoming, tepid levels of enthusiasm won't generate a book contract.

When your book is accepted for publication, you'll probably have to make revisions. You want an editor who has insight into your work, the ability to make constructive suggestions, and an understanding of what sells and what doesn't. Then you must be flexible and believe in your editor's good judgment.

Maxwell Perkins just may have been the ideal editor. He edited such literary giants as F. Scott Fitzgerald, Ernest Hemingway, Thomas Wolfe, and Ring Lardner. He was known for his ability to help writers through the tough spots, writing long, detailed letters full of suggestions.

THE IDEAL AGENT

What makes a good agent? In addition to handling the type of novel you've written and believing in your work, your agent must share your vision, understand your career goals, and be willing to support them.

You also want an agent who isn't looking for a one-book wonder. Your agent should be prepared to work with you for a career as you produce many marketable novels.

Ideally, your agent should be a member of the Association of Authors' Representatives (AAR). The AAR publishes a Canon of Ethics, and members are expected to adhere to them. One of their tenets is that AAR members are prohibited from charging reading fees. AAR members also don't charge excessive amounts for photocopying, faxing, and other administrative expenses. Legitimate agents make their money selling your work, not from collecting fees from hopeful writers.

If an agent isn't an AAR member, it doesn't mean he or she is unethical. Often new agents haven't applied yet for membership or haven't put in enough time or made enough sales to meet AAR's requirements. And some just aren't joiners, just as some writers don't join writer's associations.

To receive a list of member agents, the AAR Canon of Ethics, and a brochure describing the role of an agent, go to the AAR website at www.aar-online.org or write to them at AAR, P.O. Box 237201, Ansonia Station, New York, NY 10003. You can also make e-mail inquiries at info@aar-online.com.

Checklist for Choosing an Agent

Here's a checklist of what to consider when making your choice of agent.

- ❏ The agent is an AAR member.
- ❏ The agent handles first-time writers (anyone who hasn't published a novel).
- ❏ The agent handles—or even better, specializes in—the type of novel you've written.
- ❏ The agent charges a standard 15 percent commission for domestic sales and does not have any hidden charges and fees.
- ❏ The agent has sold books to established publishers.
- ❏ The agent's contract protects both parties' interests and includes a mutual "escape clause" for ending the relationship without penalty if that should become necessary.
- ❏ The agent will market your manuscript aggressively.
- ❏ The agent is familiar with and skilled in the auction process.
- ❏ The agent agrees to stay in touch with you on a regular basis and doesn't object to your calling occasionally.
- ❏ The agent will send you copies of all rejection letters.
- ❏ The agent will involve you in all phases of negotiations with a publisher and will not accept or reject any offers without consulting you.

- ❏ The agent's client list is not so huge that you will get lost in the crowd.
- ❏ The agent is equipped to handle subsidiary rights, such as movie options, book club deals, foreign rights, and electronic rights.

(Agent/writer contracts are covered in full in Chapter Ten.)

THE TRUTH ABOUT AGENTS

"You have to have an agent to get published," the saying goes, "but you have to be published to get an agent."

Most of us confront this conundrum when we try to publish our novels. Unfortunately, too many believe it and stop trying.

You—yes, undiscovered, unpublished, unknown *you*—really do have a chance. Editors have to produce new titles and discover new writers. They rely on agents to do it. Both get paid to say, "Yes."

Case in point: Nobody had ever heard of Mary Holmes when she set out to publish the manuscript that would become *Wild-Rose*, and she knew nobody in the publishing industry. She looked through a directory, sent her material out, landed an agent, and launched a career that spans two genres and is still going strong.

The majority of literary agents will look at a proposal from a first-time novelist. If they don't, they'll say so in their guidelines and in the directories.

What will induce an agent to take you on as a client? Jane Chelius, who heads her own agency, looks for "wonderful writers whose work I feel personally very enthusiastic about."

Have you already been rejected by an agent? Here are three possible reasons why:

1. You are mistargeting, sending your proposal to the wrong agent.

2. The agent has a full load and isn't able to take on any more clients just now. Having said that, if your query is so compelling that it knocks the agent's socks off, rest assured the agent would make room for you.

3. Your query just isn't compelling enough. It's poorly written or the material it proposes seems flat and unoriginal.

"We have to look for reasons to reject to get through the volume of submissions," Michelle Grajkowski, head of the 3 Seas Literary Agency and Marshall's agent, says. "Don't give us one."

By the time you've finished reading this book, you'll know how to overcome these obstacles. Write with all the skill and passion you can muster. Then you will find someone to love your book as much as you do. It can be done. Nobody was issued an agent at birth, and every novelist was first an unpublished novelist. Keep that in mind and keep submitting.

Agents Are Not the Enemy

BY MARY ELLEN WHITAKER

Mary Ellen Whitaker is a student in Marshall's online class, "How to Publish Your Fiction." Here she describes her initial encounters with agents.

I was sure that the process of submitting my work to agents was bound to be impersonal, painful, and demoralizing—a lesson that I'm pleased to report has proven to be absolutely false. Some writers told me you're lucky if agents even read your letter, let alone your novel. Others spoke in jaded tones about the dreaded "slush pile." I pictured each agent sitting at a desk surrounded by mountains of discarded paper, relishing the opportunity to add one more piece—mine.

Finally, despite everything I'd heard, I decided to take a deep breath and send out some query letters. Then I prepared to wait. Most agents don't promise a response before six to eight weeks after receiving a query, so I mailed over forty letters one January morning and then stopped thinking about them. I was quite surprised when I started getting responses the next week. I was even more surprised by their content.

Almost all of the responses were rejection letters, to be sure. But where were the cold, impersonal letters I was expecting? Where were the nasty remarks about my talent? Where were the recommendations that I find another hobby?

The form letters I received were in the minority, and even those were perfectly professional and cordial. Several agents took the time to write a personal note. One agent told me, "I want you to know I had a hard time saying no to your book."

After several weeks, I'd gotten back almost every SASE I'd enclosed with my queries. Finally, one Saturday, the last one arrived in the mail. I opened it as I was paying bills, giving it no more than a perfunctory once-over, when my eyes widened at a sentence I hadn't seen in any of my previous rejection letters. "I would be happy," the agent wrote, "to read the first three chapters or the first fifty pages of your manuscript."

No happier than I would be, of course! As I write this, that agent has my manuscript. I no longer fear her response. Whether it's an acceptance or a rejection, I'm sure it will be articulate and professional and tactful. You see, I've learned another very important lesson about being a writer: Agents are not the enemy.

HOW TO SPOT THE SCAMS

After mailing out your query letters, you receive a reply saying, "Your book project sounds like it might very well work for us. Send your manuscript along with a $50 (or $75 or $100 or $150 or more) reading fee." What should you do?

Toss the letter, and get your query out to other agents.

After submitting your manuscript, you receive a reply saying, "Your work shows great potential. I'd love to represent you, but you need to send $350 (or $500 or $1,000 or more!) to whip it into shape." What should you do?

Toss the letter, and get your query out to other agents.

You receive a letter that says, "Your book shows great potential but needs a professional's touch. I suggest you contact and work with the following book doctor, then send it back to us." The same day you get an e-mail from that same book doctor, assuring you that his $2,000 (or $4,000 or higher) fee can be easily charged to your credit card. What should you do?

That's right. Toss the letter, delete the e-mail, and get your query out to other agents.

Most agents and editors are honest, decent people, just as most writers are. But unfortunately, you'll find unscrupulous people in every profession. An unethical agent or editor can leave you no closer to publication but a lot lighter in the wallet.

Keep sending your query out until you find an agent who will represent you in good faith—one who makes money by negotiating a publishing contract for you, not by picking your pocket.

And keep an eye out for the following scams:

Reading Fee Scams

Some agents charge big reading fees–hundreds and even thousands of dollars–before they'll even open the envelope to read your proposal. Many of these agents make all or a substantial portion of their income from these fees.

We should note that many legitimate agents now charge modest reading or handling fees. This reflects the volume of submissions they're receiving. However, there are so many agents who don't charge any reading fees and as members of AAR are forbidden to do so.

We suggest you avoid paying even a small fee. Legitimate agents–the ones who make their money by taking a reasonable percentage of the money they earn for you (15 percent is the going rate these days)–do their job with no reading fees or other hidden charges.

Hidden Costs Scams

What are some of those hidden charges? Postage, faxes, messenger services, phone calls, and other related expenses. Basically, these agents expect you to pay for their cost of doing business.

You can expect to pay reasonable photocopying charges or else provide the agent with copies of your manuscript. Some agents charge no fee up front but cover copying costs out of any advance they negotiate for you. And if they never make a sale for you? "We simply eat the charges," says agent Kathleen Anderson, formerly of the Scovil, Chichak, Galen Literary Agency.

Here are two examples to illustrate the point.

When Blythe taught an online course called "How to Approach Editors and Agents," one of her students unwisely queried and subsequently signed on with a non-AAR agent. He came to Blythe for help when after six weeks he was given a bill for $900. The promised bidding war for his novel never materialized; in fact, it's unclear if this agent ever did anything on the writer's behalf. Blythe interceded and was hit with a verbal attack that would make even a political operative blush, but the bill was eventually torn up, and the writer and "agent" went their separate ways.

In contrast, Blythe worked with Nancy Yost of Lowenstein-Yost Associates, an AAR agency, for more than four years. During that time the agency made and sent out a huge number of photocopies of manuscripts and proposals for several book projects. They also logged many phone calls and faxes, some overseas. Blythe didn't receive a bill until a movie option sold, and then the expenses–a very low amount–were deducted from her earnings.

Hard-Sell Book-Doctoring Scams

Not every agent who recommends that you seek the services of a professional editor or "book doctor" is a scammer. Far from it. The agent could be sincerely interested in your project but doesn't think it meets publication standards yet. "Get help," she'll tell you. "Come back when you're ready." That's perfectly legit.

But some scammer "agents" actually earn a commission from the book doctor for every manuscript they refer. In less polite circles, such commissions are called kickbacks, and they're considered sleazy, if not downright illegal. In fact, the attorneys general of New York State shut down one such operation a few years ago and made them pay millions of dollars in fees back to writers. But beware: The same scammers are back in business under another name.

Soft-Sell Book-Doctoring Scams

One subtle version of the book-doctoring scam can come after an "agent" has enthusiastically accepted your work and tells you he has sent it out. Several months can go by, and then you receive a call or letter saying that the "agent" has been unsuccessful at marketing your work. The feedback suggests that your project is still "viable," but only if you get a "professional's touch." These "agents" will never produce copies of those rejection letters, instead claiming that the communications regarding your manuscript were all conducted by phone.

The "agent" will then volunteer to "fix" your manuscript for a fee. An inexperienced writer, hooked into the notion that a sale is still possible, might fall for this scam. Don't be that writer.

These scams are really a rotten deal. Those who fall for them and spend big dollars to have their manuscript edited get it back with no guarantee that the "agent" will look at it, much less agree to represent it.

Again, a referral to a book editor isn't necessarily proof of bad intentions. But it might be. Be wary.

Publishing Contract Scams

Usually getting a contract in the mail from a publisher is cause for celebration—but not always. Sometimes a subsidy publisher will masquerade as a legitimate commercial house, making no mention of money until you get to the clause buried deep in the contract that spells out the payment schedule—the dates when you must pay them to publish your book! Several of these "houses" have been under investigation for fraud and other charges.

"I Hear You're Looking for an Agent" Scams

A member of Fiction Writer's Connection, the membership association of which Blythe is director, received the following letter:

> "I heard you were looking for a literary agent. I specialize in new and un-published authors, and I would be interested in taking a look at your novel. Please send only the first three chapters and a brief synopsis. The material will be considered immediately, and you will hear from us within three weeks of its receipt. Please include an SASE. If we see promise in your work, we will ask to see the rest of the manuscript. Our agency commission is a standard ten percent. A list of my personal credentials is included. I look forward to hearing from you."

The reply to the writer's sample said that it showed "considerable promise" and asked her to enclose a check for ninety-five dollars with her manuscript. "The ninety-five dollars will be reimbursed after the sale of the manuscript to a publisher."

Agents who solicit your submissions frequently advertise in writing magazines and rent lists of subscribers for their mailings. Many of these agents solicit manuscripts simply so they can charge reading fees or refer writers to book doctors and "earn" their "commissions." They make their living off fees from writers.

Successful, non-fee-charging agents don't have to solicit clients. They don't do mailings, and they don't advertise.

Agent Referral Scams

Some enterprising folks are now charging writers to give them information they could easily find themselves.

They promise to save you hours of time by tailoring a list of "referred agents" who will be perfect for your project. After you describe your book to them, they send the "referrals"–a boilerplate list of agents culled from the same annotated directories the writer can also access.

For example, if you tell these scammers you have a "historical romance" and that you're a first-time novelist, they'll knock out a list of agents who have noted "historical romance" as one of their specialties and have expressed willingness to look at queries from first-timers.

Then they e-mail your query with their referral to the agents on the list.

It's bad enough that you've wasted your money. You've probably also ruined your novel's chances of succeeding with those agents. They're being inundated with "referred" submissions from these folks, and they've quickly learned to shoot them down on sight.

"I don't know who these people are," agent Russell Galen says. "All I can tell you is that a hell of a lot of mediocre stuff comes to me via that referral, so as soon as I see it in the subject line, I delete it without reading."

"Even if it were a division of Harvard University," he continues, "you don't want to let them send out a generic subject line on your query. If I got twenty e-mails a week that said, 'referred by Harvard University,' I would soon learn to delete all such e-mails unread, too."

You might as well be sending your precious query under the heading: "This is spam—don't bother reading."

So, how can you tell the good ones from the bad? By their fruits shall ye know them. Good agents get contracts for their clients. They make their income by taking a percentage of what they earn for those clients.

When you encounter writers who have agents, ask them about their experiences. Many publications for writers, including Blythe's newsletter, *Tidbits*, and Marshall's quarterly newsletter, *Creativity Connection*, issue warnings that list scammers by name. Stay vigilant, and if you have a bad experience, report it to as many groups and publications as you can.

When in doubt, you can ask us. We'd be glad to hear from you via e-mail. Our e-mail addresses are listed in the appendix.

Use common sense to ferret out the bad guys from the good. If you target only AAR agents, you won't have to worry about this. And always keep in mind that agents earn money by selling your manuscript to publishers, and publishers earn money by selling your book to readers, and neither of them charges the writer for doing it.

WHAT AGENTS DO FOR YOU

Agents, in essence, do the first round of selection for editors. They help screen out the weak submissions. Good agents match projects with prospective publishers, saving the editors from having to wade through material that isn't right for them. A good agent earns an editor's confidence, so that his submissions get attention.

Agents know which editor at a given house is most likely to give you a receptive reading. Marshall's second agent, Marian Young, decided to send his novel to Charles Scribner's Sons first for an exclusive look. Why? The protagonist was a convert to Catholicism and so was Charles Scribner, Jr. She figured he might give it a more sympathetic reading.

That's the sort of thing that good agents know.

"What they do is sell books, negotiate contracts, and support the writer," says author Gail Gaymer Martin, who has published with Steeple Hill, Harlequin/Silhouette, and Barbour.

"Look at the list of things an agent does," advises agent Lori Perkins, "and tell me you have the time, ability, or inclination to handle it all and won't make mistakes that may set back your career in ways you can't even imagine. Or let me put it to you another way: Only a fool has himself for a client."

Your agent will do a lot more for you than simply seek publication. Among the services a good agent performs, Perkins lists:

- sends your work to the right people

- chooses the right publisher

- negotiates the terms of your contract

- represents film, foreign, and subsidiary rights

- makes sure the publisher keeps you informed on the book's progress

- helps prepare your next project for submission

- keeps on top of financial and legal aspects of your book after publication

"Many agents are willing to handle only part of your submissions," notes Martin. "For example, you might write short stories, church plays, novellas, and long fiction. Part of your contract with an agent will be to handle only your long fiction." Some agents may offer editorial guidance, advise you about marketing trends and practices, and help you manage your writing career.

"We provide editorial support as writers work to ready a project for submission," notes Elizabeth Wales of Wales Literary Agency. "We provide whatever career support we can as we work with clients. We are a hands-on and high communication agency."

With an agent like Wales, "career support" means that your knowledgeable advocate will essentially manage your writing career with you, offering guidance on future projects, advising you on other areas or genres to explore, and even helping you with financial management.

"Looking for an agent is exhausting," Martin concludes, "but once you have representation, getting doors to open is easier."

Okay, you're convinced. You need an agent if you want a shot at getting your manuscript to the big publishers. But you also need to be aware of what an agent probably won't do for you.

How to Recognize a "Podunk Agent"

Having what Bantam Books editor Wendy McCurdy calls an "absolutely lousy, Podunk agent" can really hurt a writer. McCurdy says, "A Podunk agent is somebody from the hinterlands who hardly handles anybody but is just doing this as a hobby. Some just hang out a shingle; there's no licensing, and anyone can call himself an agent and suddenly start deluging editors with faded photocopies and bad manuscripts. [Publishers] get a bunch of junk from them, and it's a shame if you're a good writer, because I'm going to have a lot of [negative] assumptions about that manuscript right away."

Agents are supposed to work for you to sell your book, not just to take your money. "There are some reputable agents who charge reading fees, but, in general, people don't approve of that," McCurdy says. "You have to be suspicious, especially if it's exorbitant. No one should ever have to pay five or six hundred dollars to go through this process. I know there are agents who make all their money simply on charging large fees; they never publish anybody, they just make their money off of gullible people. They go through the motions, but they're not really agents."

And if you're a beginning writer, you might find you can't trust a shady agent's opinion of your work. Usually, having an agent take you on validates you, tells you you're good enough to approach publishers. But what if you're not really at that point? A new writer might not have enough experience to judge his or her own work. An agent may take on a new writer, even if there is little chance he can sell the book, knowing he can make money on fees and hidden costs. It can be crushing to find out that your agent has ulterior motives.

"You're better off on your own than to have an agent who is not reputable," McCurdy says. "Warning signs are that no one's ever heard of him or her, or he doesn't have a list of published authors." (Don't be afraid to ask for that list.)

If you're in doubt about an agent, call the editors on the reference list the agent gives you. McCurdy says she's had a few calls from writers on that subject. "One agent had put my name on his list, and a writer called to see if I had, indeed, bought anything from him. He also asked me if I thought it was okay that the agent was charging him five hundred dollars. I had the opportunity to say, 'No, it's not okay.' I might have bought something from him in the past, but I don't now. However, I haven't had a call from a writer about that particular agent for a while. I must have been taken off the reference list."

Writers are not the only people who are hurt by shady agents. Editors find them a real nuisance, taking up their time with substandard or unprofessional manuscripts.

"There's no rhyme or reason for what they're sending me," McCurdy says. "There are certain agents that if I get a submission from them, it goes right in the trash can. I don't even respond."

Another way to find a good agent is through word of mouth. "You should have heard about him and have no doubt as to his credibility," McCurdy says. "You should find other authors who have been represented by him or thanked him in the acknowledgments of their books, that sort of thing."

WHAT AGENTS WON'T DO FOR YOU

Many new writers operate under the faulty assumption that an editor's or agent's main role is to get manuscripts ready for the marketplace. These writers figure they just have to get the basic story down on paper and leave the rest–grammar, punctuation, writing style, and more–to the publishing professionals. This couldn't be further from the truth. That attitude prevents many newcomers from ever seeing their work in print.

"Most agents do not critique or line edit your work," Gail Gaymer Martin says, "although they may make suggestions as to what will work and what won't and ask for early revisions."

Agent Pesha Rubinstein acknowledges that she can't critique the manuscripts that come across her desk. "It's impossible with the volume I'm working with," she says. "I don't charge a reading fee, mainly because I don't want to spend my time critiquing when I'm really just looking for clients. If you want to learn how to write, you have to keep on doing it. Go to writers' groups, which can be wonderful; attend conferences and seminars. There are going to be a lot of false starts; you just have to keep writing."

It's important to realize that agents aren't primarily employed as writing teachers or editors. Their primary job is to sell your work to a publisher. They want to see a finished product ready to send out.

But once an agent sees potential in you, many will work with you to shape your concept and your manuscript–as well as future manuscripts–to make sure you have the best possible chance in the marketplace. Most agents want to represent career writers and will go the extra mile to help get you there. But you must be very close to the mark when you first start approaching agents. They'll help to move you further down the path, but won't be able to or want to push you the whole way.

WHERE TO LOOK FOR EDITORS OR AGENTS

Creating a salable product is only half the process; knowing how and where to market your work is the other half. Set aside a chunk of time to devote to your research. This is not something you can rush through. There are several avenues to pursue in your search for an editor or agent. Successful writers know how to take advantage of all of them.

Covered in this chapter are writers conferences, market guides, trade journals and newsletters, books by other writers, and the Internet. You will find additional resources in the appendix. Use as many of these resources as you can to give yourself the best advantage for finding what you need.

WRITERS CONFERENCES

"Meeting an agent at a conference is the best way," author Gail Gaymer Martin says. We agree.

Once you become involved in the world of writing, you hear about local, regional, state, and national writers' conferences. They're listed in magazines and newsletters such as *Writer's Digest* magazine and *Creativity Connection*. (See the appendix for more information.) You'll also find postings on public library bulletin boards and online.

There are conferences for mystery writers, romance writers, science fiction writers, and children's writers. There are some that many writers have heard of: Bouchercon, Worldcon, Maui Writers Conference, Moonlight & Magnolias, the Santa Barbara Writers Conference, and the Writers' Institute in Madison. Others are known only locally or within the state.

But with so many conferences, how do you judge if it's a good one to attend? Take a close look at the speaker list, the services offered, the topics covered, and the fees charged.

Do the Speakers Know Their Stuff?

Good conferences attract good speakers. You should be familiar with some of the names of agents, editors, and published writers on the list. You might not recognize all the names, but you should be familiar with the publishing houses or writers the agents represent.

Marshall helps put on the annual Writers' Institute, hosted by the University of Wisconsin-Madison Division of Continuing Studies. This conference attracts writers such as Elmore Leonard, Alexs Pate, Chitra Divakaruni, Gus Lee, and word-maven Richard Lederer. When you see folks like this on the guest list, you know you'll be getting good information from published pros.

If your primary reason for attending is a chance to meet agents and editors face-to-face, make sure the bios listed in the registration material reveal interests and specialties that mesh with your own.

Will You Get the Services You Need?

Again, if the most important service you're interested in is the opportunity to meet with editors and agents, make sure the conference has arrangements for these face-to-face meetings. During these editor/agent appointments, you'll get a chance to pitch your project. We cover in detail how to pitch to an agent or editor in Chapter Five.

Most conferences will set up appointments for you in advance or allow you to sign up on the spot. At a good conference you shouldn't have to worry about grabbing an editor or agent in the hall (although that can work, too).

Some conferences give you the opportunity to have an agent critique your partial manuscript. Fees for this service vary widely.

Many conferences also offer contests, with the winners usually announced there. The Writers' Institute conducts a popular "poem or page" contest, for example. Winning a contest like that means your name will come to the attention of the editors and agents attending the conference.

Do the Topics Offered Match Your Needs?

To get the most out of a conference, especially if you're a new writer, you want to make sure that the conference covers topics that suit your needs and interests. If you write mysteries, going to a conference for romance writers might not be helpful.

But don't rule out the possibility. The agents and editors who attend writing conferences often handle a variety of genres. Check out the bios. You might find that the agent who represents romance writers is also enthusiastic about mysteries, horror, and science fiction.

In addition, at the romance writers conference, though you might find the majority of workshop topics geared toward the romance genre, you'll probably find topics that apply to your writing. Conferences usually cover general topics such as point of view, plotting, dialogue, and description.

Can You Handle the Price Tag?

You obviously need to consider cost when choosing a conference. For a three-day conference, fees often range from two hundred to four hundred dollars, but some may be a lot more. Registration fees don't include transportation, food, or lodging either (although many offer a meal or meals as part of the festivities).

Additional services, such as manuscript critiquing, are usually extra. Some conferences charge extra for appointments with editors and agents. Some have special events such as banquets and public readings that may or may not be included in your registration. Read the specifications carefully to determine what you're getting for your dollar.

Attending a conference can be expensive, but the return on this investment in your writing career can be well worth it.

What to Do When You Get There

Plan to arrive early to check into your room and drop off your bags. Then find your conference registration booth, sign in, and pick up your welcome materials, which should include a printed schedule of events and locations. This is also the time to make sure your appointments with agents or editors have been confirmed.

Pressing the Flesh

With the preliminaries out of the way, it's time to put on your best smile and start meeting people. Networking is one of the biggest benefits of attending a conference. Most writers work alone, while many get very little emotional support from family and friends. At a conference, you'll be among kindred spirits, folks like you who understand how difficult, how important, and how wonderful writing stories can be. It's also a chance to gossip about agents, get referrals, and arrange for introductions.

The whole experience can be very stimulating. In a one-day seminar Blythe organized, she was in the hall when an attendee came running out. The young woman shouted her apologies, then took off toward the exit. Blythe chased after her to ask what was wrong. Out of breath, the woman managed to tell her that the speaker was so motivating, she wanted to hurry back to her novel-in-progress. Blythe managed to calm her down and talk her into staying for the rest of the day. She wanted to make sure the eager woman got her money's worth. The woman felt she most certainly had.

Former editor Michael Seidman says, "The key is networking, whether it is through classes or attending conferences or whatever works for you. If you meet an agent or an editor, you've got a leg up."

How to Be a Model Conference Attendee

Get to workshops early, sit up close, and take good notes. If a speaker or panel initially disappoints you, listen intently anyway for that one gem of information that can make a huge difference in your writing career.

Don't be shy about asking questions. Most of us learned to be good bluffers in school, appearing to understand what the teacher was saying even when we didn't have a clue. Don't revert to old classroom behaviors. If you don't understand a point, it's a good bet that half the other folks in the workshop don't either. Raise your hand at the appropriate time and fire away.

But save questions about your particular writing projects for those individual appointments or at breaks or at day's end.

After the Conference Is Over

You're back home, excited and exhausted. You want to get back to your writing, and you need to tackle all the tasks that piled up while you were gone. But don't wait to follow up on the contacts you made at the conference. You might have thank-you letters to write, sample chapters to send out, meetings to arrange, seminar material to read, and tapes to listen to. Try to get to it right away, while your enthusiasm is still high and the material is fresh in your mind.

Finally, don't start planning your next conference trip too soon. If you find yourself spending more time at conferences than at your computer, something is wrong. At one seminar that Blythe organized, speaker and successful mystery writer David Kaufelt got up to the podium, looked out over the crowd, and said, "What are you all doing here? You should be home writing." He had a point.

Ten Tips for Attending Seminars and Conferences

1. Take plenty of business cards with you to exchange with other writers and speakers. When you get your cards printed up, avoid putting *writer* or *author* next to your name (it's viewed as pretentious), unless you are a professional freelancer looking for work.

2. Make a brief note on the back of each business card you receive as a memory jogger for later. After a full day or two of meeting new people, you might not be able to connect the name with the conversation you had.

3. Make an effort to introduce yourself to at least five new people. Most people attend conferences on their own and probably feel as shy and awkward as you do. You obviously have something in common—your love of writing—so for a good icebreaker you can ask about the other person's specialty or area of interest.

4. Take a folder or tote bag with you to organize all the handouts you'll receive. Don't forget a notebook.

5. Pace yourself. Attend the sessions that interest you the most, but don't try to cram everything in. A chat with a new acquaintance over a cup of coffee in the lounge can be as informative as a string of seminar sessions.

6. Ask permission before tape-recording any of the sessions. You might be infringing upon prior arrangements between the conference organizers and a commercial outfit taping the sessions for sale of tapes later.

7. Wear comfortable shoes! You will be on your feet a lot. Dress comfortably, but appropriately. Writers' conferences are not formal affairs, but you will be meeting agents and editors in a professional capacity, and you want to make a good impression.

8. If you've signed up for an agent/editor appointment, be on time and come prepared. Have your pitch ready and your questions written out in advance.

9. Follow through on the contacts you made. Pick up the phone or write a letter or an e-mail. The networking opportunities conferences offer are as important as the sessions.

10. Do not burn any bridges. You would be surprised how many writers break that golden rule. There are always stories circulating. (A writer lost a contest, then verbally attacked the judge in the rest room. An agent was not interested in the writer's manuscript, so the writer began berating her for her lack of intelligence and foresight.) The writing community is small. You don't want to become known for your lack of professionalism.

MARKET GUIDES

No agent, editor, or writer can attend every conference. Published directories, such as *Guide to Literary Agents*, are the next best way to locate potential agents and editors. We've listed quite a few of the current market guides and directories in the appendix.

TRADE JOURNALS AND NEWSLETTERS

Writer's Digest magazine, *The Writer, FWC's Tidbits, Creativity Connection, ByLine Magazine*, and scores of other periodicals provide help in locating agents and editors. Whether through direct interviews or quotes in articles, these publishing professionals share advice and tips and will give you plenty of ideas.

Publishers Weekly, another industry bible, is fairly expensive but may be available in the reference section of your library. Here you'll find news of publishing trends, interviews, new books, hot deals, the *Publishers Weekly* best-seller list, and tons of helpful marketing and writing information. *Publishers Weekly* also maintains a Web site with some free information and information available by subscription. Visit them at www.publishersweekly.com.

OTHER WRITERS' BOOKS

When you discover a novel you enjoy (and perhaps even wish you'd written), be sure to read the dedication and acknowledgment pages, where the author is likely to express heartfelt thanks to a dedicated agent and a talented editor.

Wouldn't it be wonderful if you could have that same team working on your behalf? Maybe you can.

Chances are the book you're reading is similar in genre to yours. We tend to read what we like to write and vice versa. Add the names of those editors and agents to your contact lists. When you send your query letter to these folks—which you'll learn how to do in the next chapter—be sure to mention that you're writing to them because of your admiration for the novel in which you found their names. Approaching people you've found on an acknowledgments page is much better than hunting blindly through a directory.

If your favorite author doesn't mention his or her agent (a fairly major faux pas these days), call the publisher and ask. There are two departments likely to give you that information—public relations (PR) and contracts. Both keep records of each author's representative.

THE INTERNET

The Internet is a marvelous source of publishing information. All major houses and most of the small ones have Web sites and online catalogs. Many post guidelines for writers who want to submit. These guidelines typically provide word count requirements; plot dos and don'ts; and theme expectations (what they're looking for and what they hope never to see again).

Most literary agencies also maintain Web sites with guidelines for writers, including submission directions. Some writers' associations post databases of participating editors and agents open to new writers. Be careful, though, of the referral scammers mentioned on page 53. Don't pay for the same information you can get for free at the AAR Web site.

If you don't know a particular Web site address, you can probably find it quickly using an online search engine such as Google (www.google.com). Most writers these days are comfortable with cybersurfing, but even if you're new to this, you can complete this sort of search in under a minute.

You can also type in keywords, such as "literary agents" or "writers' associations," to uncover hundreds of potential sources of information. Also, try *Writer's Digest*'s informative Web site (www.writersdigest.com).

Use caution in cyberspace. Scammer publishers and agents have also discovered the Internet and are preying on writers who have money to spend. Remember that successful agents don't need to solicit new clients.

You'll find many legitimate offers online, of course, and cyberclasses can be a great, inexpensive way to "attend" a writers conference without ever leaving home. See the appendix for more information on Web sites for e-mail and online courses and other resources for writers.

Attending conferences, studying the market guides and trade publications, or surfing the Internet are great ways to find the right agent or editor for your novel. Once you've identified the ones you want to query, you need to turn your attention to how to approach them. The next chapter is the place to start.

Chapter Four: The All-Important Query Letter

"... say what you've got to say, and say it hot."

—D.H. LAWRENCE

When meeting new people, a bad first impression can often be turned around as we get to know the person better. But in approaching an editor or agent, you get only one chance to make that good impression and a strong query letter will help you do that.

The query letter is your calling card, the first step in approaching editors and agents, and the impression your letter makes will determine how much further you can go with that person. Simply put, the query letter is a very important piece of writing.

WHAT AGENTS AND EDITORS LOOK FOR IN A QUERY

Elisa Wares, senior editor at Ballantine Books, says, "A well-written query letter is really the unsolicited writer's best foot in the door. You want to sell yourself as well as the idea of your book. A long, involved description of the work to follow is not necessary. The letter should be entertaining, intriguing, and informative. You want the editor to read on, not stop with the initial letter. I must admit that if an author bores me in the letter, I will not read his or her submission. It sounds unfair, but writers have no idea how many queries and manuscripts editors get every day. An author has just a few minutes to catch somebody's attention."

Agent Evan Marshall would like to see a query letter describing the project and giving whatever background is appropriate. "I'm most likely to ask to see the manuscript if the letter is professional, moderate in tone, and not full of the hype I get in a lot of query letters," he says. "Most are amateurish and I never ask to see the books by those people. Some of the things they do to try to impress me are so silly. 'SEX! Okay, now that I've got your attention, here's the hottest book.' It just won't work."

Michael Seidman, former Walker and Company editor, says, "In query letters I look for calm professionalism. I want to know what the book is, who you are if that's pertinent, the length, and that's about it. Hype is beside the point; telling me my business is beside the point. So is a record of all the friends who loved your work. The best way to get my attention is to write better than anyone else, to know and understand not only my guidelines, but my editorial philosophies as expressed in the titles we release."

Literary agent/publishing law attorney Jeff Kleinman likes to see the same level of professionalism in a query as in a job application.

And agent Anne Hawkins believes, "The two important things in a query are concept and the ability to write. The funniest query I have ever seen started: 'I'm not so good at expressing myself in words, but . . .'" And that's not the kind of funny that will impress an agent or editor.

DEFINITION OF A QUERY LETTER

A query letter is a mini-proposal that aims to:
- hook the attention of the editor or agent
- describe your project
- tell the editor or agent who you are
- get the editor or agent to ask for more

The most effective query is a straightforward, polished one-page letter. It describes your novel's plot and main characters, focusing on the elements that are most intriguing or compelling, and it lists your relevant credentials and publishing credits, if any. If you've hit the mark, it will merit you a letter, phone call, or e-mail asking to see the manuscript.

JUST A QUERY LETTER?

"But how can I get interest in my novel based on a one-page letter?" you might be wondering. "Wouldn't it be best to send a synopsis, too, and sample chapters? Some of the agents and editors in the market guidebooks say they want to see the whole thing. Why bother with the query letter at all? Can't I just send in the manuscript?"

In spite of what a market listing might say, sending a one-page query letter really is the most effective and economical approach. It will get you an initial indication of interest, or lack thereof, and will save you unnecessary printing and postage expenses.

"Query first," says agent Russell Galen. "Usually, if we're interested at that point, we'll want to see the completed manuscript. I don't ever want to see a full outline or sample chapter unless I've asked for them."

Okay, you're convinced now that the query letter is the way to go. But you're probably still resisting the idea of only one page. Why not give them as much information as you can, right up front?

Again, remember you have only a few seconds to grab the attention of editors or agents. Making them plow through a long letter filled with details won't win you any points. The only excuse to write a query letter longer than one page is if you have scores of credits to mention. But then, these can be sent on a separate sheet that lists your publications and bio.

WHO GETS THE QUERY LETTER?

George Bernard Shaw said, "Literature is like any other trade; you will never sell anything unless you go to the right shop."

Send query letters to agents when you're looking for representation, and when you're seeking publication send them to editors. Whether you go it alone or seek the services of an agent, it's important to accurately target the right publishing houses, editors, and agents for your material. Nancy Bereano, former editor at Firebrand Books, says, "Before sending your work out to a particular press, do your homework. Visit bookstores and see other books that press has published; see whether or not your book seems to fit in with what that publishing house has done. Would it be at home there? Ask for a catalog. Most publishers, Firebrand included, give people catalogs for free. Look through the catalog and see whether you think your book belongs with the others there. It's not magic; it's being informed. Knowing as much as you can in advance of submitting helps make a writer feel much more powerful."

WHEN TO SEND THE QUERY LETTER

Rule of thumb: Write the novel first! Yes, it is tempting to want to get those query letters out quickly. Some of you might be thinking, "Why bother writing the novel if a query letter can let me know so easily if there's interest in my topic or not?" While this is the usual procedure with selling nonfiction books (nonfiction projects can often be sold on the basis of a proposal alone), it won't work with novels ... especially novels written by unpublished novelists. We all have to pay our dues and write the book. What guarantee is there that you'll actually be able to deliver what you promise in your query? That's the way agents and editors view it. They all know how much skill and hard work it takes to write a novel. A first-time writer has a lot to learn, and often that first attempt is just part of the learning process.

"Once a query has snagged my interest," says agent Russell Galen, "I ask for, and expect to receive, a completed manuscript. If the writer hasn't previously published a book, such a writer should never query until the manuscript has been completed."

Exception to the Rule

For every rule there is an exception, and publishing is no different. There are some occasions when an agent or editor might ask to see a novel before it's completed. But these occasions generally apply to writers with a track record or a prior relationship with the editor or agent.

Russell Galen says, "More established writers, with at least one book published by a major house, need supply only a portion and outline, or perhaps only an outline. They are actually welcome to approach us in whatever manner is most comfortable, usually a phone call."

If you're already working with an agent, perhaps for a nonfiction project, he or she might be willing to look at a partial manuscript for a novel to offer you guidance and see if you're on the right track.

It could happen for a new novelist, too, usually because of a face-to-face meeting at a writers conference. Although we caution you not to pitch your project until it is finished (see chapter five), once there, it is hard to resist taking advantage of the opportunity for feedback. Some agents and editors will tell you to send your book in when it's done; others will agree to see partial manuscripts. Agent Nancy Yost says she never asks for anything that's not complete "unless it's so fabulous I can't resist."

QUERY LETTER FORMATTING

A query should look like a business letter. Invest in letterhead stationery or design and print your own letterhead, but keep in mind it should look clean and simple.

Although desktop publishing software packages provide decorative borders and clip art, allow you to scan in photographs and intricate line drawings, give you multiple typefaces and options to vary size and even shape of letters, these are features that you, as a writer, shouldn't use.

Instead, use simple, tasteful letterhead stationery that has your name, address, phone number (very important), and your e-mail address. The last two will make it easier for an agent or editor to get in touch with you. Nothing is more frustrating than to read a good query and really want to see that manuscript—and not be able to reach the writer quickly. It's your job to make it easy for them.

The Greeting

In your first correspondence to an editor or agent, do not address him or her by his first name. Wait for a return letter to see how you have been addressed. If you get back a "Dear Joe" or "Dear Jane" letter, you can follow suit. If the reply is more formal, stick to a simple "Mr." or "Ms." "Dear Sirs" and "Gentlemen" have been out of vogue for about twenty years now. If you insist on clinging to tradition, you will annoy the large female workforce in the publishing industry. (See more on letter greetings in chapter eight.)

When addressing your query letter, make sure you include the name (spelled correctly), title (of the person you're addressing, not your book), and address of the editor or agent you're writing. You must address your letter to a specific agent or editor.

Editor Wendy McCurdy says, "There are from eight to ten editors at Bantam who handle fiction, from literary or Westerns to action/adventure to suspense. Although I would forward submissions to the proper editor if they arrived on my desk, that could add another three months to your waiting time. You should call the publisher's switchboard and ask for an editorial assistant who can help find the name of the appropriate editor for you."

Also call the publisher's switchboard if you are using market guides as a source for editors' and agents' names and addresses. Market guides can already be outdated by the time they see print. People change jobs and titles frequently in publishing. Make sure the person you are querying is still in residence.

While you're on the phone, also verify that the agent or editor you are one hundred percent sure is a male really is. We'd be willing to bet that agent Rob Cohen gets very annoyed with the "Dear Mr. Cohen" letters she probably receives every day.

Keep in mind that while creating generic form query letters might save you some time with a multiple mailing, a letter addressed "Dear Agent" or "Dear Editor" is no different than those "Dear Occupant" letters you receive in your mailbox every day. And we all know what happens to those.

Here's another reason to avoid generic letters without a name and address on them. Busy agents and editors often scribble their response right on your letter and stuff that into your SASE. How frustrating to get a "Sure, send it in" and have no idea who is requesting it. Equally important, you also want to know who is turning you down. Unless they're kind enough to sign the note in legible handwriting, you'll be left in the dark.

Paragraph Style

You have two choices when it comes to paragraph style. You can indent each paragraph about five or six spaces and leave no lines between paragraphs (this method allows you a little more room when you have one or two lines you just can't bear to cut to fit the one-page length limit). Or you can use block style, with each paragraph flush left and one line between each paragraph. When you use block style, the date, address, salutation, and closing should all be flush left, too.

You'll see samples of both on pages 88–90.

Closings

Close your letter with "Sincerely," leave a space to sign your name, then make sure you type your name as well.

Finally, don't forget to run your spell check before you print the letter. Then set it aside for at least one day before mailing it. You want the chance to go back and proofread for things the spell check won't catch: *their/there/they're*, and *here/hear*, to name just a few.

SASES

Always remember to include your #10 business-size SASE with your query letter for the editor or agent's response. If you send just a self-addressed stamped post-card (SASP), the editor or agent will not be able to enclose any guidelines they might provide as a matter of course. If you send an envelope smaller than a #10 business size, they'll have to cram their full-size response into it. And if you forget the SASE altogether, you might not get a response at all.

Before you fold the SASE into thirds, turn back the flap so the glued side isn't touching the other surface. Heat conditions in some areas will glue the envelope shut before it reaches its desti-nation, and this can be very annoying for the person on the receiving end.

Agent Susan Zeckendorf stresses the importance of the SASE. "You should always, always enclose a SASE. Unless your ma-terial is particularly captivating, if there's no SASE, it goes into the waste-basket. And don't paper clip the stamps to the envelope. They can get lost that way and it's better if you do the licking yourself." And these days all those self-adhesive stamps make it easier for everyone.

THE ELEMENTS OF A QUERY LETTER

Although there are four main approaches you can take with formulating your query letter (and we will cover all of them), all query letters should contain the follow-ing elements:

• the hook
• the handle

- a mini-synopsis
- your credentials
- your credits
- what you're offering
- the closing

Let's look at each required element individually:

The Hook

Ideally, every novel should have a hook: a special plot detail or unique approach, a twist that grabs the readers' attention and makes them want to read more. It can be something that will make them say, "Ooh" when they hear it (more on eliciting the "ooh factor" in chapter five). A hook is a concept, an intriguing idea that readers would find compelling.

If your novel has that hook, it must be evident in your query letter. If you can't identify the hook, it probably means you didn't build it in when you sat down to write your novel. It could be time to go back to the "plotting board" to rectify matters.

In Blythe's query letter for her novel *Parker's Angel*, she reveals the hook right away: "Unlucky in love, Parker Ann Bell wouldn't recognize an angel if she pulled one back to earth with her ... which is exactly what happens." Ooh.

In that one line we know what to expect from the book: romance and angels. It's a matter of taste if the topic interests you or not, but making your hook clear will help the agent or editor know right away if it's something for him.

The Handle

While the hook grabs the readers (i.e., agents or editors), the handle gives them something to hold onto. In other words, it's something they can use to determine if it's a book project they can sell.

To provide a handle, you can identify your novel's theme (e.g., unrequited love, domestic violence, or race relations) or compare your book to something that's already out there. Agent Nancy Yost wants to learn from your query letter what kind of book it is and see a comparison of your book to similar titles. "The latter piece of information always helps because it tells me they know what's out there and they're current."

Agent Peter Rubie says, "Write what you want to write and how you want to write it. And then sit down at that point and decide, 'How can I make what I have done commercial?'" When you've done that, you've provided a handle.

It could be in part identifying who your audience is. But this is another tricky part. Sometimes the audience is obvious. You don't have to go digging up statistics to tell romance editors that romance readers are female and between the ages of eighteen and ninety-eight. They already know all that. But, if you have written a book with a particular topic or theme that would be of interest to a particular segment of the population, then you should mention it.

Anne Kinsman Fisher is the author of two novels: *The Legend of Tommy Morris* and *The Masters of the Spirit.* She hit the ground running, getting an acceptance within forty-eight hours of contacting an editor. There are two things to which she attributes her success: tailoring the topic for a specific editor and providing that editor with a handle to sell the book.

"It is possible to write your book specifically for an editor so you know that you've got precisely what they want," Fisher says. "An author friend was submitting a golf book and he got rejected by HarperSanFrancisco" (a division of Harper-Collins). "The editor told him, 'Gosh, while I like your book, it's not the spiritual golf novel I've always been looking for.'

"I thought, 'Good golly. An editor who's looking for something.' I came up with an idea based on her words 'spiritual golf novel.'" And she sold it to that editor, too.

But Fisher didn't stop with just coming up with the right topic. She helped give the editor and everyone on the editorial board a handle, so they felt convinced the book would sell in the bookstores.

"I include a special section in my query/proposal on market research," Fisher says. "I tell my editor who will buy the book, specific numbers for the marketplace (e.g., for my book, women golfers are a growing audience). I include relevant articles about the popularity of my genre. I explain which other books are like mine and what they have sold. So, when my editor goes to her editorial meeting, she is prepared. Most writers worry only about getting an editor to like their work. They forget that the book actually needs to sell off the bookstore shelves."

Agent Evan Marshall says, "I really want to hear how the writer feels the book fits the market. I want to know that he has targeted his book for a certain audience, that he's done his homework. I realize that's largely my job, but I think all that has to start with the writer much more than it used to. If they are readers and are writing what they love to read, then chances are they know that the niche exists. Often the easiest way is to compare what they're doing with what's out there–a Mary Higgins Clark-type women-in-jeopardy, for example. Or they could just say they're writing a historical romance or a techno-thriller."

A Mini-Synopsis

In the synopsis part of your query you'll give an overview of your plot and introduce your main characters and their core conflict. Include a few plot high points, make the setting and time period clear, and you're done.

Sound easy?

It isn't. Many successful authors will tell you that writing the novel was a lot easier than composing a query or a synopsis. In chapter seven we cover synopsis writing in depth, and you'll get lots of helpful tips for making the synopsis section of your query letter effective.

In the meantime, just remember not to get too detailed. You can't put a complete blow by blow in two to four paragraphs. On the other hand, don't be so vague that the reader has no idea what you're offering. Hinting doesn't hook interest; it only frustrates readers.

For example, don't say, "Heroine X battles a multitude of problems before she solves the biggest one of all." This sentence includes what we call "empty phrases" and offers no information at all.

Do say, "Heroine X must cope with her husband's abandonment and a crooked judge hell-bent on revenge, before she can be reunited with the child her former husband abducted." This version gives us a much better picture of what your book is about. That's the sole purpose of the query letter's synopsis section.

Your Credentials

The purpose of the credentials section of your query letter is to convey knowledge of your subject matter and to give a little information about yourself.

Give this aspect of your submission some creative thought before you decide you don't have anything to say. No, by "creative" we're not suggesting you make things up (save that for the novel). If you're a lawyer working on a legal thriller, tell them. Been coaching Little League for thirty years? Tell them that, too, but only if your novel concerns Little League.

Agents and editors want to know who you are and how you came to write this novel. Agent Julie Castiglia says, "It annoys me when people don't include any information about themselves. What was the motivation for the book? If they want to write a book about Russia, I want to know why. Why are they qualified? Why are they interested?"

When discussing who you are, it's important not to get carried away. "Do not include your life's story, unless it's pertinent to what you've written," editor Marjorie Braman says.

Credentials could also include membership in writers' organizations, awards or contests won, attendance at writing seminars and workshops, or completion of writing courses. But here's where you need to tread carefully. Some agents and editors don't put much stock in this sort of thing. Former editor Michael Seidman says, "Telling me of the award you won from a contest is beside the point. I've judged too many of them to take them that seriously as validation. I don't think you should mention awards unless they are from professional peer organizations."

Omitting mention of your degree in creative writing might be the safest course too. Some editors and agents will be gratified to hear it. Others will try not to hold it against you.

To help you decide what to include in your credential section, agent Jeff Kleinman suggests you go to your local bookstore or library. "Take down a novel by an author you don't know. What do you immediately do? If you're like me, you'll read the flap copy, and then turn to the back and read what you can about the author. If it's a first novel, it's always helpful if the author's published in other venues or if the author has some kind of unique, interesting background that really makes this novel different. Think of those kinds of things when you're putting together your own résumé. What do you have that will make that reader think, 'Wow, I want to read what this person has to say'?"

Under the credentials section of your query letter you can also mention any access to sources you've had. Almost all fiction projects require some research. The plot may be pure fabrication, but details of setting, for example, had better be dead-on accurate. If your book is set in the Middle East and you lived there for several years, mention that. But if you have no experience in that part of the world, your book's setting will be a harder sell.

No matter what other credentials you have, and even if you can't think of a single relevant scrap of experience that might help you, your best credential, the only one you absolutely must have, is a good query sent to the right person. If you've got this one, you've got a chance. Don't let any supposed deficiency stop you.

Your Credits

If you're a brand-new writer just starting out, you might not have any credits. That's okay. Just don't bring attention to it in a negative way. Don't apologize or even mention it. That's a surefire way of pointing out your amateur status. Michael Seidman says, "If you don't mention any fiction credits in your query letter, I'll assume it is a first novel; that has no bearing on when I read it or how carefully." The recipient of your query letter will figure out that this is your first novel, and most agents and editors won't hold it against you.

Some put more stock in credits, and this could just mean that those aren't the right people for you to be querying. Some agents prefer to look only at potential clients who have a track record with published books to their credit. But any kind of credit, including publication of short stories or nonfiction in national magazines, is a step in the right direction. If you do have the credits that would interest an agent, be sure to mention them right at the beginning of the query letter. Now is the time for a little horn tooting. Don't be shy, but don't be Barnum and Bailey, either. State your truth simply and directly.

Let's look at which credits to include and which might not be worth mentioning—or might even work against you.

Of course, state the obvious. If you have any fiction credits, mention them: "My short stories have appeared in ...", then provide the actual names of the magazines.

Blythe had a student who had a slew of fiction credits, but was embarrassed to mention where they had appeared—in a series of erotica magazines. But there's no reason not to mention those. Look at Anne Rice and the work she has produced under a variety of pen names. Your shyness could read as vagueness, and your vagueness could be translated as stretching the truth or trying to hide the truth. "My short stories have appeared in a variety of magazines ..." would be hard to disprove.

If you have any nonfiction publication credits, say so. "Any writing experience at all is of interest," says agent Jane Chelius.

If all the topics of your published work are irrelevant to your novel, just avoid going into too much detail. It's enough to say you're published. Period.

But if your current work of fiction is set during the Civil War, for example, and you have also published nonfiction pieces on the same topic, then definitely get specific about that.

There might be a few credits not worth mentioning: a letter to the editor of your local newspaper, an essay posted on an online message board, or an article for your high school yearbook, for example.

The point of listing credits is to show you have a track record, that others have found your work acceptable, that you are a professional, and that you have had experience working with editors.

But don't worry if you have no credits to toot your horn about. There are plenty of agents and editors who are more than open to new writers and are always looking for fresh talent. Your writing will speak for itself.

What You're Offering

Make sure you give the title of your book, its word count, and the genre. To do that you'll need to know what category or kind of book you've written.

Basic categories of fiction include (in alphabetical order):

- action/adventure
- children's
- erotic
- espionage
- experimental
- fantasy
- gay/lesbian/bisexual
- historical
- horror
- humor
- inspirational/religious/spiritual
- military
- mystery
- romance
- science fiction
- suspense
- thriller (political/legal/medical)
- Western
- women's
- young adult (YA)

Many of these categories also have subgenres. The broad category of romance, for instance, includes subgenres such as contemporary, sweet, historical, and Regency. Within the thriller category you will find medical, political, techno- and legal thrillers. Mysteries cover a wide range, including cozies, police procedurals, and detective.

If you can't find yourself in any of these categories, you may have a mainstream or literary novel on your hands.

Defining mainstream, though, is no easy task. Agent Kathleen Anderson says mainstream novels are "books people like to read. However, mainstream can also refer to general women's fiction, for example. Mainstream women's fiction generally takes a contemporary subject such as domestic or romantic situations. But, in fact, mainstream is becoming an outdated concept. It really refers to a straightforward narrative with no poetic twists, and that is not finding a large audience these days."

Editor Elisa Wares says, "I dislike the word mainstream because you can't go into a bookstore and find a shelf for a noncategory book. So, I would say mainstream is a book that doesn't fit into a category. Unless it is a best-seller (Grisham or King), a writer should try to find a category that can be shelved. I decide what category my books fall into. If I think it has a greater or 'breakout' audience than a specific genre would have, I will assign it the general term of fiction."

When looking at the difference between category romance and mainstream romance, agent Evan Marshall says, "Category romance deals with slighter issues, and most important, centers completely on the developing romance between the man and the woman. Mainstream romance has many other things going on in the story, other subplots and issues and these issues are bigger, more momentous. It boils down to weightiness of story."

Literary fiction is difficult to define because it relies on the subjective criteria of value. Literature must stand the test of time, but there are clearly modern works that are relevant and complex as well. Literary fiction can usually be identified by the style of writing, the deep tones and textures it contains, and its subject matter, which is often more centered on character than plot and grapples with universal problems. It is usually more complex and literate than mainstream or genre fiction but still appeals to a large audience. In a way, though, to identify a work as literary fiction is a judgment call–a judgment best left to the agents or editors.

If you don't know the genre or if you're just not sure, leave it out. It is not always necessary to state it, especially if there are too many crossovers. (Blythe, for example, says her novel *Parker's Angel* falls into the mainstream/romantic/suspense/comedy/women's fiction genre with a hint of New Age, but she wouldn't tell an agent or editor that.)

In the handle section of your query letter, comparing your book to another author's can be sufficient to categorize it.

What if you have more than one book to offer? Propose only one project in a single query. You can mention that you have other books in the works (if you do), but don't go into too much detail on those in this particular query letter. Save it for later. Especially if the number of other projects you have is daunting. It's a bit unsettling for an agent or editor to read in your query that you've been writing nonstop for the last twenty years and have a closet full of unpublished manuscripts. You've been busy all right, but perhaps you've been busy writing in a vacuum. If all you're doing is writing without submitting your work, you haven't been researching the market or receiving any professional feedback. If an agent takes you on or an editor offers to publish your "first" project, you can always mention your other ones later.

The exception to the one project per query rule is if you're pitching a series. Having a series to offer can actually improve your chances. Most agents and editors are looking for career writers, not one-book wonders. "We want fiction that will appeal to the mass market, and we want writers who want to make a career," says Kensington editor Kate Duffy.

But even so, your query letter should be proposing book one of your series. Sending out a query for book two before book one has been accepted tells agents and editors that the first book didn't fly. "If you are submitting the third novel in a series to me, I'd like to know that there were two before it," notes agent Richard Henshaw. "I'd also like to know what your plans are down the road. I like to handle an author for his or her career, not by the book. If I liked the writing of this particular project but didn't find it commercial enough to take on, a good pitch on the next project might encourage me to ask for a look when it's ready."

If you hadn't thought of writing a series, it's never too late. Could the main character in your mystery novel be a sleuth for several more? Does this character have enough depth and interest to sustain more plots? As you write, keep this in mind. Leave little hints that could lead people to suspect there will be another novel. And in your query letter let the agents and editors know you're in this for the long haul.

The Closing

At the end of the query letter, offer to send the complete manuscript for a novel. Do not offer a choice of sample chapters or the complete manuscript. Offer only the completed manuscript. (You shouldn't be querying if your manuscript isn't complete.) If your query letter inspired them to ask to see your work, they will tell you what to send–sample chapters or the complete manuscript and a synopsis.

You'll find information on how to prepare your submission packet in part two of this book.

In closing your letter, less is more. Simply say, "May I send you the complete manuscript?" If you haven't made the title, genre, and word count clear earlier, you can say instead, "May I send you my completed 100,000-word mainstream novel?"

Titles, by the way, should be typed in italics in your query letters. Don't use quotation marks or all caps.

There is no need to thank the editors and agents for their time and consideration or tell them you'll wait for their response or that you eagerly look forward to hearing from them. They know that, and such sentiments just take up room.

While not crucial to your query, include the reason for selecting the editor or agent along with referrals and endorsements if they are available. Here is an explanation for each.

Reasons for Selecting an Editor or Agent

The process of selection seems pretty one-sided at this point. You're approaching the gatekeeper, submission in hand, seeking admission into the select company of the published novelists.

But you had some reason for approaching this particular gatekeeper. It may help you to tell him or her what it is. A good reason may indicate a great deal about your preparation and professionalism. If you have trouble coming up with a good reason, think back to the process when you first went through lists of agents and publishers trying to find a good home for your masterpiece.

Bad reasons include:

- "You were one of the first ten agents, alphabetically, in the directory I used."
- "I've already approached 473 agents, and I finally got to you."
- "Your name came up in an online database I had to pay to use."
- "My mother's maiden name is the same as yours, and I thought that might be lucky."

Good reasons include:

- A book you believe has special merit was represented by the agent or edited by the editor you're approaching.
- The agent or editor handled a book that you believe has notable similarities to your project.

Referrals

Many agents aren't open to new clients unless someone the agents know referred them. Even if an agent is open to new writers, a referral can work wonders. Through all your networking at conferences, you may have met a lot of other writers by now. If one suggests you contact her agent, then by all means mention that up front in your query letter.

Even if you approach editors directly without an agent, and you know one of their writers, mention it. No one likes to feel they're contacted blindly. In this situation, as long as it's true, name-dropping is an acceptable and helpful practice.

But keep in mind, knowing a successful, even a famous, writer might get your manuscript looked at more quickly, even more seriously, but nothing can guarantee you publication. It's all in your writing and how you present it.

Endorsements

You have to try to help your agent sell your work. Agent Peter Rubie says, "I love it when I can turn around to an editor and say, 'Look, I've got this first-time writer who has a promise of a quote from John le Carré.'" Wouldn't that be wonderful?

How do you go about getting such a quote? Well, you could be brazen and just send your manuscript off to your favorite best-selling author. Some of them might actually read it and answer.

Or you can canvas for a referral. "Most of the people who get published have gone through the trenches," Rubie explains. "They've studied; they've done their homework; they've written; they've attended conferences and seminars. A lot of well-known writers teach or speak at these meetings. You can contact universities or the different writers' groups and take the classes. This is how you make contacts."

Attend a conference, meet a well-known writer there and ... who knows? Maybe he or she would be willing to read your manuscript. It could happen. And a quote from Stephen King saying your stuff is even better than Dean Koontz could take you far. That's the stuff of which cover blurbs are made, a publisher's dream come true. (For agents, writers, and booksellers, too.)

QUERY LETTER APPROACHES WITH SAMPLES

The opening of your query letter is probably the most important part. It has to grab the attention of the agent or editor while being concise and professional. There are four successful approaches you can use for the opening of your query:

1. The Formal Start

2. The Summary Statement

3. The Hook Start

4. The "I've-Got-Connections" Opening

Let's look at an explanation along with a sample or two for each category.

Approach #1: The Formal Start

In this approach you mention at the start that you are seeking representation or publication for your book, and you give its vital statistics (word count, genre, title) right up front. It is a formal approach and it won't hurt you, but it also can be boring. Note that all your query letters should address a specific editor or agent by name.

FORMAL START QUERY OPENER

This opening paragraph is for a query letter that author Tracy Cooper-Posey sent to the Canadian publisher, Turnstone Press, for her novel, *The Chronicles Are Closed*. Although a formal start letter doesn't always generate excitement, it got the confetti going at this publishing house. Tracy explains: "The letter led to a phone call from a very excited editor who was already talking about contracts and publishing dates, and then, at the end of the phone call, suggested I'd better send in the full manuscript. The book was published in 1999 with the title *Chronicles of the Lost Years* and was my first published novel."

Query Opener

You can read more about Tracy's approach to getting published in chapter five.

Ms. Manuela Diaz
Managing Editor Turnstone Press
607-100 Arthur Street
Winnipeg, MB R3B 1H3

Dear Ms. Diaz,

Would you be interested in an 83,000-word historical suspense/mystery titled *The Chronicles Are Closed*? This novel is a Sherlock Holmes pastiche, and stretches across thirteen years, beginning in late Victorian London, and ending during the Edwardian period. It features both Holmes and Watson, and is in part the "real" story of Holmes' adventures in the Middle East and Asia during the three years Watson believed him dead—commonly referred to as the Great Hiatus.

Approach #2: The Summary Statement

The summary statement approach begins with a sentence or two that gives an overall sketch of the book's plot, theme, or setting. In essence, this approach provides the reader with the handle right up front.

SUMMARY STATEMENT QUERY OPENER

Query Opener

This sample paragraph is the opener for a query Michelle Collier-Johns sent to Avon Books. It resulted in a request for three chapters, but then was rejected by another editor. The editor who originally asked for the three chapters left to go to another publishing house, a not unusual occurrence. Michelle is still hard at work on her writing.

Lucia Macro, Senior Editor
Avon Books
1350 Avenue of the Americas
New York, NY 10019

Dear Ms. Macro:

When she is good, she's very, very good, but when she is bad, she's better. An old cliché, but this best describes the endearing, yet tenacious character of Liza Lee Reilly who is caught in *The Entanglement*.

Approach #3: The Hook Start

Hook start queries jump right into the plot's action, starting with a good, attention-grabbing sentence or question. The first two or three paragraphs provide a mini-synopsis of your novel's plot. The next sections highlight your credentials and credits, what you're offering, and your closing. This opening works very well, especially if you don't know the person you are approaching.

HOOK START QUERY OPENER #1

This opening paragraph is for a novel by Lucy Harmon. "The query letter," she explains, "was successful in getting requests for the manuscript from both agents and publishers. The original didn't sell, but the revision is still under consideration at Harlequin Intrigue."

Query Opener

Denise O'Sullivan, Associate Senior Editor
Harlequin Intrigue
233 Broadway, Suite 1001
New York, NY 10279

Dear Denise O'Sullivan:

What if a dying murder victim gave you $50,000? Should you keep the money or call the police? In my 78,000-word mainstream novel titled *Take the Money*, protagonist Julie Lawson has only moments to decide.

HOOK START QUERY OPENER #2

This is the opening paragraph for a query Cyndia Depre sent out to several agents and editors. Cyndia explains, "I immediately got requests for the synopsis and chapters or the entire manuscript. The requests ultimately totaled 15 to 20. Personalized rejections were encouraging, but all mentioned one plot point they didn't like. Unfortunately, it wasn't a point I was willing to change. After considering different options, I decided to sign with a small publisher, Mundania Press." *Amanda's Rib* was released in early 2005.

Query Opener

Daniel J. Reitz, Sr.
Mundania Press
6470A Glenway Avenue, #109
Cincinnati, Ohio 45211-5222

Dear Mr. Reitz,

Is Amanda Winslow a grieving widow or a cold-blooded murderer? Jack Lindsey doesn't know Amanda well; she's new in Carlisle, a small Illinois town. When Jack discovers she's recently been acquitted of murdering her husband, Michael, and confronts her with his knowledge, Amanda's cool indifference piques his curiosity. He decides to learn all he can about the killing and her trial. Jack has no idea how many secrets Amanda has, or the lengths she'll go to protect them.

Approach #4: The "I've-Got-Connections" Opening

You can take this approach if you already know the person you are contacting. Maybe you met at a conference or another writer is referring you. Perhaps you're already a well-published writer seeking a new agent or publishing house. (In this instance most agents and editors recommend a phone call as the most direct route, but if you are not comfortable with the phone, this would be the way to go.)

In this approach you should mention right up front how you happened to be contacting this particular agent or editor and include your relevant credits, then go on to summarize the book you're offering.

THE "I'VE-GOT-CONNECTIONS" QUERY OPENER

Query Opener

Although this query letter breaks many of the rules—and its author, Tracy Cooper-Posey, is aware of that—it also resulted in a contract for *Heart of Vengeance*, Tracy's ninth published novel. Says Tracy, "Normally I follow all the rules. But this was a bizarre exception. I had heard Medallion was looking for full manuscripts. Word was passing amongst authors via private e-mail, along with the address, but no name. Beth Ciotta, the connection I mention in the query, is the author who sent me the intel and is a Medallion author—her second novel came out in December, 2004. The address ended up being the private address of Helen Rosburg, the owner of the company. This "I know someone in the know" style query, netted me a frantic phone call from the publisher (not the editor, but the publisher) about four days after I dropped it in the post, and I spent the next three hours in a blur, trying to print out two full copies of the *Heart of Vengeance* manuscript in time to meet courier deadlines. It cost me over one hundred dollars Canadian to send the manuscript from western Canada all the way to Florida, but it was there by 10 A.M. the next day, which prompted another delighted phone call from the publisher. They bought the book two weeks later, once the editor had read it over. *Heart of Vengeance* was released in April, 2004.

Medallion Press
225 Seabreeze Avenue
Palm Beach, FL 33480
United States

ATTENTION: Acquisitions/HR

Dear Sir or Madam:

Re: Heart of Vengeance and Lucifer's Lover

I heard by bush telegraph (Beth Ciotta, actually) that you're considering romances in most sub-categories, but are looking for finished manuscripts. I've included in this envelope partials and synopses for two of my finished manuscripts. *Lucifer's Lover* is a long contemporary and *Heart of Vengeance* is an even longer historical romance set in England during the reign of Richard I.

FULL QUERY LETTER SAMPLE (HOOK START OPENING)

The sample query here is for the novel *Did You Get the Vibe?* by Kelly James-Enger. It's a good example of how to write a query letter that grabs interest and results in publication. James-Enger gives us the history of this query. "I originally pitched the book to Red Dress Ink, Harlequin's 'chick lit' imprint. After RDI passed, I sent a query letter to John Scognamiglio at Kensington because my agent, Laurie Harper, mentioned that she thought he acquired those kinds of books. (Laurie did read *Vibe* and thought it was good, but she usually doesn't rep fiction and told me she wasn't sure how to sell it. So I went to John on my own.) At the time, Kensington was preparing to launch its own chick lit imprint, Strapless, so it was perfect timing. I mailed the query on a Saturday; that Tuesday, John e-mailed, asking for the manuscript; and he bought it three weeks later. It was published in November 2003."

John Scognamiglio also bought Kelly James Enger's second novel, *White Bikini Panties*, released in fall 2004.

Sample Query

August 16, 2002

Mr. John Scognamiglio
Kensington Books
850 Third Avenue
New York, NY 10022

Dear Mr. Scognamiglio:

Have you ever gotten the Vibe? You know, that feeling when you meet a woman, and you know that you're attracted to each other?

Kate, 28, has based her dating life on the Vibe. If there's a Vibe there, the guy is worth pursuing—if not, forget it. The trouble is that the too-beautiful-for-her Andrew just dumped her, and now she can hardly fit into her favorite jeans. And she hates her job, but everyone keeps telling her how great it is to be a lawyer. Yeah, right.

At least she has Tracy, her best friend from law school. Both live in Chicago's up-and-coming Lakeview neighborhood. Tracy's gorgeous, smart, and has a great job, a great apartment, and a great live-in boyfriend, Tom, to go along with it all. She also has an eating disorder she's managed to keep secret from even her closest friend. Tracy doesn't believe in the Vibe—until she experiences it for the first time, and it turns her life upside down.

Will Kate find lasting love, meaningful work, and be able to squeeze back into her clothes? Will Tracy give up the man who loves her to experience sexual fulfillment—and come to grips with what she's doing to her body and her spirit? *Did You Get the Vibe?* explores the lives of these two best friends as they love, work, diet, laugh, and bond over their boyfriends, jobs, diets, and sex lives. Readers of women's contemporary fiction will enjoy their stories, and relate to their experiences, struggles, and insights.

Did You Get the Vibe? is 78,855 words and is my first novel. As a full-time freelance journalist for the past five years, my work has appeared in more than forty magazines including *Marie Claire, Woman's Day, Family Circle, Self,* and *Redbook*; I'm also a contributing editor at *Oxygen, The Writer,* and *For the Bride.* My first nonfiction book, *Ready, Aim, Specialize! Create Your Writing Specialty and Make More Money* will be published by The Writer

Books in the winter of 2003. I'm also a frequent speaker at writers conferences, and, not surprisingly, a big believer in the Vibe.

Please let me know if you're interested in seeing a synopsis and three chapters or the complete manuscript of *Vibe*.

Sincerely,

Kelly James-Enger

Main Street • Anytown, USA • (555) 422-1111 • Kelly@anyserver.com

BUILDING KILLER QUERY LETTERS

Now that you've seen some effective sample query letter openers, it's time to sit down and actually compose one. For some this might seem like a daunting task; writing the novel was so much easier. But it doesn't have to be difficult. Look at it as a writing exercise. Compose your first draft, put it aside for a while, then come back to it with fresh eyes. For your second read, replace your writer's cap with an editor's one and look for and correct any trouble spots.

What follows are several drafts of query letters written by new writers. With the query letter checklists in mind, read through them and see how many problem areas you can find. Then go on to subsequent drafts and the final, polished draft. Our comments along the way point out what works and what doesn't on each draft.

ONLY THE DEAD SURVIVE BY ED MATTINGLY, JR.

Query Letter Draft #1

Date

Mr. Mike Farris
Farris Literary Agency
P.O. Box 570069
Dallas, TX 75357-0069

Dear Mr. Farris:

I am a freelance writer, and native Atlantan, with one-hundred-plus published articles to my credit. ❶

ONLY THE DEAD SURVIVE, a novel, ❷ sends Edge McConal on a simple

---

mission of mercy: bury ex-marine buddy and all-round whack-job Jocko Murphy. ❸ Murphy, sliced and diced while in Leavenworth Prison, ❹ takes a key to the grave, but it won't unlock the Pearly Gates. ❺

McConal, erstwhile financial consultant, launches his own search for the missing key, ❻ and in the process opens a revenge-driven, anti-American can of worms. ❼

I would love to send you ONLY THE DEAD SURVIVE, which is 81,431 words. ❽ I have prepared as well a 1,250-word synopsis. ❾

Sincerely,

Ed Mattingly, Jr.

Main Street • Anytown, USA • (555) 224-2222 • Mattingly@anyserver.com

1. This is what we call a formal start query letter. And though there's nothing inherently wrong with it, it can be boring. It's better to begin with a hook start or summary statement of your novel's plot. The information in this sentence can go after your mini-synopsis in the author bio section.

2. It's better to say, "My novel, *Only the Dead Survive* (in both upper and lower case, in italics) than using this word order. This feels too abrupt.

3. Send him where? Why does he have to do the burying?

4. Not clear why he was in prison.

5. What will it unlock? Although your reference to what it won't do is intriguing and amusing, we need to know why anyone would care about this key.

6. Again, if we don't know what's so important about this key, we can't get excited for McConal and hope he finds it.

7. This is okay for book jacket copy, but this isn't what you're writing here. A query should give the reader a good idea of who your hero is and what his core conflict is. If the can of worms is his core conflict, then you need to be more specific. As it stands now, it's too vague. We can't care and get hooked if we don't know what's going on.

8. It's better to keep emotions out of this. Say simply, "May I send you the complete manuscript of my 81,000-word (here you can give an approximate word count) novel, *Only the Dead Survive*?" Don't forget to mention your book's genre.

9. This isn't important information. In fact, most agents and editors, when they ask to see a synopsis, want a one-pager only. This would be running over that limit. Offer only your completed manuscript. If they want to see something other than that, they'll let you know.

ONLY THE DEAD SURVIVE BY ED MATTINGLY, JR.

Query Letter Draft #2

Date

Mr. Mike Farris
Farris Literary Agency
P.O. Box 570069
Dallas, TX 75357-0069

Dear Mr. Farris:

My suspense novel *Only the Dead Survive* sends erstwhile ❶ financial consultant Edge McConal to Leavenworth Penitentiary on a mission of mercy. ❷ Named executor in ex-Marine buddy Jocko Murphy's hand-written will, McConal accompanies the coffin to Atlanta, where it is hijacked. ❸

Jocko Murphy–doing time on a rape charge–was sliced and diced in the Leavenworth laundry. A lifetime whack job, Murphy took a key to the grave that, instead of the Pearly Gates, opens a Pandora's Box full of a Timothy McVeigh wannabe hell-bent to vindicate the fragging in Vietnam of the father he never knew. ❹

In search of the missing key, McConal and friend Rand Hale–another ex-Marine–encounter brutality from dog poisoning to biological terror, with a little throat slashing in between. ❺

I am a freelance writer, and native Atlantan, with one-hundred-plus published articles to my credit.

May I send the complete manuscript of my 81,000-word novel, *Only the Dead Survive*? ❻

Sincerely,

Ed Mattingly, Jr.

Main Street • Anytown, USA • (555) 224-2222 • Mattingly@anyserver.com.

1. I don't like this word choice much. It sounds a bit too contrived. Keep it simpler.

2. What is the mission of mercy?

3. By whom? Why would someone hijack a coffin? And at this point, I have to say, that your book, as you are describing it, sounds more like a Tom Wolfe-style black comedy than a suspense novel. Be careful of your genre choice.

4. This sentence is long and wordy and hard to follow, as well as vague. Leave out Pandora and Timothy McVeigh and tell us exactly what the key is for.

5. Here you are including details … but the wrong details. Again, we need to know who your hero is and what stuff he's made of. Tell us his core conflict and what the stakes are if he doesn't resolve that conflict. Then tell us how he finds a resolution. You're still trying to write book jacket copy. Avoid that vague approach and give us the information that will make us like your hero and want to read about what happens to him.

6. Since you have the title here, you could delete that from the opening. Get right into your story line with some sort of hook. There's no point in repeating your title.

ONLY THE DEAD SURVIVE BY ED MATTINGLY, JR.

Query Letter Draft #3

Date

Mr. Mike Farris
Farris Literary Agency
P.O. Box 570069
Dallas, TX 75357-0069

Dear Mr. Farris:

In my mystery novel, *Only the Dead Survive*, Edge McConal, designated co-executor, ❶ accompanies the coffin of murdered ex-marine buddy Jocko Murphy from Leavenworth Prison to Atlanta. Before the funeral arrangements are made ❷ the hearse is waylaid and the driver murdered. Murphy—whack job and part-time CIA double agent—takes ❸ with him a key to a safe box whose contents could fund the next generation in biological terror.

When Edge McConal and friend Rand Hale–also an ex-marine–launch their own search for the missing coffin, they run afoul of a nut case whose taste for violence is a veritable smorgasbord. ❹ McConal's golden retriever is poisoned, lover Kaylon Early brutalized, and Hale beaten like Evander Holyfield's heavy bag. ❺ As an aperitif ❻ Hale's new love interest, Cherie Malour, has her throat slashed. ❼

The thread connecting this mayhem extends back to Vietnam, and a Marine captain "fragged" by his own troops. McConal and Hale, who conducted a fruitless investigation of the incident, now must confront the murdered officer's son, who idolizes, among others, Timothy McVeigh and all things anti-American.

I am a freelance writer, and native Atlantan, with one-hundred-plus published articles to my credit.

May I send you the complete manuscript, which runs to 81,000 words?

Sincerely,

Ed Mattingly, Jr.

Main Street • Anytown, USA • (555) 224-2222 • Mattingly@anyserver.com

1. Of what? For whom? Not clear. It's better to put the phrase "of murdered ex-marine buddy Jocko Murphy" right after the word co-executor.

2. I'd change this phrase to a simple "but." It seems that if he's accompanying a coffin heading somewhere, some arrangements would have had to have been made.

3. Although queries and synopses should be written in present tense, this action happened before the current action. "Takes" should be "took."

4. You mentioned "whack job" earlier; I'd avoid "nut case" here. It might be better to use the character's name.

5. Instead of using passive voice (which is weak and should be avoided) for the list of transgressions, change them to active voice. *So-and-so poisoned the dog,* and so on.

6. Insert a comma after aperitif.

7. Again, avoid the passive voice. Using active voice, tell us who is doing all of this.

ONLY THE DEAD SURVIVE BY ED MATTINGLY, JR.

Query Letter Final Draft

Date

Mr. Mike Farris
Farris Literary Agency
P.O. Box 570069
Dallas, TX 75357-0069

Dear Mr. Farris:

In my mystery novel, *Only the Dead Survive*, Edge McConal, co-executor for the slain Jocko Murphy, escorts his ex-marine pal's coffin from Leavenworth Prison to Atlanta. There the hearse is waylaid, its driver murdered. A part-time CIA double agent, Murphy took with him a key to a safe box whose contents could fund the next generation in biological terror. ❶

McConal and friend Rand Hale, also an ex-marine, search for the missing coffin, but in the process run afoul of Thorne Rose. Rose's taste for violence is a veritable smorgasbord: he brutalizes McConal's lover Kaylon Early; poisons the man's golden retriever; and uses Rand Hale as a heavy bag. As an aperitif, Rose slashes the throat of Hale's love interest, Cherie Malour. ❷

The mayhem's connecting thread extends back to Vietnam and a Marine captain blown away by his own men. McConal and Hale, who led a fruitless investigation of the "fragging" incident, must now confront the murdered officer's son in the guise of Rose, who believes Timothy McVeigh used too little explosive, and anti-American literature the stuff of Pulitzer Prizes. ❸

I am a freelance writer, and native Atlantan, with one-hundred-plus published articles to my credit.

May I send you the manuscript, which runs to 81,000 words?

Sincerely,

Ed Mattingly, Jr.

Main Street • Anytown, USA • (555) 224-2222 • Mattingly@anyserver.com

---

1. Now the opening is tightly written and clear, and we have a good idea of what the story will be about.

2. Because this paragraph is now well written, we're able to focus in on the writer's wonderful word choices.

3. The writer again peppers his query with a great turn of phrase here and there. Now with a tighter query letter, his writing style and story line shine through.

Notice how Ed Mattingly, Jr. took his query from a vague and too short first draft, to a tightly and well-written, intriguing proposal.

He sent his query letter to five agents, and got a request from Mike Farris for the entire manuscript. "We signed a contract within three weeks. Having said that, *Only the Dead Survive* went through thirty-five-plus publisher pink slips, and is now in revision. I've got my fingers crossed; it's a very different animal than it was almost three years ago."

THUNDERSNOW BY TODD SANDERS

Query Letter Draft #1

Date

Richard Henshaw
Richard Henshaw Group
127 W. 24th Street., 4th Floor
New York, NY 10011

Dear Mr. Henshaw:

Imagine witnessing your brother killed by a child-murdering snow demon who not only controls the winter storm you're trapped in, but who moves through the snow like a shark through water. Imagine seeing this when you're five years old ❶ and escaping only with the help of a Native American boy who can shape-shift into animal form at will. How would you feel when you discover that no one believes your story? And how would you feel twenty-two years later when the storm returns and they still don't believe you, and this time it's your child that vanishes? ❷

For twenty-eight-year-old Brooke Daniels, the answer is furious . . . and panicked. ❸ In a race for time ❹ where every second counts, ❺ she must locate the Native American who saved her as a child, the only person who will believe her. He alone can destroy the demon and save her daughter. But where do you find a man who spends half his life as an animal?

Thundersnow, an approximately ❻ 100,000-word horror novel, follows Brooke's search for the one man who can help her, and their combined pursuit of the demon, which they catch in a valley high in the Rocky Mountains–the same valley her brother died in so many years before. ❼

From the cave she hid in as a child, they watch the beast as it prepares to dine on the unconscious form of Brooke's daughter. Having gone so long without the nourishment of youth, the demon is in a rare, vulnerable state when they attack. Brooke's drive to protect her daughter, plus a need to revenge her brother, combined with the man's matured shape-shifting skills, prove too much for the demon. A bloody battle marks the demon's end, and a century old curse is forever silenced. ❽ ❾

Should you find *Thundersnow* interesting, the completed manuscript is available upon request. ❿ For your convenience, I have enclosed an SASE. ⓫

Sincerely,

Todd Sanders

Main Street • Anytown, USA • (555) 222-2222 • Sanders@anyserver.com

---

1. This more or less repeats how you opened the query. You can insert the age in the top line "Imagine at five years old witnessing . . ." and delete this line here.

2. This opening is basically okay, but could be tighter. It's too long of a build up and you are using too many questions. When you ask too many questions, it can take the reader off the path of your query to start thinking about possible answers.

3. We can figure out how she would feel. It's best not to ask this question and then answer it. We'd rather know what she does than how she feels. Stick to your plot action.

4. Avoid clichés.

5. Should be "when" not "where." But this is repetitive. It copies what "in a race for time" tells us.

6. Delete "an approximately." It's awkward.

7. Once you've given us the title and the word count, you're signaling that the synopsis part of the query is finished. We expect you to move on to other query sections. Don't pick up with more plot details at this point.

8. Delete this entire paragraph. As noted above, you ended the query in the last paragraph. Now move on to other information here.

9. You need some sort of bio section next. If you have no credits, at least mention you have experience with the setting. Or why you are querying this particular agent. Are you familiar with something he's represented that's similar to your book?

10. Close simply by saying, "May I send you the completed manuscript?"

11. Delete this sentence. He'll see the SASE.

THUNDERSNOW BY TODD SANDERS

Query Letter Final Draft

Date

Richard Henshaw
Richard Henshaw Group
127 W. 24th Street., 4th Floor
New York, NY 10011

Dear Mr. Henshaw:

Imagine at five years old witnessing your brother killed by a demon who not only controls the winter storm you're trapped in, but who moves through the snow like a shark through water. Imagine escaping only with the help of a Native American boy who can shape-shift into animal form at will. But no one believes your story, and the body of your brother is never found. So what do you do twenty-two years later when the storm returns and it's *your* child that vanishes, and still no one believes you? ❶

Twenty-seven-year-old Brooke Daniels races to find the Native American who rescued her as a child, the only person who can destroy the demon and save her daughter. By her calculations, he should be thirty-two years old now. And there's only one place to look for a man who spends half his life as an animal: the same valley she's avoided for twenty-two years—the one where the demon has been waiting for her to return. ❷

Thundersnow is a 100,000-word horror novel set in the Rocky Mountains of southern Colorado, where I have lived for the past several years and spend much of my time exploring the higher elevations and the several hidden valleys there. The plot is in a similar vein to the Dean Koontz novels *Hideaway* and *Lightning*. I am approaching you specifically, Mr. Henshaw, because of your interest in horror, your experience with leading agencies, and the fact that you have chosen to remain a small, personable agency. ❸

May I send you the completed manuscript?

Sincerely,

Todd Sanders

Main Street • Anytown, USA • (555) 222-2222 • Sanders@anyserver.com

1. This paragraph is much tighter now with fewer questions.
2. We now have a clear sense of what the heroine's conflict is and what she must to do resolve it.
3. The writer has added a well-written paragraph that shows his ability to handle his novel's setting, gives the agent a good handle for the plot and style, and makes it clear that he has chosen to approach this particular agent for several good reasons.

Although there were a couple of other query drafts addressing minor issues, Todd Sanders started with a basically sound first draft—which made getting to the final draft a fairly painless process. He has an excellent query ready to go out, but he's letting it sit until he has finished the novel and is sure that it's ready to be submitted.

Query Letter Checklist

Here's a checklist of items to watch for and fix:

- ❑ Weak lead sentence
- ❑ Wordiness
- ❑ Awkward phrasings
- ❑ Lack of clarity
- ❑ Illogical paragraph organization
- ❑ Repetitiveness
- ❑ Weak verbs (avoid the verb "to be")
- ❑ Clichés
- ❑ Lack of rhythm (read your material aloud to see how it flows)

❏ Overusing adjectives and adverbs

❏ No transitions (or weak ones) between paragraphs

❏ Weak plotting (as related in the query)

❏ Incorrect punctuation, grammar, and spelling

BACK TO THE PLOTTING BOARD

Writing a good query letter can often be a revealing exercise. If it's proving to be overly troublesome–you can't seem to find the hook or identify your main character's conflict, for example–the problem might be a flawed plot. The hook or conflict just isn't in your novel to identify. This is a hard but incredibly valuable lesson to learn. It means putting the query letter aside and going back to the plotting board. A revised novel with a clear-cut hook and conflict will lend itself to a much easier query letter and will be much easier to sell.

SLOW AND STEADY OR THE BLITZ APPROACH?

Let's say your novel and query letter are finished and you're ready to get started hitting the marketplace. It is important to consider how many query letters to send out at a time. Say you have identified forty possible agents who handle the genre in which you're writing. Should you fire up the printer and mail your query to all forty at once? Probably not.

Say that all forty agents reject your manuscript so you decide to do a rewrite. You may end up with a better book, but where will you send it now? You've already queried your top forty choices of agents, and chances are they aren't going to want to look at something they've already rejected. Your blitz has left you with no good options.

To avoid eliminating all potential agents or editors, start by sending out your query to five at a time. If feedback comes back with rejection letters, then you have the opportunity to revise and still have fresh avenues to which you can submit.

This brings us to a common question new writers ask: "But if I have revised the novel so completely that it's almost unrecognizable from its former self, and it's definitely so much better, and I have a new query letter to go along with it, why can't I query the same people again?"

Sometimes you can. With a completely revised book and query letter proposing it, the passage of time and a new title to boot, you might get away with it. (The new title is important. Most agencies and major publishing houses log all submissions into their computer by author, date, and title. If the same title were to come around again, it would show on the computer and you'd be found out.)

Not all agents will remember your first query letter. Agent Richard Henshaw says, "The truth is that I receive so many queries that if one didn't make an impression the first time around, in a month or so I'll probably be able to read it with a fresh eye. So, yes, I will reconsider queries, but there's a good chance I didn't pass on it because the query wasn't effective. It might just not be the sort of story I'm looking for at the moment."

Other agents have excellent memories and will remember a query letter they previously rejected. Unless an agent or editor has suggested (or implied) willingness to take a second look at a revised work, there's not much point in querying about a book to the same people again.

SIMULTANEOUS AND MULTIPLE SUBMISSIONS

Sending a query out to more than one agent or editor at a time is called a simultaneous submission. This is often confused with a multiple submission, which means sending more than one project at a time to the same editor or agent.

In the midst of the slow and steady approach or, if one couldn't resist, the blitz approach, many new writers wonder if they should be announcing their simultaneous submission tactics to the agents and editors they are approaching. There are different schools of thought on this. Many agents and editors ask to be informed. They say it will spur them to get to your work faster if they know there's competition.

Others don't want to bother with simultaneous submissions; they don't want the pressure of the competition. Nor do they want to invest the time it takes to read your query, scribble a request for more across it, then stuff it into your SASE, only to learn later you've been snapped up by another agent or your book found a home at another publishing house.

Our feeling is this: Say you start writing a novel at age thirty-five, finish it at age thirty-seven. You send out one query letter, wait six weeks for a reply. Now let's say that reply is positive. You send in your manuscript and wait another three months for a reply. If that response is negative, you send out another query letter and start the process all over again. Now you're thirty-eight. By the time you approach the forty agents on your list, you'll be what, fifty-three?

Unless you want to spend the rest of your life trying to sell your first novel (never mind the second or third or fourth), sending out simultaneous query letters is the only way to go, and we don't think there's any need to announce your approach tactics.

The rules differ for simultaneous submissions of manuscripts, though, and we've covered that topic for you in chapter six.

No Smelly Queries

Michelle Grajkowski, president of the 3 Seas Literary Agency, says she once received a query letter that smelled so bad, she and her staff were afraid to open it. So they didn't. They tossed it out. Which leads us to other helpful dos and don'ts for query letters.

QUERY LETTER DOS

1. Your query letter's writing style should reflect the writing style of the project you are proposing.

2. Make sure you state your novel's word count. Some editors have a fixed word count they can work with and it helps to know right up front if yours falls inside those parameters.

3. Pitch only one project at a time, unless it's a series. If you've got a multitude of finished but unpublished novels on hand, this will trigger alarm bells. If you find interest for the one book, you can mention the others later.

4. Always include an SASE.

5. Be specific when describing your plot. Hinting will not hook interest. It will only create reader frustration.

6. Be nice. Arrogance and demands are turnoffs. Agents and editors want to feel they'll be able to have a good working relationship with you.

QUERY LETTER DON'TS

1. Avoid mentioning how many people have read and loved your book. The opinions of your in-laws or your hairdresser won't help build your case.

2. Stay clear of self-glorifying adjectives (save those for the book reviewers). Don't give into the temptation of describing your work as dazzling, dramatic, exciting, fast-paced, or funny. Say, "My book is an account of …," not "My book is a fascinating account of …"

3. Avoid predicting your book's climb up the best-seller lists (no one can predict that) or stating that you're the next major literary writer of your generation. The grander the brag and boast, the bigger the turnoff.

4. Don't show your desperation. You've been trying for years to get it published; you're out of money and your spouse is threatening to leave. This certainly is a scary place to be ... but it's of no interest to an agent or editor and will only hurt your chances. If so many other people have seen and passed on your material, why should anyone you're querying now take it? Don't say anything to provoke that reaction.

5. Don't put yourself down in a query letter. Ever. Don't say it's your first novel—unless you've been writing and publishing articles and nonfiction books. Then they can know you're adding to your areas of expertise. If you have no credits, they'll figure it out. In the same vein, don't say you hope they'll like it. Of course, you do.

6. Don't tell editors or agents their business. While you need to be market savvy and show you know the market for your book, there's a fine line to walk here. Unless you have actual current sales statistics at hand, don't go out on an unsupported limb.

E-MAIL OR SNAIL MAIL?

Don't send your query to editors and agents via e-mail unless you are sure this form of communication is acceptable. Although more and more agents and some editors are willing to consider electronic submissions, most still prefer the old-fashioned way.

E-mails can so easily go astray, be diverted by spam filters, or be deleted by a quick stroke on the keyboard. And e-mails, when read, invite a fast reply–maybe too fast. Speed is great for positive responses, but it's much too easy to make a snap decision to turn down an e-mail query.

As an example, although some agents at Lowenstein-Yost Associates accept e-mail queries (a specific format and e-mail form is provided at their Web site: www.lowensteinyost.com), agent Nancy Yost, herself, is not a fan of e-queries. "If they are sent to my personal work e-mail (not the official query address), I'm likely to delete them without even reading them. If they don't have anything in the subject line, I'll delete those, too. And I delete anything that's from an address I don't recognize."

Yost provides her reasons for not liking e-queries: "(1) First of all, I've tried to post in as many places that I prefer hardcopy queries, so those submitting haven't done their research. (2) I have limited space in my e-mail, and the queries and attachments clog the space/memory. (3) It's my experience that ninety percent of electronic queries are sent as a mass mailing, and not targeted to my specific 'list.' (4) For the most part, I don't get the sense that e-queriers really want me to represent them—it seems as if it takes no effort to send and they don't know what I do. Who can get excited by that kind of first impression? It's the literary equivalent of a shrug.

"I will say that I respect the queries that come after a posting on Publishers Lunch," Nancy Yost adds. "At least someone is paying attention and is savvy enough to know that PL exists." (For more information on Publishers Lunch, see the appendix.)

Danielle Egan-Miller, president of Browne & Miller Literary Associates, says, "We are receiving more and more queries via e-mail. The very nature of e-mail—quick, kind of casual—seems to give authors license to ignore some of the standard query protocol. I see many more spelling mistakes and errors, often formatting problems, and lots of times the e-mail itself is hard to read."

There seem to be a lot of reasons not to query electronically—but if you insist, there are certain rules and procedures you should be aware of and observe.

THE NEWEST ART: E-MAIL SUBJECT LINES

How you label your e-mail can affect whether it gets read with enthusiasm or deleted without opening. Says agent Russell Galen, "I can tell you that on the basis of idiotic subject lines, I delete many e-mails without ever opening them. I open others with a feeling of foreboding and irritation (although sometimes I'm pleasantly surprised when I read the body of the e-mail). In other, rare cases, the subject line grabs my attention, and I open the e-mail pre-convinced I'm going to want to see the manuscript."

Here are four things Galen looks for (or tries to avoid) in an e-mail subject line:

1. My least favorite subject line lets me know that the sender has been referred by an online database, fee-charging site. A lot of mediocre stuff comes to me from those kinds of referrals, so at this point, as soon as I see it in the subject line, I delete it without reading.

2. Many writers anticipate the general problem of e-mail subject lines, and thus they say in their subject line, "Published writer seeks agent."

The problem is that I soon come to realize that in almost every case the author has been published by a vanity press, Internet publisher, or the like. I've become inured to this subject line and I now almost immediately assume the writer lacks real credentials.

3. In the short space the subject line allows, it's a good idea to insert some evidence that you have serious credentials, such as "Random House author seeks agent" or "Yale professor seeks agent."

4. If you don't have such credentials, it's probably best to label the query simply "Query" or "Submission." More often than not the attempt to create a peppy, attractive, noticeable subject line backfires and makes the sender look like an amateur.

Galen concludes, "Although e-mail and hardcopy queries are very similar in content, there is one specific difference about the e-mail medium: In e-mail, the agent sees the subject line first and forms a judgment about the e-mail before he begins to read it. Thus, the only new skill writers must learn is to perfect the art of the e-mail subject line."

The thing to keep in mind, in either case, says literary agent/publishing law attorney Jeff Kleinman, is that agents tend to make snap decisions based on a couple of paragraphs. "So be sure that the writing of any query letter is really strong. No matter how you send it."

In summary, you want to send a professional, strong, to-the-point query letter (whether via e-mail or snail mail) that avoids hype or gimmicks. A commercially viable idea presented concisely will get you requests for more.

In later chapters we'll show you how to compose, format, and submit that "more," but first we'll tell you how to bypass the query letter step altogether. Turn the page.

E-mail Query Letter Checklist

Just because you are sending a query via e-mail instead of snail mail, doesn't mean there aren't rules to follow. It is still a formal letter with the goal of creating interest in an editor or agent.

- ☐ Just as with snail mail queries, make sure to put the name of the person you're querying in the salutation. "Dear Agent" is guaranteed to get you deleted—it's the equivalent of junk mail.
- ☐ Make sure your subject line is filled in and appropriate.
- ☐ Do not include any attachments with your e-mail. Most people are wary of viruses and won't download attachments from strangers.
- ☐ Do not refer agents or editors to Web sites to read sample pages. No hyperlinks in your e-mail queries.
- ☐ Run your spellchecker before hitting "Send."
- ☐ Agent Anne Hawkins adds one more caution: "Never, ever query an agent via an instant message!"

Chapter Five:
The In-Person Pitch

"All my books literally come to me in the form of a sentence, an original sentence which contains the entire book."—RAYMOND FEDERMAN

Now that you've learned how to write a query letter, we'll show you how you can sometimes bypass that step and get straight to an agent or editor requesting to see your manuscript. This can happen at writers conferences, which often feature agents and editors looking to share their knowledge and find new talent.

We discussed conferences in some detail in chapter three, but now it's time to focus on that ten-, fifteen- or twenty-minute appointment. This is your chance to pitch your novel to an agent or editor face-to-face, find out if there's interest, and forego the query letter stage.

If your idea is a hit, the agent or editor will ask you to send material—perhaps sample chapters, perhaps the whole manuscript—after the conference.

Don't expect agents or editors to read your manuscript on the spot or take it home with them. They'll be meeting with a lot of writers and couldn't possibly carry all that material back on the plane. Don't worry; they won't forget you. In part two we show you how to prepare your solicited submission package, including the cover letter, which serves as a reminder to the agent or editor of where you met.

ARRANGING THE AGENT/EDITOR APPOINTMENT

You don't have to sidle up to an agent or editor at the bar or break through a crowd of schmoozers to schmooze yourself. (You certainly can try these approaches if you want, but never, *ever* interrupt them in the restroom. During meals check first if they want to talk shop or if they want a break.) Most conferences offer the option on the registration form to sign up for an appointment. When you get to the conference, you'll be told the time and place of your meeting.

Some conference sponsors will wait until the first day of the conference to post sign-up sheets. In that case, come early to grab a slot with the agent or editor of your choice.

WHO CAN PITCH?

Anyone who has signed up for a conference and laid down the money is entitled to pitch to an agent or editor. But some agents and editors prefer your work be completed before taking up their time.

Agent George Nicholson says, "At conferences, I've met some wonderful writers who eventually became my clients. At one conference, though, a guy had an appointment to meet with me for twenty minutes. I read his submission, which was just awful. I asked him how long he had been writing for children and he said since last night. I had to laugh, but it was hard for me to take this guy seriously. He had paid his money, so he was entitled to his twenty minutes. It was very frustrating, because instead of spending that twenty minutes talking to a serious writer, I spent that time guiding him to the books he should be reading."

That's an extreme example. Most people don't decide the night before a conference they want to become writers. Many conference attendees are in the middle of a project and come to get feedback on their idea, to see if they're heading in the right direction, and that's fine. You can have an appointment even though your novel isn't completed. Just make sure you let the agent or editor know that. They can tell you if your project interests them. The feedback could be invaluable for revising your book. And when you're done, you know you have an interested party to approach. That knowledge can provide wonderful motivation for finishing the project and making it your best work ever.

BATTLING NERVES

When it's finally time for your appointment, you may find yourself more nervous than you thought possible. Your mouth is dry. Your hands are clammy. You'd rather be anywhere but here.

Relax. Take several deep breaths. Remember, agents and editors are just like other people. You'll hit it off with some of them. Some will help you feel comfortable. Others won't. Just be yourself, and look for a kindred spirit. Concentrate on your message–your book–rather than on yourself.

If you're still nervous, say so. You might be surprised at how understanding agents and editors can be. Your confession might just break the ice.

Author Tracy Cooper-Posey admits to being "so nervous I thought I'd puke on her shoes" when she met with an agent at a conference. "But I'd honed my pitching skills," she says, "so I managed to keep it together."

She must have. The agent listened to one pitch and asked for more. Cooper-Posey went home from the conference with the agent's request to see full manuscripts for five novels!

Keep in mind why agents and editors are at this conference. They're not doing you a favor. They don't like flying any more than you do. Like you, they have plenty of other work they could and should be doing. They're at the conference because they're looking for new stars–the next John Grisham, Mary Higgins Clark or Stephen King–or at least a solid, steadily selling author. And you just might be that person. The agent is psychologically disposed toward liking you, toward liking your project. So is the editor. You've got the edge. You might be the next writer to hit the best-seller list.

Best-selling author Tom Clancy sums it up well: "What do you suppose editors do? They look for new talent. My editor was an editor when we started together. Now he's editor-in-chief and publisher. His replacement will get there by discovering new talent, too."

INTERVIEWING AGENTS

While the agent evaluates you, you're also evaluating the agent and finding out how he works. Come prepared with questions of your own: Does he have any publishing houses in mind where your book might fit? Does he make simultaneous submissions? Does he work with a contract? Ask whatever you need to know. You might decide that this is not the agent for you, even if the agent expresses interest in you. The conference appointment should be a give-and-take dialogue. The agent should come away with a good sense of your book, and you should feel that you know the agent's working style.

BE PREPARED

Have your pitch polished. Be ready to describe your book concisely. If you ramble, the agent or editor may figure you do the same in your book. How you present your project will influence the way the agent or editor views your work.

Also anticipate questions the agent or editor might ask you for further clarification.

Arrive on time, and don't keep the agent over the allotted time. Other eager writers are waiting for their turns.

You'll probably introduce yourself and shake hands, sit down across from each other, perhaps exchange business cards. You can write the name of your book on the back of the card as a reminder.

Then the agent or editor might say, "How can I help you?" It's time to pitch your novel.

You Need to Know Your Story's "Beat"

BY CHRISTINE DESMET

Christine DeSmet teaches writing and publishing for the University of Wisconsin-Madison, Division of Continuing Studies. In addition to being a published novelist, she has written award-winning screenplays.

I'm often asked by writers, "How can I possibly get my 400-page book summarized for a five-minute pitch?"

Here's how: Start your pitch with your logline, that sentence that summarizes the book. Next, tell the agent the theme, what's at stake in the book.

Then the agent wants to know your character's major personality weakness or flaw and his or her big strength. We read to see characters triumph over their weaknesses, so mentioning the weakness and strength is usually crucial in a pitch. Stick to one of each. A focused writer reflects a focused story.

Finally, in a short pitch session, the agent wants to know the major plot points. Write them on a cheat sheet if you need to. Agents don't care if you read, and pitch sessions aren't memory tests.

Try to touch on these major points:

- Why does your character desperately need to go on this story's journey?

- What inciting incident pushes him or her into the story?

- What happens in the middle that almost makes him or her turn back?

- What motivates or forces the climax and the dark moment of the story?

- How is the crisis resolved?

These days I recommend to the writers I coach that they know what the term "story beat" means. Savvy agents and editors appreciate the writer who knows the lingo, and you don't want to be caught off guard if they ask you.

The term comes from the world of screenplay writing. A story beat is any point in the story where the character's emotional journey and action plot changes significantly for better or worse. Beats cover both action plot and emotional plot. A story changes beat by beat. Some might call the beat a "moment." Whatever you call them, we build our stories on them. And a novel will have twenty, forty, even sixty or more beats.

THE ANATOMY OF A PITCH

You have only a few minutes to make it clear what type of book you're offering, its theme, and basic plot essentials.

You also want to make your novel sound fabulous, of course. But you shouldn't brag and boast shamelessly about your book. "I don't like it when someone tells me their book is great," agent Rob Cohen says. "Some of the best writers I know think their own work is terrible."

Stick to the facts, but make those facts fascinating.

Begin with the title, genre, and approximate word count.

Next comes your one-sentence pitch line, the concept underlying your novel. You'll need to prepare this in advance and practice it until you can deliver it confidently and naturally. It's the hook, the angle, what Hollywood types call "the premise." It needs to be compelling and intriguing. The best pitch lines elicit the "ooh factor." It makes the listeners say, "Ooh, I want to read that book."

The pitch line can be jazzy, but it doesn't have to be. It does have to contain the most important element in your story—the main conflict. Your pitch should reveal the primary problem your protagonist will face.

Here are a few examples of effective pitch lines, for books that were on the best-seller list when we wrote this chapter.

> "The largest think tank in the world is behind a series of mysterious deaths, and the young widows of two of the victims must stop them."
> *ARE YOU AFRAID OF THE DARK?* BY SIDNEY SHELDON

> "When a grizzled war veteran dies on his 83rd birthday, he finds himself in heaven, where the five people who mattered most to him explain the meaning of life."
> *THE FIVE PEOPLE YOU MEET IN HEAVEN* BY MITCH ALBOM

> "A group of strangers, isolated in the Greek village of Agia Anna, must confront everything they have run away from when an explosion on a local tourist boat rocks their world."
> *NIGHTS OF RAIN AND STARS* BY MAEVE BINCHY

> "In nineteenth century England, a partnership between two brilliant conjurers is threatened when one heedlessly pursues the shadowy magic of the Raven King."
> *JONATHAN STRANGE & MR. NORRELL* BY SUSANNA CLARKE

Here are two examples of effective pitch lines for popular novels of the last couple of decades:

> "Recent law school grad is offered a job that seems too good to be true—and it is."
> *THE FIRM* BY JOHN GRISHAM

"Best-selling writer needs to be wary of his Number One Fan; she's psychotic and is bent on keeping him her prisoner."

MISERY BY STEPHEN KING

WHAT COMES AFTER THE PITCH LINE?

You're not done yet. After you've delivered your pitch line, be ready to:

- summarize the rest of the plot
- compare your book to similar novels
- describe the setting

Agent Kathleen Anderson says, "You should be sure, wherever possible, to be specific about setting in your pitches. Instead of a small town, say *what* town; instead of Africa, *where* in Africa."

Allow the agent time to ask you questions. Try to structure some give-and-take into the conversation.

After the appointment is over and you've taken a deep breath, make a quick note of what the agent or editor said. You might be meeting with several. You don't want to confuse what they asked to see or how they asked for your material to be submitted.

OTHER USES FOR YOUR PITCH LINE

Conferences aren't the only time you'll use your pitch line. There are lots of other times to have one ready:

1. If you create your pitch line before you actually write the novel, it can guide your writing and keep your plot on track.

2. Friends and family may ask what you're writing about. Try your pitch line out on them as a good way to get practice and feedback.

3. Your pitch line can be your query letter's first sentence. In fact, agent Susan Zeckendorf recommends it. "In your letter state in one sentence what the book is about," she advises. "You have to catch the agent's eye right away."

4. If you already have an agent from a previous project, use your pitch line to launch a discussion of your next book before you write it. Your agent can give you great ideas and feedback on the marketability of your idea. Take the time to craft a compelling pitch line. It will serve you well.

You and Your Agent Can Work a Conference Together

BY TRACY COOPER-POSEY

These days, I coordinate with my agent so that we'll both attend many conferences together, and we work the room. She collars editors and tells them about her wonderful author, Tracy, and then draws me into the conversation.

"I was just telling Jenny here about your novel," she'll say. "Perhaps you should tell her about it."

That's my cue. I go into my pitch, while my agent wanders off to find another editor to chat with. I get a few precious minutes to schmooze with the editor, talk about her needs, and pitch other books that might fit those needs. (I, of course, edit my pitch to suit her requirements.)

Soon my agent is tugging at my elbow again, with another editor for me to meet. We make a great team.

Part Two:
The Package

pages, or chapters one through three. Design your chapters so they end in the right place. You can always reorganize them later and divide them up differently. But knowing what you'll be asked for can help you prepare in advance how you lay out your book.

What about that pesky prologue you've written for your book? Does that count as part of the first fifty pages? Would a request for the first three chapters mean the prologue, too? If they ask for only the first chapter, should you send the prologue or chapter one?

If you've set your prologue in a completely different time or place than the rest of your novel, don't send it. In the prologue for William Peter Blatty's famous novel *The Exorcist*, a religious figure wanders through an unspecified desert. The setting and tone are diametrically opposed to the contemporary Washington, DC, established in chapter one. In a case like this, we suggest you leave the prologue home and submit the first three chapters.

If your prologue is an integral part of the story, set in the same time period and in the same location as the rest of your book, then count that as part of the first fifty pages.

Why do agents and editors just ask for samples? Why don't they request the whole thing? "When I ask for just sample chapters, it's not because I'm less interested than I might be with someone else's query," agent Kathleen Anderson says. "It's because the success of the story for me will lie in the writing, and I can usually judge whether or not the writing works for me by just a few chapters."

Complete Manuscript

Many agents and editors agree with Kathleen Anderson, but not all. Some feel that once they've started reading those first three chapters and are hooked, they don't want to have to wait for the rest of the manuscript. Those agents and editors will always request you send in the complete manuscript, the finished product.

"I prefer to see the entire book," says agent George Nicholson. "For me, one or two chapters aren't enough to tell whether the book is salable. Besides, the less busywork I can get involved in, the better. If I receive only a partial, and I'm interested enough to ask for the whole book, requesting the rest of the book means more work on my part. But it's different for every agent."

SASE

"A good many young writers make the mistake of enclosing a stamped, self-addressed envelope, big enough for the manuscript to come back in," Ring Lardner once noted. "This is too much of a temptation to the editor."

Lardner's wit aside, you must enclose a #10 business-size SASE with your submission package. You hope the agent or editor will use it to send an acceptance letter, but it obviously may carry a rejection letter. It might seem like negative thinking to send it along, as if you're inviting rejection, but send it along you must. If your acceptance comes by phone, the agent and editor will either dump your SASE or use it to send your contract.

If you want your manuscript returned, you must enclose a larger, self-addressed, stamped mailer. But in these days of laser printers and relatively low photocopying charges, many writers prefer not to pay the extra postage. They include a small note at the end of their cover letter, sometimes in a postscript, that the manuscript is recyclable and need not be returned.

Agents and editors want to feel as if they are the first to read your manuscript. To help foster that feeling, it's a good idea to send only a fresh manuscript. As careful as agents and editors try to be, a coffee ring or a splotch of jelly may end up your pages. Even if it doesn't, paper becomes "tired" from handling. Why waste the return postage for a manuscript you're just going to have to recycle anyway?

Most agents and editors are accustomed to this practice and think nothing of tossing the manuscript into the recycle bin. Agent Evan Marshall has a different slant, though. Take this into consideration when deciding how to approach this issue. "I think people should care that their work be returned to them," he says. "They should think that this is their baby, even if it comes back dog-eared and unusable. Whenever I send something to an editor, I ask for it back. No agent tells an editor to throw it away. You're sending a subliminal message that this is valuable. It wouldn't make me not take someone on, but everything I have taken on has come with an envelope to send it back."

Cover Letter

Although they might not ask you to send a cover letter with your submission, not sending one is like making a phone call and refusing to speak when your party picks up.

Use the cover letter to reintroduce yourself briefly (you made your initial introduction through your query letter or at that writers conference) and identify what you're submitting. You can't assume that the recipient of your submission knows what's inside or will want to figure it out by going through the material. For more help with cover letters, turn to chapter eight.

Synopsis

A synopsis is a concise summary of your book's story. Agents and editors often request a synopsis with your submission package. Some will read it first before settling down with your manuscript; some even use it to decide if they will read your manuscript at all. Others save the synopsis until they've read your manuscript. Writing a synopsis is a task even successful writers dread. The good news is that the more successful you get, the less often you have to write a synopsis. Even better news is that in chapter seven you'll see that writing the synopsis doesn't have to be painful.

Chapter Outline

Although the term *outline* is often used synonymously with synopsis, these are separate entities. Some agents or editors request an outline, which expands the synopsis and gives a running summary of your novel, chapter by chapter. You'll learn more about the chapter outline in chapter seven.

PRESENTATION, PRESENTATION, PRESENTATION

Although what you write and how you write it is the most important consideration, the presentation of your overall submission package will also make an impression. The trick is to make a good impression.

"I don't like submissions that are sloppily put together," editorial director John Scognamiglio says. "Whatever you submit should be professionally presented. It should be neatly typed, with margins and a nice cover letter. The presentation is what first catches my eye."

While a package that follows all the standard conventions won't guarantee you representation or publication, one that breaks the rules will probably hurt your chances.

Jack Kerouac wrote the manuscript that would become his classic novel *On the Road* on one continuous scroll of paper, 120 feet long, with single-spaced text, no commas, and no paragraph breaks. He showed it to many publishers, insisting that he would only let them publish it if they left it unrevised.

Not surprisingly, they all turned him down.

Kerouac spent the next several years working on other novels, but finally, in 1957, he created a revised and more accessible version of *On the Road* and found a publisher. Proper presentation really does pay.

That said, we must add that in 2001, the original scroll version of *On the Road* sold for $2.4 million at auction to Jim Irsay, owner of the Indianapolis Colts.

FOLLOWING THE RULES

Some writers are tempted to pull out all the stops when submitting their manuscript. They resort to gimmicks and even gifts. They don't realize that the writing alone is what will get a foot in the door–and the gimmicks and gifts will slam it shut.

"Sometimes I get a fancy package with the manuscript bound together like a book, tied with ribbons and that sort of thing," says John Scognamiglio. "I need loose pages. I carry the manuscripts around with me. Or maybe I need to make a copy of it so somebody else can read it."

"There are the people who send chocolates and other little gifts," says editor Ginjer Buchanan, "which might be cute but won't make the least bit of difference in the evaluation of your manuscript. The one that has gone down as legend, though, is the writer who sent his manuscript in a hand-tooled leather binder inside a hand-carved wooden box. He didn't even send return postage, and he was from Canada. Apparently he thought fancy packaging would get our attention. It got a reaction, but not the one he was hoping for. His ploy couldn't disguise the fact that the manuscript wasn't very good. So don't send us distracting gifts or manuscripts on strange paper or in fancy boxes. If your writing is good, if your ideas are fresh, and if it is appropriate for us, then your work will get noticed."

"I get things on pink paper with perfume sprinkled over them and wrapped with ribbons," agent Evan Marshall says. "I get things printed on both sides of the page."

He gets them, and then he rejects them.

MANUSCRIPT FORMATTING

1. So that your manuscript won't be rejected because of improper formatting, follow our step-by-step guidelines: Use good quality, 8 ½" x 11" (22cm x 28cm) white paper (no onion skin).
2. Print on only one side of the page.

3. Double-space your manuscript. (One-page query letters and synopses should be single-spaced, but anything over one page must be double-spaced.)

4. Indent each paragraph, and do not insert an extra space between paragraphs. You can, however, leave an extra space between scene changes.

5. Use a good laser printer with sufficient toner.

6. Place your name, book title, and page number on the first line of each page. It should look like this:

Brown/THE DA VINCI CODE   3

Most word processing packages have a heading function that can do this for you.

7. Leave ample margins (½" to 1" [9cm to 2.5cm]) on all four sides of all pages.

8. Do not justify your manuscript's right margin; leave the edges ragged.

9. Drop down a quarter or half page to start a new chapter.

10. Include a cover page with your manuscript. Put your name, address, phone number, e-mail address, and approximate word count on the cover page. See the sample cover page on page 122.

11. Type "The End" on the last page.

12. To protect the last page from getting soiled, place a blank piece of paper at the end.

A WORD ON COPYRIGHT

There is no need to display the copyright symbol on your manuscript. You also don't need it on your cover letter, your synopsis, your chapter outline, or your sample chapters. The copyright laws automatically protect you before your work sees print. Generally, the publisher takes care of filing the copyright notice for you, inserting the copyright formula in your book, and registering your book with the Library of Congress. Most standard publishing contracts call for the copyright to be issued in your name.

As an aspiring author, you should know all this. Including the copyright notice on your submission marks you as an amateur. Also, it might send a most unwanted, negative message: "I don't trust you." That's no way to start a conversation, especially not when you're asking someone to risk time, money, and reputation on you.

Cover Page

Your Name ❶   Word Count ❷
Street Address
City, State, Zip Code
Phone number, e-mail address

Title

By

Your name

1. Your contact information is placed in the upper left-hand corner.

2. The word count is placed in the upper right-hand corner.

3. The title and your byline are centered halfway down the page.

ADAPTING TO MEET THE NEED

Long before Elmore Leonard became one of North America's most popular and prolific novelists, he wrote a treatment for a Western yarn he called *Legends* and tried to sell it to the movies. "I would write a book on spec," he says, "but not a screenplay." He had been immersing himself in Western lore and was able to write the treatment without much new research.

The treatment failed to sell as a film, but Marc Jaffe, an editor at Bantam Books, asked Leonard to do a Western novel, and Leonard used the *Legends* treatment to write the book. "Emmett Long" from the treatment became "Dana Moon" in the book. "If I wrote any more Westerns," Leonard explains, "I planned to use Emmett Long as a pseudonym." Something he never did.

The treatment for *Legends* doubles as a synopsis, and a compelling one at that–a good plot in an authentic setting, rendered crisply and with a good dose of Leonard's famous dialogue for flavor. It's long, but it reads short. And it shows how you can turn the sawdust of a failed project into gold. Although Leonard uses past tense, we recommend that you use present tense for your synopses.

The *Legends* treatment is reproduced here.

TREATMENT FOR *LEGENDS* BY ELMORE LEONARD

Elmore Leonard/LEGENDS   **1**

Two riders came down out of the Sierra Madres and re-crossed the Rio Grande with their prisoner: a one-eyed renegade Nimbre Apache named Lobo, who had jumped the reservation at San Carlos and was said to have taken part in the White Tanks massacre. They brought in Lobo and a young white woman, Carla Wells, the Apache had been dragging along with him since White Tanks. (They said they had to keep the young woman away from Lobo or she would have caved his head in with a rock.) They set the young woman free, returning her to what was left of her family, and delivered Lobo to the military lockup at Fort Huachuca.

For their trouble, both men were kicked out of the Army.

Emmett Long–a stringy cowboy turned contract guide, who was accepted as a brother by his Apache trackers and could read sign right along with them–was fired on the spot.

Sample Treatment

Brendan Early–after ten years on frontier station, 2nd Lt. Of Cavalry ("the Dandy 5th") and after telling the Department of Arizona what he thought of their candy-ass procedures–was forced to resign his commission.

They had gotten their man, but "without written authority to cross the border into Mexico to undertake an extended campaign ... and without the necessary complement of troops."

So there they were: loose, easygoing Emmett Long and Brendan Early, the long-haired swashbuckler, sitting in a saloon in Contention, Arizona, looking out at the desert. Em got talking to a man who was district superintendent for Hatch & Hodges, the stage line company, and found out they were expanding their services and needed a steady supply of fresh horses. So Em rounded up some of his White Mountain trackers and went into the horse business as a mustanger, halterbreaking green mounts and delivering them to the company's line stations.

Bren Early tried organizing and guiding for hunting parties–taking rich Easterners out for a look at the Wild West and a chance to shoot big horn and mule deer. The trouble was, Bren's temperament got in the way. He could stand hip-cocked and show them how to fan a six-shooter and keep a bean can jumping. But he didn't have the patience to wait on tourists, no matter how much they paid him. So Bren quit the hunting guide business and went into holding up Hatch & Hodges stagecoaches, the same company that was supporting Emmett.

Bren was caught at it and sentenced to ten years of hard labor at a work camp out in the desert, where convicts lived in cages and busted rocks building roads to nowhere.

Em, in the meantime, had gotten something going with Carla Wells–the young lady they'd rescued–and finally married her. She was a cute little thing, but salty talking and with a hard bark on her. Yes, she'd marry Emmett, but she wasn't going to live in any horse camp. She had him buy her a boarding house in Contention. That was where he could find her when he wasn't out in the bleak lonesome busting his ass.

Elmore Leonard/LEGENDS   **3**

Emmett was out there with his White Mountain boys one day when he happened across his old buddy Brendan Early chopping rocks on the road gang.

Bren said, "Sweet saving, Jesus, get me out of here, will you?"

Em thought it was pretty funny. The head guard, a son of a bitch named Brazil, didn't think it was funny at all and got mean with Emmett and ran him off with shotguns, scattering Em's herd. The head guard shouldn't have done that.

Emmett plotted and figured out a way to spring Bren loose without anyone getting seriously hurt. Bren promised to lead a pure life and not get in any trouble again. He went off prospecting for gold.

Emmett, about this time, was contacted by an official in the Department of the Interior and offered the job of Indian Agent at the Stone River Reservation. The money wasn't much, but Em was offered good land, too, the opportunity to develop his own spread, and Carla said it was OK with her. So Em got into the business of supervising life on an Indian reservation—handling serious human rights situations as well as petty squabbles—while operating a horse ranch on the side, keeping on his White Mountain Apaches, a good bunch to have in a tight spot.

Bren Early the gold prospector staked out claims in the mountains and hit pay dirt a couple of times. His trouble was not only impatience but holding onto his money. Bren was a big spender, and so eager to find gold he didn't realize right away he was sitting on a bonanza lode of copper. When this was discovered, the big-big company Dorado Mining moved in, gave Bren full treatment with booze and broads and visions of vast wealth. As a result, Dorado was able to buy a controlling interest in Bren's holdings and set him up as a company vice-president in charge of local operations.

Emmett Long had been dealing with a minor problem ever since he became an Indian Agent. Some of his charges had left the reservation to live up in the nearby mountains, where they were able to irrigate and develop rich plots of farmland—holdings that were small but adequate to their needs. Along with the reservation Indians in the mountains, there was a scattering of Chicano homesteads and even a small community of Black people.

The spokesman for the Chicanos was a revolutionary type named Santana who was always bitching about something–the encroachment of the
Indians–or looking for the Big Cause, some way he could be martyred.

The elder of the Black community was an ex-Tenth Cavalry sergeant
named Billy Goss, who was an old friend of Emmett's. The two of them liked
to track up into high country for a few days at a time, hunt mule deer and
drink whiskey and get away from their women.

Everything was going fine until the Bureau of Indian Affairs informed
Emmett that he had to get his people down out of the mountains and back to
the reservation.

What for? Nobody owned the land or was using it. But that's where he was
wrong. Dorado Mining had taken out leases on large tracts and they were
going in there to dynamite and test for copper lodes.

Shit, well let them test and if they didn't find any copper then let them
get their equipment out of there. No, the Bureau said, the Indians had to get
back on the reservation anyway.

But what about all the other people living up there? Well, if they didn't
clear out it was tough shit if somebody got hurt.

You know who the first one was to get it. Emilio Santana. He wouldn't
budge, took a bullet in the chest and died smiling.

Then the Black community was hit in a brutal raid that left several innocent people dead, including Billy Goss.

Emmett wired the Bureau, but they'd washed their hands of the situation. It was a local matter now, under the jurisdiction of the District Court.
Emmett went to court, but what kind of suit could he file? His people were
trespassing and the legal owners had the right to protect their property.

By this time, skirmishes were going on in the hills, both sides sniping at
each other, people getting killed. It became known in the press as the Dragoon Mountains War.

Next, Emmett rode to the Dorado Mining Company offices in Contention
and asked to see the man in charge. When they told him to leave and tried
to throw him out, he kicked the door down and there stood face-to-face with

Brendan Early. So they drank whiskey and discussed the situation, and Emmett didn't like the tone of it at all. Bren's attitude was: Why should Emmett worry? Those people didn't mean anything to him. Emmett said they had years staked in their land and the dynamiting was messing up their watersheds and running off their livestock. The chances were the company wouldn't find any ore; they pull out and leave the poor people ruined. It wasn't fair.

So when was life fair? Bren said. It was too bad, but that's the way it was.

On the way home, Emmett was stopped by a couple of company gunmen. They tried to have a little fun with him, scare him. When Emmett didn't flinch or back down, they got uglier and Emmett was forced to pull his gun and kill one of them. The next day he was arrested, charged with murder and placed in Contention jail.

It bothered Bren that he couldn't help Emmett and call off his dogs. But now his allegiance was to the company, and money. When Emmett was arrested, thought, it gave Bren the opportunity to return a favor and even their account. He told Emmett he could bribe a deputy and spring him loose if he wanted. Emmett said fine, but if he was allowed to walk out, he was going to ride up into the hills and finish this business, one way or another.

Emmett returned to find his house burned down, his herd scattered and Carla hiding in the woods. If he had any misgivings before, they were gone now. He got his wife, rounded up his White Mountain boys and rode up into high country.

Bren Early found he didn't have the clout he thought he did. When he tried to get the company to ease up, he was told his office had nothing to do with public relations. The man in charge of that job was a known gunman by the name of Sundeen, who had little or no respect for Bren Early, vice-president or not. So there was Bren with his house, his money, his ladies; but feeling pretty rotten and not able to rationalize his way out of it. What the hell was he supposed to do?

Emmett knew what to do. It wasn't even a matter of choice now. The fact that in the long run he couldn't win and probably would be shot dead was not a consideration. He'd stand with his people and the big company was going to suffer great pain and expense before it was through.

He said to Carla, "What do you think?" And she said to him, "When you're right, honey, stand up and kick ass." She was a sweet girl and would be there with him because there was no sending her away.

The Company posted a $5,000 reward for Emmett Long, dead or alive. Bren Early resented it. How come Emmett was getting all the attention?

Newspaper people came out to Contention and roamed the countryside trying to get a glimpse of the Dragoon Mountains War. They took pictures of reservation Apaches, peaceful Navahos and Lipans, holding old Army Springfields and muzzle-loaders. They posed Sundeen and his bunch in front of the Gold Dollar, getting them to display every weapon they owned and borrowed a few more, sticking the revolvers in their belts.

Sundeen ate it up ...

Until Emmett, with a big-bore .50 caliber Sharps, blew Sundeen out of his saddle at 480 measured yards, shattering the man's right arm and breaking some ribs. Sundeen went home, wherever that was.

Still, there were plenty of shooters to be hired at $25 a week who would take their rifles and some chuck and go up into the high country. Some of them did not come back. Those who did shook their heads and said there wasn't anybody up there–as though Emmett Long and his White Mountain boys were sitting on stumps waiting to be seen.

The mining company dynamite crews didn't see them either, thought they'd wake up to find all their powder and stores had disappeared in the night. How could you fight a man who didn't show himself? Armed men would sneak up on a rancheria and there wouldn't be a soul there or anything worth burning. They'd get back down to the draw where they'd left their horses and find them gone.

Meanwhile Emmett and his ghost band had hit another mine camp and put the fear of hell in men waking up bug-eyed in the night.

When the newspapers began laughing at the big important company, somebody at the company said, "Enough, get it done." So they mustered a couple hundred hard cases and hoboes in Contention, fed and armed them, and sent them up to kill that worrisome son of a bitch once and for all. Kill him or don't come back.

Bren Early said good-bye to the good life and rode out an hour ahead of them—rode out of Contention as he had ridden out of Cairo, Illinois, twenty-two years ago, to join in the Indian Wars before they were over. What in the hell had he been sitting on the fence for when Emmett was getting all the glory? What was important in life anyway?

Bren placed $500 in bets at the Gold Dollar that Emmett Long would never be shot dead nor taken alive ... left an envelope in the local newspaper office marked "PRINT AT ONCE" ... and lashed a case of good bourbon to his pack animal in case Emmett had run out of corn.

The message the newspaper typesetter took out of the envelope and put on his machine said: $10,000 REWARD—DEAD OR ALIVE, and the name under it, specified in even bigger letters, BRENDAN EARLY.

Emmett welcomed Bren with a feeling of apprehension. He trusted him, but ... what was going on? What was Bren so tickled about if he'd come over to join the doomed? Emmett wondered if Bren had put himself in this fight-to-the-death situation for the sole purpose of regaining his self-respect. Was that how Bren looked at it? It gave Emmett a strange feeling. Like they were putting on a show just for Bren.

Emmett knew the mining company army was on its way. He'd already sent his scouts to act as decoys, to lure the ragtag army into a box canyon. Emmett believed the plan had a slim chance of working and could save their lives if it did. But to lure them in so easily—he couldn't believe it when the two hundred armed men, under some fool who thought he was a general, marched eagerly into the canyon and stood there under Emmett's gun like they were anxious to be killed.

"A gesture," Brendan said. "The company wants out, but they can't do it with an egg on their face, so they send these rummies and drifters, thinking to smother you with numbers."

Emmett had settled his mind about dying if it was to come. But he wasn't going to shed blood for a company press release—for the newspaper people and photographers climbing up to his position, wanting to get pictures, they said, of both sides of the action.

Or for the man in tailored buckskins and white whiskers who came up to Emmett and said, "Sign here. If you get through this, Mr. Long, I want you in our Real and Authentic Rip-Roaring Wild West Show."

Emmett's White Mountain Apaches and the tough Chicano farmers and the hard-eyed survivors from the Black settlement, they all looked at him. What was going on? Brendan Early drew matched revolvers and said, "Come on. Let's get to it."

Not yet aware.

Now Carla was looking at him. She said, "What are we doing here?"

Emmett said, "I don't know. I didn't see it happening, but it's over."

The White Mountain boys had already felt it and were disappearing, moving off one by one. The Chicanos and the Blacks stood looking at Emmett a little longer. Now they began to walk away.

Emmett turned to Brendan Early. He said, "You're too late for your glory." He looked up to see all his people gone. "And I've stayed too long."

It stopped Brendan. What, never again face death and feel the kick of his six-shooters? It took Bren a minute or so to readjust; not much longer than that.

He looked at the man in the tailored buckskins and white whiskers, thought a moment, then looked at Emmett. "We're paid up," Bren said, "rode hard and lived to tell about it. That's worth more than something. You want to stoop in a cornfield or walk tall down the main drag?"

The man in the tailored buckskins was waiting.

Emmett thought hard and said to Carla, "It wouldn't hurt to see the sights, would it?" Carla said to him, "You're the sights. You and your partner." But she'd go along. What the hell.

Emmett looked over at Brendan. He said, "Let's see what's next."

AGENT AND EDITOR ETIQUETTE (YOURS, NOT THEIRS)

Once you've sent in the requested "more," the wait begins. We admit that this can be difficult to deal with for some people, and in chapter nine you'll find tips to help you through it. But now is a good time to look at a few more important rules that you might be tempted to break at this stage of the process.

Believe it or not, some new writers, with no track record and no reason to think they could get away with it, are demanding, overbearing, aggressive, and just plain rude. They make unpleasant phone calls and write unpleasant letters.

The quality of your work is not the only element evaluated by an agent or editor considering a business relationship with you. Successful relationships are long term; no one wants to work with someone who is arrogant.

While brewing new plots and honing your craft takes time and effort, providing a turnoff is quick and easy.

But avoiding one is easy, too. Here are some examples of blatant turnoffs to steer clear of.

Turnoff #1: Inappropriate Phone Calls

There are times you can call to check on your manuscript. If it was solicited material and you haven't heard within the response time reported in the market guide listing, adding another week of waiting time, then making a polite call during business hours is appropriate. But there are inappropriate times and ways to call.

THE MIDDLE-OF-THE-NIGHT PHONE CALL

Kent Brown, founder of Boyds Mills Press, reveals the worst experience he ever had with a writer:

> 3:25 a.m. my phone rang. The voice on the other end said, "Kent Brown?"
>
> I said, "Yes."

"Kent L. Brown?"

"Yes."

"You work at *Highlights for Children*?"

"Yes."

Now, I have three children. And this sounds to me just the way the state police would contact you when they have a cadaver that belongs to you. I was beginning to get very stressed.

Then the caller said, "I need to get published."

I said, "You can't call me in the middle of the night," and hung up.

And she called back.

I went into the other room and said, "Okay, tell me what your name is."

She did, then said, "You won't hold this against me?"

I said, "I certainly will," and hung up. I believe that is the only time in twenty-eight years I ever hung up on an author.

THE "BUT WHY? BUT WHY?" PHONE CALL

Editor Wendy McCurdy says calls from writers asking why their work was rejected turn her off. "That always puts me in an awkward position, because I will never say to a person that I rejected something because it was terrible," she says. "So what does that leave me to say if that was the case? All I can say is I get so many submissions, I just don't remember. I don't want to be responsible for affecting a person's life that way."

"Arguing with my decision doesn't help," former editor Michael Seidman says. "In fact, it's only going to work against you with future submissions. Editors are only human (although some are willing to accept deification). If I had a sleepless night, I'm not going to be in a good mood. So, stay cool and professional, show the respect that anyone deserves (as we try to show you that respect by reading what you send), and keep your fingers crossed."

THE "DID IT GET THERE YET?" PHONE CALL

"I dislike writers who call and ask if I received their manuscript," agent Nancy Love says. "This can easily be remedied by sending a self-addressed, stamped postcard along with the manuscript."

Former Firebrand editor Nancy Bereano says, "Don't call to follow up on a manuscript. If a publisher has a reputation for not losing manuscripts and for responding, and the publisher says she will get back in two to four weeks, then just assume the publisher will do that. I won't talk to people on the phone about why we rejected their manuscript or how soon we'll get back to them."

Turnoff #2: Gimmicks

Resist the temptation to use strange colors (or even shapes!) of paper for your synopsis. Don't dab perfume on your romance novel chapter outline. Forget about tucking a pinecone into the envelope with your query for a novel starring a forest ranger. Such gimmicks certainly get an agent's attention, but the attention is usually negative.

Evan Marshall says, "I get a lot of books with the hero named Evan. This has happened too often for me to think it's coincidence. In these days of 'find and replace,' I picture all these writers sitting at their computers, changing the main characters' names depending upon the agent to whom they are submitting."

And, if you're writing science fiction, for example, don't think you'll impress an editor or agent by claiming you've visited other planets. Although you might get a laugh, you probably won't get an acceptance.

Turnoff #3: Hard-on-the-Eyes Manuscripts

Before an agent can decide to represent your novel, she's got to be able to read your query and synopsis. Legibility is critical. Make sure your toner is fresh, so that you have maximum contrast between black print and white paper. Select an easy-to-read typeface.

"I prefer to be sent clean copy," agent Nancy Yost says. "It doesn't have to be on a laser printer, but handwritten ones are out. And I hate to admit it, but there's always a bit of a psychological prejudice against manuscripts produced on an old typewriter. All that Wite-Out®. You want to feel your writers are current, using computers."

Turnoff #4: Improper Manuscript Formatting

"Be sure that the manuscript is double-spaced and that the pages are numbered," agent Susan Zeckendorf says. "These are things that people don't necessarily do."

Agent Pesha Rubinstein says, "Manuscripts *must* be double-spaced. You wouldn't believe how many projects get submitted to me that are still single-spaced. It's hard on the eyes; you can't read it."

Proper formatting means double-spaced copy; ½" to 1" (2cm to 2.5cm) margins on top, sides, and bottom, and each paragraph indented with no extra space between paragraphs.

Turnoff #5: Overdone Manuscript Packaging

Again, common sense must prevail. You want to make sure your manuscript is well protected in transit so that it arrives at the agent's office crisp and clean. But you also want the agent to be able to open the package without having to use a blowtorch.

"In any industry there are rules you usually follow, and not to [do so] shows you're an amateur, not aware of the conventions," says Evan Marshall. "I get things packed so tight that it's like a Brink's truck. My secretary and I hack away at it with sledgehammers and axes to get it open, and by the time it's open, we barely want to look at it. All you really need to do is put your manuscript in a box and then put it in a simple mailer and staple it four times. You don't need rubber bands, bubble wrap, duct tape, newspaper, or jiffy bags with stuffing so we have to vacuum every day."

Turnoff #6: Queries and Submissions Via Fax and E-mail

"Faxes are a turnoff," Evan Marshall says. "It's never going to look as good as a nice crisp letter. And of course an SASE can't accompany a fax."

"We don't want manuscripts by e-mail," editor Kent Brown says. "Most of the manuscripts get read in somebody's bed or armchair. So far, it's easier to read black type on paper than it is on a computer screen."

Imagine the turnoff when a new writer sends a ZIP file of his manuscript via e-mail. He or she obviously expects the agent or editor either to pay for the toner and paper and take the time to print it out, or sit there at the screen and read a whole novel. Either way, it won't work.

Now, having said that, once you have a contract and you're delivering a finished product, some editors will ask for ZIP files or disks. But it's rare for that to happen with the first read.

The way you prepare and submit your manuscript can make a good impression or turn an agent or editor off. While not all transgressions are major, and many do border on overly picky, they can add up to convey an unfavorable image. There's certainly humor in some of them, but unless you're a comedy writer, you don't want an agent or editor laughing at your unconventional approach. The idea is to be taken seriously.

Getting published is hard enough; don't make it more difficult for yourself. Learning the conventions and following through with them might even impress the person you were thoughtful enough not to annoy.

Submission Dos and Don'ts

Do remember to enclose a #10 SASE for the reply, a large SASE mailer for the return of the manuscript, and a self-addressed, stamped postcard so the agent or editor can notify you that he or she received the manuscript.

Do your homework before sending anything out. Know whom you're submitting your work to. Request guidelines, sample copies or catalogs.

Do learn the jargon. Know the difference between a multiple submission and a simultaneous submission (see chapter four for an explanation).

Do send your work to reputable publishing houses and literary agencies. Know the scams and what to avoid. Don't pay reading fees or sign a contract that asks you for money.

Do show from your correspondence or phone conversations that you are an agreeable, flexible person. Agents take personality into account when deciding whom to represent. Editors can be put off from accepting a book if the writer is impossible to deal with.

Don't bind your manuscript. You can place one large elastic band around it to hold the pages loosely together.

Don't use staples on any submissions.

Don't overwrap your manuscript.

Don't send your manuscript registered or insured. Requiring agents or editors to sign for packages is an inconvenience for them.

> ***Don't*** send your only copy.
>
> ***Don't*** call a few days after sending your package to ask the agent if he or she received your manuscript.
>
> ***Don't*** make costly mistakes such as calling your work a "fictional novel." (All novels are fiction; the redundancy shows amateur status.)

SIMULTANEOUS SUBMISSIONS

We pointed out in chapter four that it's okay to submit query letters simultaneously. Submitting manuscripts simultaneously can be okay–but not if an agent has asked for an exclusive read–many do nowadays because of the pressure of competition. Although it takes little time to respond to a query, a lot more effort goes into reading an entire manuscript, and it's understandable if an agent requires an exclusive read.

Most agents include their need for an exclusive read in their market guide listings. If you don't want to lose the time that would involve, don't query that agent.

Even if this requirement isn't listed, they'll tell you about it if and when they respond positively to your query. Now you have to decide if this is an agent you'd really like to work with. (If not, you really shouldn't have bothered querying in the first place.) If so, it's worth your while to grant the exclusive. You can (politely) provide a four- to six-week time limit for the exclusive. If the agent goes over that time limit, and you have others waiting, then follow up with a note or phone call.

What if your manuscript is already out elsewhere on an exclusive read when the request for another exclusive comes in? Simply wait to hear back from the first agent before you send the manuscript out again. No one is waiting impatiently for your manuscript to arrive. They've put the request in the mail to you and gone on to other things. There's no need for you to write the second agent and tell her or him it will be a couple of weeks before you can send the material.

New writers often ask us, "But what if I send my manuscript to four or five agents, and all of them want to represent me? Or what if more than one publishing house wants to accept my book?"

It *could* happen–but it probably won't. If it should, go with the agent you feel will represent you best and write polite letters declining the others' services.

If more than one publisher is vying for your book, call the agent you want to represent you. The agent will conduct an auction to get the best contract for you.

Final Submission Checklist

When those requests for more start coming in, be ready. Here's a checklist to help you keep organized.

- ☐ Photocopy several sets of your first three chapters as well as your complete manuscript.
- ☐ Have your one-page synopsis ready to go.
- ☐ Make sure the cover letter you've prepared to accompany your submission packet is personally addressed to the agent or editor, reminds her that your material is solicited, and states your genre, word count, and a one- or two-line description of the plot.
- ☐ Prepare enough #10 SASEs to include in your submissions. Either mention in your cover letter that it's not necessary to return the manuscript or enclose a large postage-paid mailer for the manuscript's return.
- ☐ Keep a list of all agents and editors you've queried, the dates you heard from them and sent the requested material, and an itemization of what each submission packet contains.

Chapter Seven:
Successful Synopses

"I just sit at a typewriter and curse a bit."—P.G. WODEHOUSE

If all goes well with the querying or pitching process, the agent or editor will ask to see more. In addition to sample chapters or your complete manuscript, more almost always includes a synopsis.

So, what is a synopsis? It's a summary with feeling. It's a good read with strong narrative writing in the present tense. And it's an important tool for getting an agent or publisher for your novel.

It is *not* a blow-by-blow, scene-by-scene outline. Some agents or editors may use the terms "outline" and "synopsis" interchangeably, but don't be confused. Unless the agent specifically asks for a chapter-by-chapter outline, you'll use the synopsis for your initial submission.

While a chapter outline may run to dozens of pages, your synopsis must be short. You'll need to summarize your story in just a few pages. Many agents and editors require a synopsis of no longer than a single page!

Don't panic. You can give them exactly what they want. You're learning to create pitch lines and queries. A synopsis draws on those same skills.

And if you find the prospect of writing a synopsis daunting, you're in good company.

Robyn Carr, author of *Mind Tryst* and *Informed Risk*, says, "My agent says she can tell how good a novel will be on the basis of a short synopsis. My editor says she can, too. But I can't, and I'm the one who has to write the blasted novel."

Mega-best-selling novelists like Dean Koontz and Stephen King no longer have to write a synopsis to sell a novel. Their names do the selling. "I send 'em the book; they publish it," King says. "It's a great deal. And give me credit for this: I'm smart enough to be grateful."

But until you reach the level of a Dean Koontz or a Stephen King, the synopsis is an essential tool for selling your novel.

Why Dick Francis Has Never Had to Write a Synposis

Dick Francis told us how he managed to publish a series of best-sellers without using a selling tool we've been telling you is crucial. Here's his story, in his own words.

"The first book I had published—in 1957—was my autobiography, *The Sport of Queens*, based mostly, up to that time, on my life as a young rider of ponies and horses and, ultimately, as a successful steeplechase jockey. I was persuaded to try my hand at this by an author's agent, Englishman John Johnson. Our mothers were friends, and on one occasion, when John had driven his mother to have tea at my mother's London apartment, he happened to be walking around the apartment looking at photographs on the walls while the two old ladies were conversing about something of no importance. Suddenly, John came across a photograph of the Queen Mother's horse, Devon Loch, collapsing with me in the 1956 Grand National when many lengths in front of any of our rivals, and with only about twenty-five to thirty yards of the race still left to run. It was one of the greatest disasters, not only in racing but in the whole sporting calendar.

"John immediately got my address and telephone number from my mother and suggested to me that the 'Devon Loch disaster' was an ideal peg on which to 'hang' an autobiography, and why didn't I try my hand at it? After much persuasion from John—and my wife, Mary—I first put pen to paper during the summer of 1956 and finally handed the completed manuscript (which I got permission from Her Majesty to call *The Sport of Queens*) to John during the spring of the following year.

"John said he would take it around the London publishing houses and see if any of them were interested enough to publish, and after I had suggested to him that I had been lucky enough to ride—and win!—on some racehorses owned by publisher Michael Joseph, he immediately took the manuscript to the Joseph publishing house.

"This was followed by Joseph saying that if I wrote one, or perhaps two, more chapters he would be only too pleased to publish. This he did in December 1957, and I'm glad to say it was an immediate success. I had, by this time, retired from being a jockey, this career being immediately followed by that of racing correspondent for the Sunday Express, a successful London newspaper.

"One of the conditions of *The Sport of Queens* contract with Michael Joseph Ltd. was that if I ever wrote anything else, Joseph must have priority in seeing the manuscript before any other publisher. So, in late 1961, John Johnson submitted to them the manuscript of my first novel, *Dead Cert*, and this they accepted, and published in the spring of the following year. My second (*Nerve*) and third (*For Kicks*) novels were published in the springs of 1964 and 1965, but on submitting the For Kicks manuscript, Joseph said that in order to get me into their 1965 'Christmas Sales' list, they would very much like to have a second manuscript for publication that year. I duly went to work very hard, and the submission of the *Odds Against* manuscript was achieved in time to meet this said list.

"Since then, there has been a new fall Dick Francis novel published in London by Michael Joseph Ltd. and in New York by G.P. Putnam's Sons every year without interruption. I have also done (1986) the biography of the highly successful British jockey Lester Piggott. In London it was titled *Lester* and in New York, *A Jockey's Life*."

So, if you want to be a famous novelist, first become a successful jockey?

That's not the lesson here. Nor is the notion that if you wait long enough, you'll be discovered. But if you write with the skill and insight of Dick Francis, your novel has a chance of finding a publisher and an audience. If it can happen for a man who rode horses for a living, it can happen for you.

WHY WRITING A SYNOPSIS IS SO DIFFICULT

Here are three very good reasons why a synopsis is difficult to write:

1. A Synopsis Is Different From a Novel. As a novelist, you tell stories–long stories. You use narration to create compelling scenes. You've learned to show, not tell. Now you're faced with the prospect of having to summarize your story.

If you'd wanted to write summaries, you'd have gotten a job writing study guides, right?

2. A Synopsis Should Read Like a Novel. You must summarize your story in a few brilliantly chosen paragraphs but avoid reducing it to bloodless "synopsis speak." If it reads like a series of "and then he ... and then she ... and then they ... ," you won't like writing it and, worse, an agent or editor won't like reading it.

If they don't like reading it, they simply don't read it.

3. A Synopsis Leaves Out a Lot of the Story. You'll probably try to tell too much. You created the story. To you every scene is important, or you wouldn't have included it. But now you must select only the high points for your synopsis, perhaps leaving out entire subplots.

It's a tough job, but not nearly as tough as writing a novel. Apply your creativity, your determination, and your craft to this new format, and you'll come up with an effective sales tool to help your novel find its audience.

Once you understand the purpose for your synopsis and the elements it should include, you'll be able to do a fine job.

WHEN TO WRITE THE SYNOPSIS

When is the best time to write the synopsis, before or after you write the book? Either will work.

If you write your synopsis before you begin the novel, the process will help you create and smooth your plot, and the synopsis can guide you while you write.

The book will probably take on a life of its own as you write it, and you may depart from your synopsis. When that happens, simply go back and rewrite the synopsis.

Once you have an agent for one book, writing the synopsis first for the next book makes a lot of sense. When discussing future projects, you can present your ideas in the one-page synopsis format to get your agent's feedback. If there are any problems with your plot, your agent can make suggestions before you invest your time, energy and creativity in writing the book.

Many writers plan on (or put off) writing the synopsis until after they finish the manuscript. Just as with writing the novel, the process of creating a synopsis varies with each writer. You'll need to find the best way for you.

Kate Hoffmann, author of *Love Potion #9* and *Lady of the Night*, does a great deal of plotting before creating the synopsis. "Before I begin writing, I develop the characters, story goals, and setting," she says. "Often, I choose the hero's and heroine's story goals so that they are in conflict with each other. After that, I work out motivation and external conflicts. Then I work on the internal conflict–what keeps the characters from falling in love. Once I have these well in hand, I begin my synopsis."

"A synopsis is one of the last things I do when writing a book," says Kiel Stuart, author of *Magic in Ithkar* and *Tales of the Witch World*. "Usually I don't think the sort of scribble I do when beginning a novel from scratch (clustering, character and plot sketches) counts as a synopsis."

SYNOPSIS FORMAT

Keep it simple. Forget cover pages and binders, illustrations and borders, novelty fonts and colored ink. Your characters and conflicts, plus your strong narrative writing, will sell your project. Still, the presentation must be professional.

In the upper left-hand corner, single-spaced, provide the following:

- title
- genre
- approximate word count
- your name
- one-sentence pitch line (optional)

Just as with your query and cover letters, you should single-space your one-page synopsis. If the synopsis runs longer than one page single-spaced, then double-space it. Indent paragraphs but don't leave extra lines between paragraphs.

Select a readable typeface. Don't go smaller than ten-point type, trying to squeeze more words on a page. Use black ink on white paper. Legibility is the key to the physical presentation.

ELEMENTS OF A SUCCESSFUL SYNOPSIS

"The goal is not to explain the entire book," says James Scott Bell, author of *A Greater Glory* and *A Higher Justice*. "The goal is to get the editor, agent, or reader hooked enough to read the sample chapters and to see the market potential."

You need to convey a clear idea of what your book is about, what characters we'll care about (including the ones we'll hate), what's at stake for the main character(s), and how the conflict comes out.

"Basically, we're reading for a sense of characters, conflict internal and external, and some indication of the setting," says editor Karen Taylor Richman.

Understanding these key elements "can help potential authors write brief but effective synopses instead of dry plot summaries," Bell says.

Your synopsis should include:

- the opening hook
- quick sketches of the main characters
- plot highlights
- core conflict
- the conclusion

Let's look at each section of a synopsis.

1. The Opening Hook

Author James A. Ritchie reminds us of just how important a good beginning is. "It's the first chapter that matters most," he says. "And perhaps the first page of the first chapter matters most of all. I have a hunch many editors stop reading if the first page or two doesn't hold their interest. So I work on this above all else. Get the opening sentence perfect, make it ask a question the editor/reader wants answered, and you're well on the way to selling a novel."

And as with the novel, you must start strong with the novel synopsis. Agents and editors want to be engaged when they're up late at night, plowing through submissions. If they don't like the opening, they won't get through the rest of it.

"Open with a hook, just as you would in a novel," says Marilyn Campbell, author of *Pyramid of Dreams* and *Worlds Apart*. Your opening sentences should pull the editor or agent into the synopsis, just as your first scene must pull the reader into the novel.

The hook you create for your synopsis may or may not be the opening scene in your novel, but it has to be every bit as involving and engaging as that opening scene. You might use the same opening hook that you provided in your query letter.

Barbara Parker, author of *Suspicion of Guilt* and *Suspicion of Innocence*, gives her editor a double hook–"a super short spoonful you can gulp down in ten seconds" and then "an expanded version to nibble on."

Here's her "super short spoonful" for the novel *Blood Relations*, published by Dutton:

The woman whom attorney Thomas Gage loved, then abandoned over twenty years ago, begs him to defend her daughter, a young fashion model charged with murdering the owner of a South Beach nightclub. Then another murder occurs, and Tom has to confront his past and the recent suicide of his only son to discover the truth.

We've got two murders, family conflict, and backstory all in two crisp sentences, fifty-seven words.

John Tigges, author of *The Curse* and *Evil Dreams*, doesn't waste any time getting to the action with his hook for the synopsis of *Monster*:

Mal and Jonna Evans, in an effort to save their marriage, which has been jeopardized by Jonna's extramarital affair, go backpacking near Garibaldi Provincial Park, British Columbia. On their first night, while preparing their evening meal, a Sasquatch barges into their camp and grabs Jonna.

And we're off.

In the first two sentences, we've got exotic setting (Garibaldi Provincial Park, British Columbia), conflict (a marriage at risk), backstory (Jonna's extramarital affair), and, oh yes, the monster.

Robert W. Walker, author of *Cutting Edge* and *Unnatural Instinct*, uses this grabber for *Darkest Instinct*:

FBI Medical Examiner Dr. Jessica Coran must stare into the oldest and darkest instinct known to mankind–murderous rage–to unmask a vicious, phantom killer who leaves his victims in the water, mangled and mutilated. The monster has turned loose his venom against young women in seaside towns and cities along Florida's coastal waters, turning dark the sun. A population is terrorized, unsure when or where the Night Crawler will strike next.

Karen Wiesner, author of *Degrees of Separation* and *The Fifteenth Letter*, offers this hook for *Tears on Stone*, one of the erotic thrillers in her Falcon's Bend Series:

MaryEmma Gold, someone Pete's older brother Jordan knew and loved as a boy, is secretive and on-edge. She and her sister are in hiding. But from what? When Pete offers to do his brother a favor by digging into her background, he uncovers murder in the form of a conspiracy that both horrifies him and confronts him with the age-old question of "Is murder ever justifiable?"

Finally, here's Eva Augustin Rumpf's hook for her new campus satire, *Prot U:*

Mike Carter, a hard-working commuter student and editor of the campus newspaper, just wants to graduate and get a good job. But his investigative instincts are sparked when he uncovers a costly secret plan underway on the campus and reveals it in the student newspaper. The administration cracks down on the paper, and Mike is faced with the agonizing choice of compromising his journalistic principles and losing the admiration of protégé Jenny Lofton, or defying the administration and jeopardizing his carefully planned future.

2. Character Sketches

You need to provide a sense of your main characters' motivations, especially those that will bring the characters into conflict with one another. Most writers simply weave these motivations into the plot summary. Others provide separate thumbnail portraits of their characters.

"The characters' physical descriptions are not vital, but their motivations are," Marilyn Campbell says.

Here's how Barbara Parker describes her *Blood Relations* protagonist:

Like many successful men who have hit forty-something, Thomas Gage found out how hollow his success really was. By the time Matthew died, Tom was already about to topple. Losing Matthew sent him in the wrong direction: toward disintegration. A second chance with Susan will help to turn him around. He betrayed her love for him when they were young. Now he has to make her believe it isn't too late.

Here's how Kate Hoffmann describes the heroine for her novel *Wanted: Wife:*

Elise Sinclair is in love with love—perfect qualifications for a wedding consultant. From a crumbling Victorian townhouse in Chicago's Old Town, Elise runs her wedding consulting business, A Tasteful Affair. In addition to dealing with tasteless clients, Elise's happiness is hindered by a leaky roof, a temperamental heating system, inconsistent cash flow, and two demanding and aloof Persian cats named Clorinda and Thisbe.

She is, Hoffmann tells us, a "hopeless romantic"–a characteristic Hoffmann will reveal in the novel through action and dialogue without ever labeling her.

Blythe begins her synopsis for *Broken Connections*, which earned her a television movie option, with this quick sketch of her heroine's backstory:

> Twenty-six-year-old Julie Hampton, author of several gardening books, has returned to her native Boston from California after separating from her philandering husband, Joel Gregg. Julie had fled to California seven years earlier to attend UC Berkeley and to put as much distance as she could between herself and her mother.

Karen Wiesner doubles up on this character sketch for her Falcon's Bend Series:

> Melody and Cherry, identical twins, grew up in different families, each traumatized in her own way. Melody is Andre's wife, and yet, she's the only woman who hasn't fallen for his charms. Her sister Cherry is a dancer at Andre's club and the one who refuses to do anything to betray her boss.

3. Plot Highlights

Once you've captured interest with an effective hook, you must sustain it with the body of your synopsis. Your hook has made a promise; now you must make good on that promise.

"Detail the beginning and ending scenes and one or two in the middle that give an indication of the kind of emotional intensity or type of action to be expected," Marilyn Campbell says. "Be clear about the type of action in your book. If your story contains explicitly graphic sex or violence, that should be obvious in the synopsis."

Kate Hoffmann says, "I try to present each major scene in the book by following this form: incident, reaction, decision."

Ah, but which are the major scenes? Here are two guidelines to apply in auditioning a scene for possible inclusion in the synopsis:

1. Do I need this scene to make the primary plot hang together?

2. Do I need this scene for the ending to make sense?

Barbara Parker has a simple rule for picking out plot highlights: "I have gone back to my first rule of novel writing, which is 'How can we make the protagonist(s) suffer?'"

Your synopsis reveals how much and what kind of trouble your poor protagonist is going to encounter. In the next section, you'll learn how to show that in even more detail.

4. Core Conflict

If you don't have a conflict, you don't have a story to tell or to sell. That's why you need to make sure your book's core conflict is clear in your synopsis.

Ideally, your hook will contain your conflict. In Barbara Parker's "super short spoonful," quoted on page 144, we have protagonist Thomas Gage's double conflict made clear while solving two murders; he must also confront a past love and the suicide of his only son. In the same way, the opening sentences of John Tigges's synopsis establish an emotional conflict (saving a troubled marriage) and a physical one (the sudden appearance of the monster Sasquatch).

If your conflict isn't implicit in your hook, spell it out. As with your pitch line, you should be able to state your core conflict in a single sentence.

For practice, take a few novels you've read recently and see if you can put the core conflict of each into a sentence. If you're familiar with these classics of American literature, try the same exercise with each of them:

> *To Kill a Mockingbird* by Harper Lee
> *The Adventures of Huckleberry Finn* by Mark Twain
> *The Old Man and the Sea* by Ernest Hemingway
> *The Great Gatsby* by F. Scott Fitzgerald
> *Invisible Man* by Ralph Ellison
> *Gone With the Wind* by Margaret Mitchell
> *One Flew Over the Cuckoo's Nest* by Ken Kesey

Did you give them a try? The more you practice, the better you'll get. Here's how we would state the core conflicts for the classic tales:

To Kill a Mockingbird by Harper Lee: Attorney Atticus Finch fights the bigotry of the small-town South to defend a Black man falsely accused of rape.

The Adventures of Huckleberry Finn by Mark Twain: A boy must choose between upholding social mores by turning in an escaped slave or risk hell by letting his friend escape.

The Old Man and the Sea by Ernest Hemingway: Aging fisherman Santiago battles to save his great catch from sharks.

The Great Gatsby by F. Scott Fitzgerald: Millionaire Jay Gatsby remains hopelessly in love with his married ex-lover, Daisy Buchanan.

Invisible Man by Ralph Ellison: Young Black man struggles to define himself in a racist society that insists he deny his authentic self.

Gone With the Wind by Margaret Mitchell: Headstrong, spoiled Scarlett O'Hara loves her cousin Melanie's husband, Ashley Wilkes, and is in turn loved by the opportunistic and dashing Rhett Butler.

One Flew Over the Cuckoo's Nest by Ken Kesey: Brash inmate Randall McMurphy fights the oppressive Big Nurse Ratched for control of a mental institution.

You'll have an easier time developing and defining your core conflict if you think in terms of one or more of these four traditional categories:

1. person vs. person

2. person vs. nature

3. person vs. society

4. person vs. self

Your core conflict may, of course, overlap categories and could even touch on all four. Here's an example:

> Tortured by grief and loss (person vs. self) and fleeing a wrongful conviction for a crime he didn't commit (person vs. society), Dr. Richard Kimble struggles to survive (person vs. nature) while fleeing the relentless lawman who pursues him (person vs. person).

That, of course, states the core conflicts for the successful television series and movie *The Fugitive*.

If you can't come up with a core conflict to describe your novel, the problem may be with the book rather than the synopsis. Your book must have conflict. If you can't find the conflict in your novel, then neither will an agent or editor.

5. The Conclusion

A synopsis is not a quiz or a puzzle. Don't close with a cliffhanger. Revealing the ending to your novel won't spoil the story for the editor or agent. It will show that you've successfully finished your novel.

"Make sure every loose thread is tied up and never leave an editor guessing about anything," Marilyn Campbell says.

"Cover all the important bases to show that you can bring the story to a satisfying conclusion," says author Gail Gaymer Martin.

"Don't try to be cute and leave us guessing what is going to happen in the story," editor Karen Taylor Richman says. "The whole purpose of this process is to determine if the story is anything that might work for us."

Literary agent Pesha Rubinstein stresses this point. "I cannot stand teasers saying, 'Well, you'll just have to read the manuscript to find out what the end is.' I need to know the whole story in order to see if it makes sense."

If your novel is one of a series, your ending can point to the sequel, as Robert W. Walker does in his outline for *Darkest Instinct:*

> Santiva then tells her about another case he wants her to attend to, one that will take her to London, where a madman is killing people for their eyes. She'll be working alongside the man who helped them track Patric Allain.

Notice when you read Marshall's one-page synopsis later in this chapter (on page 152) that he also alludes to the next book in the series.

HOW TO STRUCTURE YOUR SYNOPSIS

After having worked with editors at five different publishing houses in three different genres–contemporary, paranormal romance, and contemporary category romance–Marilyn Campbell says she's learned that "there are no set guidelines for the perfect synopsis."

Develop a format that best lets you tell your story.

Most synopses, especially the shorter ones, weave character and conflict into a tight narrative. Each paragraph must flow naturally from the paragraph before it.

Some writers deal with the conflict in one paragraph; plot highlights in a second paragraph; a paragraph for each major character; and then the resolution.

Kate Hoffmann uses this basic outline for each synopsis:

First paragraph: hook; story setup

Second paragraph: heroine's story goal; motivation; physical description; internal and external conflicts; backstory

Third paragraph: hero's story goal; motivation; physical description; internal and external conflicts; backstory

Following paragraphs: story development; conclusion

Carla Anderson, who writes Silhouette romances such as *Into the Sunset* and *Montana Man* as Jessica Barkley, devotes a tight paragraph each to:

- the setting
- the heroine

- the hero
- the beginning
- the romance (internal conflicts)
- the external conflict
- the complication
- the ending

Whatever format you use, if you've enclosed the first three chapters in your submission packet, don't begin your synopsis at chapter four. Let the agent or editor get an accurate sense of your story from the beginning.

FOUR WAYS TO AVOID "SYNOPSIS SPEAK"

Your synopsis is not the place for promotional-style book jacket copy, a medley of adjectives and adverbs, or every possible scene and background detail. But don't settle for a dry plot summary. If your synopsis is flat and stilted, the agent or editor will assume that your manuscript is, too.

Here are four ways to make the synopsis sing:

1. Select the Right Tense and Person. No matter what choices you've made for the novel itself, write the synopsis in present tense and third person. ("Ahab harpoons the whale.") Third person works well for summary, and present tense creates immediacy and drama.

2. Use an Appropriate Writing Style. Stick with the same writing style you use in your novel. Dark, brooding novel? You want a dark, brooding synopsis. A chatty, upbeat novel begets a chatty, upbeat synopsis.

Dull, plodding novel? Rewrite the novel.

3. Choose Effective Nouns and Verbs. Make strong action verbs and specific, concrete nouns carry the weight. Use adjectives and adverbs sparingly.

Remember, the synopsis is not a book review, and it's not a book jacket blurb. Eliminate opinion words and phrases ("in the next scintillating plot twist, which will have the reader on the edge of his chair ..."). Just tell your story. Let the editor or agent judge if it's scintillating or not.

4. Use Dialogue Sparingly ... If At All. Many successful synopses contain no dialogue. Include dialogue only if it's essential to reveal character or further the plot or create dramatic intensity.

HOW LONG IS LONG ENOUGH?

"The length of the synopsis depends on the complexity of the story's premise, background, and motivations," editor Paula Eykelhof says.

"As long as I know where the story is going—the beginning, the middle, the end—I'm not concerned with its length," editor John Scognamiglio says.

But editors and agents agree that shorter is generally better. They want to be able to see at a glance what your book is about. And regardless of the length of the synopsis, it should be concise. Make every word count.

"Once the synopsis is written, go through it again and ask yourself if this fact, sentence or phrase is important," Gail Gaymer Martin advises. "Things like 'the next morning,' 'two days later,' and 'wearing a dark suit' aren't important to a synopsis. Details are not important. What the editor is looking for is GMC—goals, motivations, and conflict—then the resolution."

"I recently heard a great description of a synopsis," editor Michael Seidman says. "Make it read as if you were explaining a movie to a ten-year-old. The more complex you make it, the more holes will open."

Agent Russell Galen looks for about 1,500 words. Karen Taylor Richman wants two to three pages, double-spaced. Editor Jennifer Brehl wants a synopsis of no more than "three pages for the entire book, beginning to end."

A one-page synopsis is often the best bet. It's a chance to show how tight your writing is; it won't put them to sleep; and the shorter the synopsis, the easier it is to keep from making mistakes. The better you get at mastering this challenging format, the more success you're likely to have selling your novels.

But a one-page synopsis just won't do the job in many contexts. Your agent or editor might prefer a longer, more detailed synopsis, or even a full chapter outline. As in all things, follow our basic philosophy: Give them what they want—no more, no less.

Marilyn Campbell's synopsis for *Pretty Maids in a Row* is actually very long. Is it too long? It worked, so we'd say it was just long enough.

TWO SHORT SYNOPSES

Here are two examples of the short synopsis: first Marshall's summary for his mystery, *Murder Over Easy*, and then a slightly longer synopsis of Blythe's novel *Parker's Angel*. You'll notice that Blythe's bends one of our rules; she intentionally leaves one of the elements in the ending ("another angel") vague. But the synopsis does its job, and it got her an agent.

Murder Over Easy
A 60,000-word amateur sleuth mystery
By Marshall J. Cook
Pitch line: *A weekly newspaper editor tracks a killer and uncovers a town's sordid secret when someone murders the owner of the local diner.*

Short Synopsis #1

Everyone in town loved Charlie Connell—with the obvious exception of the person who beat him to death.

Like everyone else in the little town of Mitchell, Wisconsin, Monona Quinn is shocked and saddened when Charlie's mother finds his body at the foot of the basement steps of his diner. The presence of a County deputy sheriff videotaping Charlie's funeral and the glimpse she catches of the stairway where Charlie supposedly fell make Mo suspect that Charlie was murdered. Her interviews with townsfolk for a tribute to Charlie for the Mitchell *Doings* deepen her suspicions.

Sabra Farnum, one of "Charlie's Angels" who waitressed at the diner for years, offers a potential suspect, a young man named Pete, whom Charlie had hired as a dishwasher and who hasn't been seen since Charlie died.

Mo's husband, Douglas Stennett, discovers a possible motive: Charlie had recently taken out a large loan on the diner. Why did he need the money, and where is it now?

Nikki von Thoreaux, owner of the Monde Theatre and a one-woman show on and off stage, tells Mo that some in town hated Charlie because he was a homosexual—which is news to Mo. Dan Weilman, owner of the Starlite Video Rental, says he saw Charlie arguing with a short, thin man in a stocking cap the night Charlie was found dead.

After her self-defense class in nearby Madison, Mo gets the coroner's report from Sheriff Roger Repoz. Off the record, Repoz admits Charlie would have had to throw himself down the stairs several times to account for the severity of the bruises, and no fall could account for the strange mark on his forehead. Mo also investigates the files of the local afternoon daily and finds that Charlie was once arrested for indecent exposure.

Mo tracks down the mysterious Pete, who has a partial alibi, and learns from Charlie's mother that the "missing" loan money had gone to buy land for a new home for her. Even so, Mrs. Connell is convinced that someone murdered her son.

Mo revisits the high school wrestling coach, Norb Hopkins, whom she had previously interviewed for her story, and Hopkins admits he banned Charlie from having contact with members of the team after Charlie exposed himself to an athlete years before.

Repoz makes an arrest, a current member of the high school wrestling team, Marcus Trevin. His girlfriend, Cindy Kramer, admits that Marcus argued with Charlie outside the diner that night but insists Marcus left Charlie alive and went to see his coach.

Mo discovers a subbasement in the diner and there finds a pile of sunflower seed husks that seem to place Coach Hopkins in the room. She also finds the probable murder weapon, a square-cornered bottle from the old Mitchell Brewery.

Hopkins finds Mo alone at the *Doings* office and attacks her, but her self-defense training enables her to fight him off.

When Mo breaks the story of Hopkin's arrest in the *Doings*, the national media pick it up. Mo assures her husband that she wants nothing more to do with murders and detective work, but the brutal killing of Mitchell's gentle parish priest will soon plunge her into another mystery.

SYNOPSIS SAMPLE #2

Short Synopsis #2

Parker's Angel
A 94,000-word paranormal romance
By Blythe Camenson

Parker's Angel is a mainstream romantic suspense novel in a similar vein to the movie *Ghost*. It takes a tongue-in-cheek look at near-death experiences and America's ongoing fascination with angels. With a whimsical Beatles motif running throughout, it is also the story of a young woman, Parker Ann Bell, who must learn to trust and love again.

Unlucky in love (in a prologue one year prior to the beginning of the story, Parker walks in on her fiancé with another woman), Parker wouldn't recognize an angel if she pulled one back to earth with her. Which is exactly what happens. During the renovations of her new bookstore, the Scene of the Crime, Parker is electrocuted trying to help a workman in trouble. It takes her a few moments to understand why she's floating inches from the ceiling, her own body lying on the floor beneath her. She views the bright light ("Hey, you're supposed to be embracing me, not toasting me"), the tunnel, and the faceless angel at the end of it with a healthy skepticism, but after she is brought back to life, a series of events become impossible to explain away in earthly terms.

She finds herself studying each new person she meets for signs of an otherworldly nature, especially the uncanny Hemingway look-alike, who is the proprietor of the New Age bookstore next to hers, her new suitor Desmond, and Molly Jones, her recently hired assistant manager.

But Parker doesn't really believe angels exist. She tries to convince herself that her NDE was a dream or the result of a brain starved for oxygen. Desmond doesn't help matters; he keeps insisting he's an angel who has loved Parker from afar. Parker can't figure out if he's an accomplished flirt and kidder or if he really believes what he's telling her. She discounts the possibility he might be exactly what he claims. He takes her to a tavern (an angel hangout, he calls it) where she finds Molly singing with the band. A few days later she returns to investigate and discovers a derelict building where the lively nightspot had been.

But trying to find out if there's really an angel in her life is not Parker's only problem. Parker's bookstore is one of eight due to open soon on Boston's Harris' Wharf. The stretch of converted warehouses, unofficially dubbed Readers Row, is having financial problems, and Parker might lose everything before she even gets started.

Virginia Harper, proprietor of the Book of Love, and a woman with a penchant for pink and a good head for business, puts together a deal to save the Row, but Parker has to come up with extra money to be included. When the exact amount she needs shows up in a forgotten bank account, Parker is convinced Desmond is behind the unexpected windfall, even though he denies having anything to do with it.

A little bit of mind reading, blue lights whenever Desmond kisses her, events mimicking the lyrics of a Beatles' song ("Ob-la-di, ob-la-da, life goes on ..."), surfacing memories of a previous NDE, and miraculously healed injuries received during an attack (while an angel was sleeping on the job?) all push Parker toward believing. But by then it's too late. Parker has fallen in love with Desmond, but he claims he has to return to his heavenly responsibilities. A villain emerges intent on payback time and Parker finds herself in the tunnel again. Wondering if it's three strikes and she's out, she finds there is yet another angel who can put everything right.

Synopsis Checklist

Here is a checklist of elements to look for in the following synopsis drafts and in your own.

- ❏ Strong lead sentence
- ❏ Logical paragraph organization
- ❏ Concise expression of ideas with no repetition
- ❏ Introduction of main characters and their core conflicts
- ❏ Plot highlights
- ❏ Narrative writing in the present tense
- ❏ Transitions between ideas
- ❏ Strong verbs
- ❏ Minimal use of adjectives and adverbs
- ❏ Correct punctuation, grammar, and spelling
- ❏ Specific conclusion to the story

BUILDING YOUR ONE-PAGE SYNOPSIS

In chapter four we revised two query letters to demonstrate how writers can shape and sharpen their work. Now we'll do the same with a synopsis by one of Marshall's students, Kelly Fitzpatrick. Read through the first two drafts of Kelly Fitzpatrick's synopsis carefully, noting our suggestions to the author. Then read the final edited synopsis and see why it works so well.

DILIGENCE UNDONE BY KELLY FITZPATRICK

Diligence Undone ❶
Mystery, 117,000 words ❷
By Kelly Fitzpatrick ❸

The Game Plan: Anne Fischer embarks on a dangerous journey to stop an unseen, unknown force threatening a high-stakes acquisition. She risks the revelation of her own secret and, in the process, discovers herself. ❹

The Stakes: During a national information security crisis, ❺ the FBI suspects Anne of being the culprit. Anne is concerned about the FBI digging into her history because in college she formed a Robin Hood-like white-collar crime-fighting group. ❻ Although it started with small steps, it quickly got beyond their control, making them a legend. Their identities must remain a mystery because the group sometimes cultivated proof using illegal means.

The Players: On the surface, Anne is an unlikely FBI suspect. The feisty information systems manager has it all–a fast track career, a steady relationship, a wide circle of family and friends, and a fixer-upper townhouse that consumes her free time. ❼

Anne uncovers revenue skimming inside Serena Tonelli's acquisition. After taking credit for Anne's work, Serena gives her a seemingly impossible assignment ❽ in the top-secret Albuquerque lab, hoping to destroy her career. Anne's mentor, Roger Albright, is the founder and CEO of Confirmed Identities (CI). Being a life-long chess aficionado, he uses chess as a metaphor for teaching business strategy. ❾

The Gambit: Years ago, Roger hid assets from his ex-business partner, Martin Zarkin. Then he parlayed them into a multi-million dollar business. Now Zarkin competes for the same customers and wants to win back what he feels is rightfully his–his part of CI's technology as well as access to CI's customers, the major corporations and governmental agencies of North America.

Synopsis Draft #1

The Playing Field: The FBI searches for a notorious hacker dubbed Cracker Jack, who leaves nasty surprises inside companies' servers. ⑩ When Anne becomes the FBI's leading suspect, she is concerned that they will uncover her secret past. ⑪ Anne is trailed by the FBI from Chicago to Phoenix, Albuquerque, and Santa Fe, and is stalked by a pocked-faced, hooded man, while she uncovers an intricate web of political intrigue, corruption, and murder. ⑫

The Strategy: Anne is taunted by a hacker and fears it is Cracker Jack. She assembles clues and deduces the hacker is playing chess, using employees as pawns. She must make judicious moves to remain on his imaginary chessboard, not only to save her career but also simply to stay alive.

Capture: Using chutzpah and her rusty hacking skills, Anne matches wits with the hacker, beating him at his own game. She discovers the hacker is not Cracker Jack, but the CEO's son. ⑬

End Game: Anne uncovers traitors who are employed by Zarkin but driven by revenge—revenge against her nemesis, Serena. Anne also finds out her ex-boyfriend is Cracker Jack. ⑭

Checkmate: Anne confronts Serena in a final boardroom showdown. Using her newfound courage, she has a heart-to-heart with Roger about the impact of being beaten by his son at his own game. ⑮

1. Many folks will pick up on the reference to "due diligence," but many more probably won't. Consider a new title for the novel.

2. Be more specific: amateur sleuth, cozy, police procedural, etc.? And have you done your research on word count for your genre? Most mysteries come in much under 100,000 words.

3. Before you plunge into the synopsis, you could provide a one-sentence pitch line.

4. You need to reveal what's being acquired, what the revelation consists of, and how she discovers herself. You should be telling the story here, not talking about the story.

5. Name it.

6. Good. There's the secret.

7. Nice economical character summary.

8. Do we need to know the specific assignment?

9. Ah. That's why you've organized your synopsis around chess terms. If chess is not really

the controlling metaphor for the book, I'd dump the terms here. If it is important, introduce chess right away so we know what you're doing. In any case, avoid headings for each section. Use transitions so paragraphs flow from one to another logically.

10. Say this the first time instead of using general words like "crisis."

11. Your format has forced you to repeat yourself. You need to reorganize. Avoid repetition.

12. This is vague cover blurb copy. You must tell us what happened. Give specifics.

13. Good stuff, told with economy.

14. That sounds like a fairly crucial plot element. How does she find these things out?

15. Do we need to know the specifics of the heart-to-heart? Make sure you haven't left anything untold here.

This is good and very close. We've made suggestions about the format and about getting more specific about certain plot elements, which Fitzpatrick implemented.

Here's her next draft, along with our comments. (Remember that in actuality, this would be on one page, single-spaced.) She's made tremendous improvement and now has a concise, powerful synopsis. With a few more relatively minor changes, she'll be ready to send it off. Will she land an agent and get published? Nobody can predict the ways of agents, editors, and markets, but she's giving herself a wonderful chance by presenting an effective, professionally written and formatted synopsis.

DILIGENCE UNDONE (RENAMED *IN PURSUIT OF PROOF*) BY KELLY FITZPATRICK

In Pursuit of Proof ❶
Mainstream Fiction, ❷ 117,000 words
By Kelly Fitzpatrick

Synopsis Draft #2

Pitch line: *In a chase from boardrooms to back alleys, Anne risks revealing her own deeply hidden secret when she embarks on a dangerous journey.* ❸

On the surface, Anne is an unlikely FBI suspect. She's an information systems manager who seems to have it all—a fast-track career, a steady relationship, a wide circle of family and friends, and a fixer-upper townhouse that consumes her free time. She's on the cusp of getting her dream job while her employer, Confirmed Identities (CI), pursues its largest acquisition. ❹

Meanwhile, the FBI is searching for a notorious hacker, dubbed Cracker Jack, who leaves nasty surprises inside companies' servers. ⑤ When Anne becomes the FBI's leading suspect, she is worried that they will dig into her past, uncovering a well-guarded secret. In college Anne was a founding member of a Robin Hood-like crime-fighting group. Although the group started with small white-collar crimes, their successes quickly accumulated, making them a local legend. Since the group sometimes cultivated proof ⑥ using illegal means, ⑦ their identities must remain anonymous.

Anne's mentor is Roger Albright, founder and president of CI. A chess aficionado, Roger uses chess as a metaphor for teaching business strategy. His Chief Operating Officer, Serena Tonelli, is determined to unseat him and become the next CEO. She undermines his leadership at every opportunity and will destroy ⑧ anyone obstructing her path to the corner office, including Anne. ⑨

After a hacker deletes an important file, Anne digs deeper and uncovers revenue skimming. Serena pushes for the acquisition and suspects that Anne is in cahoots with Roger, attempting to thwart her acquisition. ⑩ Serena gives her a seemingly impossible assignment ⑪ in Albuquerque, hoping ⑫ to destroy Anne's career and end Roger's reign.

Unknown to Anne, ⑬ Martin Zarkin, CI's top competitor, is also determined to destroy Roger. Zarkin suspects ⑭ Roger hid assets years earlier when they severed their partnership and then parlayed the assets into his current multi-million dollar business. Now, Zarkin plans to win back what he feels is rightfully his—his part of CI's technology as well as access to CI's customers, the major corporations and governmental agencies of North America. He hires CI insiders who lie in wait within CI.

A hacker posts some of CI's top-secret design notes on the Internet, blaming Anne for the security breach. Fearing the hacker is Cracker Jack, Anne assembles clues ⑮ and deduces ⑯ the hacker is playing chess, using employees as pawns. She must make judicious moves to remain on his imaginary chessboard, not only to save her career but to stay alive.

Anne is trailed by the FBI and stalked by a hooded man as she travels from Chicago to Phoenix, Albuquerque, and Santa Fe. She dodges police dogs and hovering helicopters to track a late-night interloper, until he disappears into the side of a mountain near Santa Fe. Using rusty hacking skills, Anne matches wits with the hacker, beating him at his own game ⑰ and discovers the hacker is not Cracker Jack, but the CEO's son. She uncovers ⑱ CI's traitors are paid by Zarkin and driven by revenge–revenge against her nemesis, Serena.

In a boardroom showdown, Anne uses her newfound courage ⑲ to prove her innocence and reveal the traitors are Serena's long-time secretary and Anne's predecessor, who had been forced out by Serena. Anne helps Roger deal with the impact of being beaten by his son at his own game. ⑳

Anne becomes CI's new Director of Information Security. Having peeked beneath the shiny corporate façade, Anne knows she needs more than technical knowledge and managerial skills. She must use her determination to manage the political undertones, especially with Cracker Jack remaining at large. ㉑

1. You did change the title. We like this one much better. It's concise, and the alliteration is catchy.

2. Since this project doesn't fit any conventional category, you applied the label of "mainstream." That also solves the problem of the word count, since many mainstream novels are this length.

3. The synopsis now includes a pitch line. We like "boardroom and back alley" a lot. But be more specific about "hidden secret" and "dangerous journey."

4. You stripped out the chess apparatus and use a straight narrative style here. It's more direct and gets us into the thick of things quickly.

5. Can you get more specific about "nasty surprises"? And "companies' servers" is awkward.

6. Now you reveal the secret when you first mention it, eliminating a vague plot element and the need for repetition. But "proof" of what?

7. "Illegal means"? Be more specific.

8. The synopsis should be consistently in present tense. We need "destroys" if she's actually doing it or "seeks to destroy" or "is willing to destroy" if she hasn't.

9. Notice how the character sketch is integrated into the plot.

10. Although it's okay to shift point of view within a novel-length narrative, signaling the shifts with chapter breaks or a transitional element, it's best to keep the short synop-

sis in a single point of view. We should keep this in Anne's perspective—don't switch to Serena's viewpoint.

11. We need to know what that impossible assignment is. If an explanation won't fit the one-page format, it's better to delete the reference.

12. Here is another point-of-view switch to avoid.

13. If Anne doesn't know it, how can we know it? Delete the phrase to preserve a unified point of view for the synopsis.

14. Sometimes a point-of-view switch is unavoidable. Otherwise, this important information would have to be deleted.

15. You can't list all the clues in a short synopsis. For that reason, simply delete mention of them.

16. Plain old "figures out" would be better here.

17. A double helping of clichés.

18. One of the great benefits of keeping within a single point of view in the synopsis: We always know who's doing the uncovering. You don't need to mention it.

19. You've had no previous indication that Anne lacks courage.

20. Another cliché.

21. With Cracker Jack at large you have provided for the possibility of a sequel.

The second draft is much better than the first, but still needed some smoothing out.

Here's the final draft, addressing all of the issues we raised. Kelly Fitzpatrick now has a tight, fast-paced synopsis. She hasn't been able to reveal everything, of course, but she has economically developed her primary plot, including conflicts and motivations.

**_DILIGENCE UNDONE_ (RENAMED _PURSUIT OF PROOF_)
BY KELLY FITZPATRICK**

Final Synopsis Draft

In Pursuit of Proof
Mainstream Fiction, 117,000 words
By Kelly Fitzpatrick

Pitch line: *In a chase from boardrooms to back alleys, Anne risks revealing her past as a Robin Hood-style sleuth when she attempts to discover the identity of a dangerous computer hacker.*

On the surface, Anne is an unlikely FBI suspect. She's an information systems manager who seems to have it all–a fast-track career, a steady re-

---

lationship, a wide circle of family and friends, and a fixer-upper town-house that consumes her free time. She's on the cusp of getting her dream job while her employer, Confirmed Identities (CI), pursues its largest acquisition.

Meanwhile, the FBI is searching for a notorious hacker, dubbed Cracker Jack. When Anne becomes the FBI's leading suspect, she is worried that they will dig into her past, uncovering a well-guarded secret. In college Anne was a founding member of a Robin Hood-like crime-fighting group. Although the group started with small white-collar crimes, their successes quickly accumulated, making them a local legend. Since the group sometimes broke the law, their identities must remain anonymous.

Anne's mentor is Roger Albright, founder and president of CI. A chess aficionado, Roger uses chess as a metaphor for teaching business strategy. His Chief Operating Officer, Serena Tonelli, is determined to unseat him and become the next CEO. She undermines his leadership at every opportunity and vows to destroy anyone obstructing her path to the corner office, including Anne.

After a hacker deletes an important file, Anne digs deeper and uncovers revenue skimming. Serena pushes for the acquisition and sends Anne on assignment to Albuquerque, with the goal of destroying Anne's career and ending Roger's reign.

Martin Zarkin, CI's top competitor, also tries to destroy Roger. Zarkin suspects Roger hid assets years earlier when they severed their partnership and then parlayed the assets into his current multi-million dollar business. Now Zarkin plans to win back what he feels is rightfully his—his part of CI's technology as well as access to CI's customers, the major corporations and governmental agencies of North America. He hires CI insiders who lie in wait within CI.

A hacker posts some of CI's top-secret design notes on the Internet, blaming Anne for the security breach. Anne figures out that the hacker, whom she fears is Cracker Jack, is playing chess, using employees as pawns. She must make judicious moves to remain on his imaginary chessboard, not only to save her career but to stay alive.

> Anne is trailed by the FBI and stalked by a hooded man as she travels from Chicago to Phoenix, Albuquerque, and Santa Fe. She dodges police dogs and hovering helicopters to track a late-night interloper, until he disappears into the side of a mountain near Santa Fe. Using rusty hacking skills, Anne goes against the hacker and beats him. The hacker turns out to be the CEO's son.
>
> In a boardroom showdown, Anne proves her innocence and reveals the traitors—Serena's long-time secretary and Anne's predecessor, who had been forced out by Serena. Anne helps Roger deal with the impact of being beaten by his son.
>
> Anne becomes CI's new Director of Information Security. Having peeked beneath the shiny corporate façade, she knows she needs more than technical knowledge and managerial skills. She must use her determination to manage the political undertones, especially with Cracker Jack remaining at large.

You can create an equally compelling synopsis if you aren't afraid ot look at your drafts critically and to make revisions. If you can write and revise your novel, you can certainly do the same with your synopsis. Taking care with your revisions is well worth the time and effort you put into it. You'll be thankful for your hard work when an agent calls wanting to represent you.

THE LONGER SYNOPSIS

Sometimes you'll need a longer synopsis or even a chapter-by-chapter outline. We've provided two successful, longer synopses, the first for Gail Gaymer Martin's *Secrets of the Heart*, and then our heavyweight champion, *Pretty Maids in a Row* by Marilyn Campbell.

Marilyn Campbell's synopsis is definitely long, but it moves rapidly, with characterization woven into the action throughout. See if you can stop reading it once you start.

Although Martin's synopsis is a lot longer than most, and longer than we recommend you use, it did the job, getting Gail a publishing contract with Steeple Hill. You know our philosophy: give them exactly what they want, no more and no less.

SECRETS OF THE HEART BY GAIL GAYMER MARTIN

Secrets of the Heart
An Inspirational Romance, 62,000 words
By Gail Gaymer Martin

"And the secrets of his heart will be laid bare."

–1 Corinthians 14:25

When social worker Kate Davis agrees to share a house with a co-worker, she doesn't realize that she'll wind up also sharing with the co-worker's brother, Doctor Scott Ryan. Kate is captivated by his friendly warmth and open concern for people. Yet as their lives intertwine, a dark secret stands in her way of a long-term relationship. While Scott struggles with his own past, he senses Kate's growing reserve. And when Kate learns that someone from her past is searching for her, the situation only worsens.

The Characters

Kate Davis, thirty-four, grew up in a Christian home with loving parents. She longed to be popular like her attractive older sister. Misguided by her longing, she was deceived by a popular boy, and her young life was devastated when she learned she was pregnant from her one sexual encounter. Sent away to a home for unwed mothers by her horrified parents, Kate gave birth to a daughter who was placed for adoption. Finishing high school, Kate was compelled to help hurting children and became a social worker, anything to make retribution for her sin. Though saddened by her past, Kate looks for the positive in all things.

Scott Ryan was an adopted child, raised by an affluent, Christian family who gave him love, confidence, and to their surprise, a baby-sister conceived after his adoption. In college, Ryan studied biology, but entering his master's program, he realized his true calling was to be a doctor and switched his major to medicine. Now at thirty-two, Scott is completing his residency at County General Hospital. Though appreciative and filled with familial love, Scott harbors a deep sense of abandonment and has the hidden desire

---

to find his birth parents and to understand why he was given up for adoption. Though warm and genial, Scott struggles with the serious side of his personality that focuses on the negative aspects of life.

The Story

Kate Davis hears a piercing scream and, thinking the worst, darts to her friend's aid, only to find Phyllis Ryan welcoming her brother at their front door. Doctor Scott Ryan has returned to the Detroit area to do his residency at a local hospital. Without an apartment, Phyllis suggests he stay with them until he finds his own place. Always helpful, Kate agrees.

Though she likes most things about Scott, Kate is troubled by the negative memories he evokes, dredging up the sorrow and guilt of her troubled teen years. With her past serving as a career catalyst, Kate works as a social worker at Children's Haven, located in a northern Detroit suburb. Daily, she interacts with hurting children and is driven to making their lives better. Her work is the one place Kate feels she is in control.

As a physician, Scott, too, has compassion for human well-being and believes he is doing God's will to make life better. But as well, he is driven by his personal desire to be independent and to succeed, a gift he wants to return to his adoptive parents for their love and support.

Scott is intrigued by Kate's paradoxical, upbeat, yet cautious, personality, and he enjoys her company as she helps him search for an apartment. But Scott has avoided forming romantic relationships. His conscious reasons are his devotion to his career and the rigors of medical school. But subconsciously, Scott is scarred by a college romance that left him embarrassed and uncomfortable with his staunch feelings of chastity. Pulling himself from his time-consuming studies, Scott dated a young woman, opening his heart to his belief of chastity until marriage and knowing his conviction was uncommon compared to many of his cohorts. When he learned that she had deceived him and was pregnant, he felt betrayed and believed that most modern-day women would scorn him for his conviction. Instead of taking a chance, he turns his energies to his career.

But God has other plans. While Scott spends time with his sister, he is also in Kate's company. Thinking of her as a friend, he is relaxed and enjoys Kate's dedication and good humor. Without guarding his heart, Kate gets under his skin.

When six-year-old Amber arrives at Children's Haven, Kate struggles to keep her personal feelings in line. The child's physical characteristics trigger thoughts of her own daughter, adopted at birth many years earlier. Kate has never talked with anyone except her family about this sad and horrible experience. Her parents in Florida and sister in New York plucked at her guilt and shame, but with all of them away from Michigan, Kate has been able to keep her secret and emotions buried. Now Amber drags them out of hiding.

When Scott asks Kate to help him hunt for an apartment, she is busy with a church activity called Helping the Elderly Live Proudly (HELP). On a lark, he joins her and enjoys spending the day and evening with Kate.

Ashamed of her past, Kate has steered clear of male companionship, but her unbidden feelings grow toward Scott. She is no longer a virgin, and Scott has expressed his attitude about the importance of chastity before marriage. Kate longs for a man that she cares about as much as Scott, who will understand and forgive her sin.

During a conversation with Scott and Phyllis, Kate is startled to learn that he is adopted and his sister has never mentioned it. Scott and Phyllis have a closer, warmer friendship than she and her birth-sister have ever had. With their strong Christian upbringing, she could never confess her shame to Scott or Phyllis. And if she told Scott the truth, she believes he would never respect her, let alone love her. Kate's blossoming feelings can never flower into a permanent relationship.

But Providence brings them together even more when Scott is sent to Children's Haven to work temporarily. Scott admires Kate's energy and devotion to the children and senses that his choice of family practice is a good one. When Amber comes down with measles, Scott notices a sizeable burn scar on her back. He finds no explanation in her medical records and shares the information with Kate.

As they discuss the plight of children at the center, Kate longs to tell Scott of her deep-seeded hurt as a parent placing a child for adoption, but she fears his disdain and rejection. Kate finds herself in a dilemma–to avoid the truth or chance losing Scott–and seeks God's counsel.

While Scott continues to volunteer in the HELP program, he admires Kate's interaction with the elderly and her giving without expectations, an experience he has never had. His giving to others has always been accompanied by an awareness of his growing success. But in time, he learns from the seniors' wisdom and finds their joy contagious. Through their family stories and counsel, he comes to understand the importance of human relationships–especially a Christian marriage and children. Also, while working at one senior's home, Scott recognizes a serious health problem of an elderly woman and is instrumental in saving her life.

Concerned for Amber, Kate takes action and makes an unapproved visit to the gravely ill grandmother in County General. Unable to communicate with the comatose woman, she witnesses severe burn scars on the woman's hand and arm. Realizing the same fire might have caused Amber's burns, she asks Scott to help her learn the facts, thinking it might reveal important information about Amber. But he refuses to seek information regarding a case in which he is not involved. His career is too important to push aside proper medical protocol.

Despite their personal struggles, Kate and Scott know their hearts are not following their heads. When Thanksgiving nears, Scott invites Kate to attend a Thanksgiving Eve harvest celebration and share his family's holiday meal. Though she has known his parents through Phyllis, this year it is Scott who invites her, not Phyllis, and this raises uncomfortable questions. Is she being invited as a friend or as a potential wife?

Cornered without an adequate excuse to refuse, Kate accepts his invitation, although it heightens her fears. Scott, younger than Kate, is inde-

Gail Gaymer Martin/SECRETS OF THE HEART 5

pendent, successful, and a Christian with strong moral values. She feels inadequate and undeserving of him. But as the day progresses, the experience proves pleasant, and Kate enjoys his family, though their warm, loving relationship pokes at her envy.

Released from Children's Haven, Scott's newest assignment is to provide medical treatment at Madonna House, a Christian home for unwed mothers. At Christmas, he is invited to a holiday party at this facility. Wanting to show support to the young women, he asks Kate to accompany him, having no idea Kate once resided in the facility. She is disconcerted.

Asking God for help, Kate forces herself to attend but is overwrought with memories. When they leave, Scott's comment about the importance of being chaste sends Kate reeling and validates her belief that nothing can ever come from their friendship. But her attachment to him keeps her from ending their relationship.

During the Christmas holidays, Scott observes Kate's visiting parents and sister. He senses tension and lack of warmth in their relationship. As well, Kate's sister, a glamorous divorcee, flirts with him, and Scott senses Kate's parents' disapproval of both her sister's behavior and her divorce. He wonders why Kate arouses similar criticism from them. The incident provides insight into Kate's wavering feelings of self-worth.

Embarrassed by her family's behavior, Kate is sure Scott will question their innuendos, and her sister's obvious flirtation triggers her childhood feelings of inadequacy.

When Scott questions Kate, she offers evasive answers. He seeks the Lord's guidance on how to proceed with his growing love. Visiting one of the elderly, Scott seeks her counsel. When he leaves, he is confident that Kate loves him, having stuck by his side despite her apprehension. Testing the waters, Scott hints to Kate of his desire for commitment.

Recognizing Scott is about to propose marriage, Kate does all she can to discourage him, short of ending their relationship. She prays she can resolve her anxiety.

Gail Gaymer Martin/SECRETS OF THE HEART   6

Adding to Kate's stress, Amber's grandmother dies, and Kate learns the girl will be placed in a foster home. With Kate's personal investigation, she has learned that Amber's family died in a house fire, and since then, she has helped the child rid herself of most of her nightmares and fears. Kate longs to take Amber into her home. When Kate tells Scott, he dissuades her, reminding her of the difficulty of being a single, working woman. But Kate hears God's Word: "Whoever welcomes one of these little children welcomes me." The responsibility would be difficult, but she yearns for the motherhood of which she has been deprived.

Struggling with her decisions about Amber, she recalls her birth child and believes Amber is God's blessing, a visual sign of the Lord's forgiveness of her sin. Yet she continues to keep her secret from Scott and grapples with her dishonesty.

Realizing that a successful career does not guarantee a happy, fulfilled life, Scott faces his emptiness and proposes to Kate but is startled by her hesitation. Her rejection shakes his faith in romance and in their relationship. Confused, Scott clings to God's guidance and is determined to learn the unknown factor that stands in their way.

When Kate and Scott talk, he solicits for his plan that she could more easily be a foster parent to Amber if she were married. He suggests that Kate become his wife and that whatever she fears about their relationship will pass with time.

Amazed at his devotion and ashamed of her avoidance, Kate finally releases her secret and tells him about her parent's shame, her anguish at Madonna House, and the devastation of placing her child for adoption. With her revelation, she fears that their relationship will end. And it does. Startled and confused, Scott leaves, and Kate is left behind, miserable and saddened that she had trusted him and he let her down.

When Scott storms off, he is hurt that Kate did not have enough faith in him to confide her secret earlier. But when he reviews his attitude, he is ashamed of his anger, realizing his comments may have motivated Kate's silence.

Gail Gaymer Martin/SECRETS OF THE HEART   6

Days pass, and Phyllis tries to comfort Kate, but to no avail. Only the news that Amber will be placed with her in foster care gives Kate shadowed joy, gaining Amber, but losing Scott. She takes a step backward with the new situation.

But one day, the telephone rings and Scott, filled with sorrow, asks to see her. Though Kate wants to refuse, her heart and God prod her to agree. Scott asks Kate's forgiveness and tells her his life will only be whole and complete with her at his side. She expresses her love for him and asks his forgiveness for hiding the truth. With a new understanding and shared forgiveness, he proposes again, and this time, Kate accepts.

Ten months later: Scott stands in the front of the church, his heart filled with love for Kate and affection for Amber, who is dropping rose petals down the white runner. As his gaze sweeps the faces of family and friends, he smiles at his loving, adoptive parents.

With joy and sense of wholeness, Kate beams as Amber precedes her down the aisle. God has given her the opportunity to mother the little girl, and in that gift, Kate finds forgiveness and healing. As her gaze locks with Scott's, she offers thanks that God impelled her to release the secret of her heart and gave her peaceful assurance that her daughter has been raised by a loving Christian family. At the altar, Kate and Scott join hands and hearts as they gaze toward Amber, soon to be their adopted daughter.

PRETTY MAIDS IN A ROW BY MARILYN CAMPBELL

Pretty Maids in a Row (Villard Books)
Mystery/Suspense
By Marilyn Campbell

Long Synopsis #2

"I move we cut his balls off and be done with it." Those vicious words are the first Holly Kaufman hears as she enters a hotel suite in Washington, D C, where a meeting is already in progress. Over the years since college, Holly's longtime friend April MacLeash had tried to convince Holly to join The Little Sister Society, but Holly had never been a joiner, and

Marylin Campbell/PRETTY MAIDS IN A ROW   **2**

she wanted to forget, not be continuously reminded of the past. She is now thirty-three and a successful environmental lobbyist. A television newscast a few days ago brought the past back with a vengeance, and she gave in to the impulse to call and meet the others that April had told her about.

Already in the suite are four of the five members of The Society. April, who is now an IRS agent, she has known since their freshman year of college, when people kept confusing the two girls because of their appearance. They are both of medium height, with light blond hair, blue eyes and lush figures. April's Tennessee accent and Holly's Pittsburghese quickly differentiate them, however.

Holly vaguely remembers Bobbi Renquist, a psychologist whose mousy coloring and demeanor hide a brilliant, analytical mind.

April introduces Holly to Rachel Greenley, a tall, muscular woman who is an agent of the Federal Bureau of Investigation; and Erica Donner, an aggressively competitive redhead who aspires to loftier heights than her present position as vice-president of a major hotel chain. The absent member, Cheryl Wallace, was one of the people featured on the newscast, and thus, could not be present at this meeting.

It was Rachel that had spat out the move for violence. She has been drinking, much to the others' dismay. They have each had to deal with addictions of one kind or another over the years, and Rachel had been clean for some time, but the same newscast that disturbed Holly gave Rachel a push off the wagon. Drinking makes Rachel mouthy–and potentially dangerous. Bobbi explains that the original reason they formed the group back in college was because of what they had in common. After graduation, they agreed to meet twice a year as a sort of self-styled therapy group. Part of recovery is talking about one's problem, both with others who understand from similar experiences and with those loved ones who have been indirectly hurt because of it.

The women each relate their personal nightmares to Holly. Fourteen years ago, they were all victims of a cruel game perpetrated by eighteen fraternity brothers. The object of the game was for a brother to fill up his "dance

Marylin Campbell/PRETTY MAIDS IN A ROW 3

card" with as many names of female conquests as possible. It had become a traditional competition in that fraternity, but that year, the contest turned brutal. Seduction and willingness on the part of the girl were no longer necessary. Plying a girl with alcohol and drugs, trickery and rape, by one or a dozen brothers at a time, became acceptable methods of adding names to the cards.

Holly is stunned. She had left school after her ordeal, and not being part of a sorority, had not been aware of how bad it truly was. She had always refused to talk about that time, even when April had urged her to. Still not ready to talk about it, she declines to share her tale, but she promises to think about what they've said.

April tells her there's more she can do to heal the pain. Each of The Little Sisters had been victims of the game, until they changed the rules. After they graduated, they were all preoccupied with launching their careers and, in April's and Erica's cases, establishing marriages as well. It took a while to realize that talking to each other was only going so far to help them deal with their problems. Ten years ago, the purpose of The Little Sister Society changed from comfort to revenge, and the results have been most satisfying.

The eighteen men were secretly investigated and tracked, with an eye to finding a way to wreak havoc on their lives. Because of the careers the women had chosen, they were able to exact revenge in a number of ways without having to make any of their identities known. Only a card signed "With the compliments of The Little Sister Society" let the men know their downfall was no fluke.

Timothy Ziegler's appointment to the U.S. Presidential Cabinet changed that. The Society had not been able to find a single flaw in his lifestyle after he left college. All five of the members' names had appeared on his dance card, but Cheryl Wallace had the least to lose by stepping forward to object to his appointment at the confirmation hearings. Public embarrassment would not affect her career as an artist or touch the fortune she had inherited from her family.

Marylin Campbell/PRETTY MAIDS IN A ROW   4

Unfortunately, Cheryl was being raked over the coals by several of the Senators and her credibility was waning under stress.

It had been agreed at the outset that Cheryl was the only one who would testify in order to preserve the secrecy of The Society. They still had important work to do, and besides, the way the hearing was progressing, it was beginning to look like Ziegler's appointment would be confirmed, even if twenty women testified against him.

Holly admits her name would have been on Tim's dance card also. That was why the newscast was so upsetting. But he was not the one who had set her up for a trip to hell. She asks the women if Jerry Frampton was one of the eighteen boys, and what, if anything happened to him.

April tells her his is one of the five names left on their hit list—not because he's squeaky clean like Ziegler, but because he's such a sleazebag. He's now the publisher of a men's magazine, and disgusting secrets that have been revealed about him, past or present, have only made his magazine more popular. Nothing he's done has landed him behind bars, however. Even his financial records appear to be in order.

Rachel suggests they turn his file over to Holly. A new tidbit of information had turned up that she hadn't had time to track down. All Holly would have to do is leak it to one of the hungry reporters she knows in Washington, follow that person's progress, then report back to Rachel. Holly is hesitant, but they talk her into at least taking Frampton's file and reading it over—for her own good. They also give her the three other names on the list besides Frampton and Ziegler in case she learns anything of interest about them. She scribbles the names on the inside of the folder, but doesn't agree to do any more than look at the reports inside.

From a chair in the hotel lobby, investigative reporter David Wells had watched four professionally dressed women between the ages of thirty and thirty-five enter the private elevator to the penthouse suite within a half hour of each other. Two hours later, the same four came down, one at a time. David had been trying for two days to interview Erica Donner, the vice-president of the corporation that owns this hotel and a string of others. He was only attempting to get some details for an article he was working on about the latest buyout she was negotiating, but her evasive tactics caused his nose to twitch. Since she refused his request to meet with her, and having nothing more pressing to do that day, he had decided to hang out in the lobby in hopes of catching her on her way in or out.

As the fourth woman exits the elevator with a slight stagger, his curiosity is piqued. He follows the woman to the building that houses the FBI, but loses her after she goes inside. Exuding a considerable amount of his boyish charm on a female guard gets him the woman's identity: Special Agent Rachel Greenley.

He has no idea why an FBI agent would have been meeting with Erica Donner, and he doesn't yet know the identities of the other three women. But his reporter's instincts tell him there's a story here.

After the meeting broke up, Holly went for a long walk rather than return to her office near the hotel. She needs time alone to digest everything she's learned. Listening to those women brought back every detail of what Jerry did to her ...

She was a nineteen-year-old sophomore, an outstanding student and a shy virgin. Jerry Frampton had slithered into her life in the guise of a jock who needed tutoring. After all his other efforts to have sex with her failed, he talked of marriage and forever. Naïve child that she was, she believed him. Her mother had convinced her that her virginity was a special gift from God. It could only be given away one time, and she should be absolutely certain the recipient was deserving of the honor. She decided Jerry was the man she had been waiting for, the one she would give the ultimate gift of her love.

At the end of their next date, Jerry talked her into playing a game. He wanted to see if shutting out two of their senses would enable them to communicate mentally. She assumed it was another of his attempts to get her into bed with him, but since that was her intention that night anyway, she went along with him. Blindfolding her before they entered her apart-

Marylin Campbell/PRETTY MAIDS IN A ROW 6

ment, Jerry made her promise to abide by a no talking rule. He led her into her windowless bedroom, where it was so dark the blindfold was unnecessary.

The night became a sensuous journey into womanhood for Holly. The next morning, however, after switching on the light, she turned to awaken her future husband with a kiss–and froze in shock.

The naked lover in her bed was a stranger.

Before she could gather her wits, someone pounding on her apartment door demanded her attention. The early morning visitors were Jerry and one of his fraternity brothers. Suddenly she remembered having seen the man in her bed before–at Jerry's frat house. His name was Tim Ziegler. On the edge of hysteria, Holly managed to absorb the fact that she was the victim of a fraternity prank.

Jerry was so furious for putting out to Tim instead of him, he hit her, then shoved her down on the floor, intending to get what he deserved. Tim made an attempt to stop him, but the other brother dragged Tim out of Holly's apartment so that Jerry could rape her in peace.

The pain has not lessened in fourteen years. The inhuman treatment by the college counselor and security people she had complained to and the cruel taunts and subtle threats of her classmates in the days that followed had been more than she could cope with. She had quit school and gone home to her parents. Bernie and Vivian Kaufman had never insisted that she tell them what had happened to drive her away from school, even when she inflicted on them her depression, temper tantrums and tranquilizer addiction. Foolish or not, she was afraid that, like the others, they would believe she had somehow been at fault. Holly recalls the advice Bobbi had given her about discussing the incident and decides the time has come to have a long overdue talk with her parents. Perhaps if she could make amends with them, she could begin to forget. Before she can lose her nerve, she heads home to Pittsburgh on the next airline flight. She should have known what their reaction would be to her story, but self-doubt had blinded her. As the only survivor of three children, Holly has always been the center of the universe to them. She finally realizes she didn't tell them before for fear of losing that cherished position. Instead of blaming her for poor judgment, they respond as if they had been stabbed in the heart that very day.

Vivian cries and shares the heartache of her daughter's lost innocence. Bernie vows to kill both the bastards who hurt his baby, or at least castrate them. He seems sincerely disappointed when Holly tells him she doesn't want him to do anything on her behalf.

The visit lifts one of the weights from her conscience and convinces her there is another person she owes the same consideration as she gave her parents–Philip Sinkiewicz, her employer, friend and onetime lover. Holly met Philip and his wife, Cora, while working in her parents' restaurant after she had moved home. They were friends of her parents and closer to their age bracket than Holly's. One evening, Philip drew Holly into a conversation that gave her the final shove back into the real world. Philip had finally secured the funding he had been seeking to establish Earth Guard, an organization devoted to political lobbying for environmental concerns. He informed Holly that the fledgling lobby would be needing all the help it could get from intelligent, young people. They would have a place for her if she would like to move to Washington, D C. Within a week she had decided to take him up on his offer.

Philip and Holly spent a great deal of time together setting up Earth Guard. His zealousness about saving Earth's resources was contagious, and she soon found herself caught up in his interests as well as the faced-paced life of the Capitol. He recognized her genius and untapped talents and urged her to finish college in order to give herself every advantage in the competitive city. She chose a school in the D C area so that she could continue to work with him.

As the years went by she realized his feelings for her went beyond that of a close friend and employer, but he never acted upon his obvious desire. He was a man who took his wedding vows seriously, regardless of how difficult that marriage was for him. Even if he had not been married, however, Holly never wanted another man in her bed.

About seven years ago, Philip's wife was diagnosed with cancer of the brain. For two years he suffered along with her as she underwent surgery and treatments, unspeakable pain and forgetfulness. As his closest friend, Holly was always there for him and shared his every frustration. Understanding Philip's confusion of and grief and relief after Cora's funeral, Holly cared too much to add to his distress by denying him the comfort he sought in her arms. Temporarily setting aside her vow of celibacy, she spent the night with him, but learned that compassion and friendship are not sufficient motivation for physical lovemaking. Either that, or her ability to enjoy the experience was killed the morning after she had discovered it.

That loss, and the inability to return the love of a man as wonderful as Philip, compounded her hate—and her guilt. She had done her best to put it behind her and had almost convinced herself it didn't matter. Bobbi may have been right when she said, "A rape victim tends to continue to be a victim until she learns to fight back."

Holly goes directly from the airport to Philip's home. After the one time, she turned down his gentle hints to repeat the intimacy, but that never seemed to bother him. Over the years, he was always respectful and attentive, clearly devoted to her and no other woman. He often tells her how much he loves her and, once a year on the anniversary of their night together, he asks her to marry him, or at least share his home.

But she likes things the way they are. Without relinquishing her independence or privacy, she has as good friend to be her escort when she needs one and to act as a buffer between her and other men. Philip may want more, but he has never demanded anything beyond being her steady companion. Knowing that he has no competition for her affections seems to be enough for him.

She realizes there is a good chance that he might one day run into Ziegler, and Philip might feel the need to say something embarrassing to them all.

Therefore, she tells Philip a vague version of her experience without revealing exact details or the names of the boys.

Philip's face contorts with rage, and for a moment Holly fears he is angry with her, but he calms down almost immediately and expresses his sincere sympathy. Philip now understands her fear of the dark, the way she jumps when someone touches her unexpectedly, her distrust of men and her distaste for sex. He wishes he could send the men involved to perdition for the damage they did to such a sweet, innocent girl, and for preventing her from having a normal relationship with him. He loves her all the more now that he's aware of the reasons behind her behavior.

He gives her a hug and an undemanding kiss, then asks her where she's been all day. She tells him about the reunion with some women she knew in college and her unplanned visit with her parents. He is sorry she didn't let him know about that, since he would have enjoyed seeing Bernie and Viv also. He says he will have to give them a call. Before leaving, she goes to the bathroom and, as she walks back into the room, she sees Philip thumbing through the folders in her briefcase. When she questions him, he scolds her for taking too much work home.

Two days later there is an announcement that the news that Timothy Ziegler's appointment has been confirmed. Cheryl Wallace had not convinced the Senate Committee that he should be disqualified. Someone watching the broadcast is furious with the turn of events. This person determines to personally punish Ziegler for his crimes of years ago.

The next day, David Wells is having lunch with his friend and mentor, Harry Abbott, when a gorgeous blond and an older, white-haired man enter the deli. Not only does the woman catch David's attention because she has all the attributes he is normally attracted to, but he remembers her from the hotel. He hasn't been able to let go of the feeling that there's a story right under his nose that no one else knows about.

David pretends to recognize the man to wrangle an introduction, but he is very protective of his lady. And the lady never once meets David's eyes.

David is not foiled, however. He sees the name on the man's charge card–Philip Sinkiewicz–and knows what to do with that. One phone call to the newspaper's society columnist, Christine Manning, gets him more information than he needs. It also gets him invited to a fund-raiser dinner where Christine is certain Holly and Philip will be the next night.

Christine tells him of Holly Kaufman's reputation for shooting down would-be suitors. If he wants to get close to her for any reason, it will have to be through Philip and for business purposes only. David's well-known seductive skills will get him nowhere with her, but Christine is anxious to watch him try.

As Christine predicted, Holly seems immune to his smile, but responds to the bait of an article about Earth Guard. By the end of the evening, they have an appointment to meet at her office.

Until that night, Holly had avoided picking up Frampton's file. The same reporter turning up twice seemed a strange coincidence, and she recalls Rachel's suggestion that she turn the Frampton lead over to a hungry reporter, then follow his progress. It sounded easy enough, and the information in the file certainly warranted such action.

A knee injury ended Jerry Frampton's promising football career, and his limited talents narrowed his choices for the future. He has since become the publisher of a popular men's magazine focusing on sports and women. The last notation in the file states that it has just been discovered that during the time when he was launching his magazine, Jerry Frampton had been closely associated with Mick Donley, a convicted child pornographer. If Frampton still had his fingers in the pie of the illegal side of smut, it could finally mean his ruin.

As Holly goes to sleep, someone enters the Ziegler bedroom and places ether-soaked cloths over Tim's and his wife's faces. When the intruder is certain they will not awaken too quickly, a gag is stuffed in Tim's mouth, and he is stripped. The intruder then hauls the naked unconscious man out into the backyard and ties him to a tree upright. When Ziegler comes to, he is told it's payback time. He doesn't understand until his captor picks up a large

pair of hedge clippers from the ground. Ziegler's muffled screams and pleading eyes do not slow the progress of the blades of the giant scissors as they
are positioned on each side of his genitals, then swiftly brought together. As
Timothy Ziegler's lifeblood drains from his body, a sign is hung around his
neck with stick-on letters that read:

JUST PUNISHMENT FOR A RAPIST

The next morning the news is filled with speculation about the reported
murder of the just-confirmed Secretary Ziegler. The police are not releas-
ing details, other than that is was a home invasion, and the wife and children are in seclusion.

Rachel Greenley is informed by her superior that she will be part of the task
force working with the local police on Ziegler's murder. She can barely con-
strain her laughter at the incredible irony of it all. Holly was upset by the way
the hearing ended, but she still feels sympathy for the wife and children. The
hearing itself had to have been a difficult ordeal for them, but this was so
much worse.

Before her meeting with Wells, she checks on him through a friend. David
Wells is an up-and-coming journalist, hungry and aggressive, yet scrupu-
lously honest with his stories. Gossip has it that he has cut a wide swath through
the female population of D C, but shows a decided preference for buxom,
blue-eyed blondes like herself. That could make dealing with him difficult,
but other than that, he sounded perfect for what she was planning to do. If
Earth Guard got some publicity out of it at the same time, so much the better.

When David requests a postponement of their appointment until dinner,
Holly hesitantly agrees. Throughout dinner, they interview each other. She
asks several questions about where he gets his leads and how he decides what
tips to investigate. He eventually questions her about what she was doing at
the hotel last week and she refuses to say more than "meeting some friends."
He does learn that she is leaving in a few days for a three-week tour of the
United States. She will be addressing city governments about taking advantage of new environmental conservation laws and how to apply for grants to

Marylin Campbell/PRETTY MAIDS IN A ROW   **12**

get started. David senses she is playing with him, and his charm becomes a weapon to demonstrate his greater experience with the game. Before they part, he lures her into a seductive kiss, then insults her.

Holly is shocked by his ability to arouse feelings she believed were dead, but has no intention of experimenting further. His devastating kiss and well-aimed insult make Holly realize that she is no match for him. She backs away, intending to find another, more malleable instrument of the press.

David is somehow shocked at his own ill-mannered behavior with Holly. Everything about her aroused and annoyed him simultaneously. He figures he owes her an apology, but he has a dislike for telephone communication, besides having a personal rule against using it with women he's interested in. And he's definitely interested in Holly Kaufman. Besides intriguing the hell out of him, he knows she has a secret or two, and the meeting at the hotel has something to do with it. He tells himself if he pursues her, it will be mainly because of that secret and not because she holds any special attraction for him.

David has moved up through very traditional ranks. One of five children raised by an overburdened father whose laborer wages were supplemented by welfare, David's first job was a newspaper route. Later he got hired as a copy boy and was taken under the wing of Harry Abbott, a tough-talking, soft-hearted sportswriter. With the help of a newsboy scholarship David worked his way through college. For years his pieces were relegated to the middle pages, but he has recently risen above the mediocre by uncovering scandal in the Department of Housing and Urban Development. A good-looking, thirty-five-year-old bachelor with a charismatic personality, David is accustomed to making feminine conquests with little more than a wink and a grin. Women quickly discover his intention to remain single, but that knowledge does not deter their vying for his companionship, and even seems to make him more sought after.

David's mother taught him at an early age not to put his trust in the female gender. She walked out on her husband and brood of young children and never looked back. David enjoys women, but abides by the advice Harry

Marylin Campbell/PRETTY MAIDS IN A ROW **13**

Abbott gave him: "When you're up to bat, go for a homer, and when you're not, play the field."

*　　　　*　　　　*

Tim Ziegler's murderer is disappointed at first by the lack of information made public, but decides it could be beneficial. The next execution will take a little longer to plan. After that one, they will know Ziegler was not an isolated incident, and they won't be able to keep it quiet. The world must be shown what a rapist's punishment should be. In the meantime, it will be interesting to see if Holly comes up with anything substantial on Jerry Frampton before the plan is in place.

*　　　　*　　　　*

David convinces his boss that he's onto something big and gets himself assigned to cover Holly's tour that begins on the West Coast then meanders eastward. After that, it's a simple matter to reserve the seat next to her on the long flight. At first Holly is very upset at seeing him. His sincere apology makes her feel somewhat better, but when he reveals his very real terror of flying and she is able to help him through it, the tension between them rapidly dissipates. Within a few days however, a new kind of tension has built between them. Only hours of raw, passionate sex, the likes of which Holly had no way of knowing about, satisfy their mutual needs.

More surprising is that they actually grow to like each other as well. Nevertheless, they both assume this is a temporary infatuation that will go away once they're back in Washington. After they return, thinking he is in danger of falling under Holly's spell, David stays away from her for several days. He must continually fight his own desire to pick up the phone and at least talk to her, but that in itself tells him how close to the edge he got with her.

Holly is both angry that he could set her out of his mind so easily and relieved that her one detour into passion's parlor is over. She tells herself it was an interesting experience, but now her life will return to its normal, predictable state. She's proven wrong when she enters her office one morning to find David waiting for her. They both know instantly that the fire between them is still raging.

Marylin Campbell/PRETTY MAIDS IN A ROW   **14**

A few minutes later, Philip comes into Holly's office to speak to her. Although she and David are across the room from each other, he suspects something. David cannot resist letting Philip know that he had covered Holly's tour. After Philip leaves them alone again, Holly berates David for pulling such a macho trick, but he's as angry with himself as she is. When he explains he's never been jealous before and didn't realize how stupid it could make him, she forgives him and agrees to meet him for lunch. Philip confronts her the moment David exits. His own jealousy is barely contained as he warns her about what a womanizer David Wells is. She should know better, he reprimands her. She's already been damaged by his kind. Not ready to admit there is anything serious between her and David, and not wanting to hurt Philip, she tells Philip she is only talking to David because of the article he's doing on Earth Guard. Philip wants to believe her badly enough that he accepts what she tells him.

At lunch, Holly decides to give David the information on Frampton, without revealing how she came upon it. The reminder that she is still keeping a secret irks him, but he takes the bait and is soon headed out of town again. While he is gone, Holly goes out to dinner with Philip, fully intending to tell him about her relationship with David. Before she can begin however, he lets her know how badly she could hurt him if she ever left him and how worried he was about her involvement with Wells. Seeing his very real distress, Holly decides to wait a little longer before telling him. After all, this whole thing with David could go away in a few weeks, and she would have broken Philip's heart for nothing.

What David expects to be a preliminary fact-finding trip to Florida becomes a dangerous interlude with the pornographer, Donley. David ends up being the key figure in a deadly FBI sting operation to arrest Donley and confiscate his illegal films. The feature move of the collection is a snuff film in which a prostitute was beaten to death. What makes it doubly valuable is the moment when the cameral focuses on a familiar face, a man who had been offstage until he realized the actor had gone too far. The face belongs to Jerry Frampton. He was an accessory to murder.

Marylin Campbell/PRETTY MAIDS IN A ROW   **15**

During Holly's weekly phone conversation with her parents, her father tells her he is gratified that Ziegler is dead and Frampton's been arrested, but it will be even better if he gets the electric chair. Holly is taken aback by his extreme bitterness when her own has been diminishing with every one of David's kisses. When he asks how things are going between her and Philip, she promises to talk to them about that at another time. She knows her father would be extremely happy and relieved if she would marry Philip and "settle down."

David comes home after his near brush with death, ready to make a commitment to Holly. Just as they admit their love for one another and they are taking their relationship to a deeper level, the telephone rings. Holly decides to let the answering machine pick it up, never imagining it could be anything she didn't want David to hear. Unfortunately, it's April, calling to congratulate Holly on a job well done and for picking the perfect reporter for the job.

The only way Holly can explain is with the whole truth, but David feels too betrayed to listen rationally. They end up having a fight about the definition of rape and Holly orders him out of her life.

One disappointment is followed by another. Jerry Frampton gets off due to a technicality. But one person sees it as a sign to strike again. On his way home, Frampton is abducted and brutally butchered, just as Ziegler was. This time details of the murder are revealed plus the similarity to the Ziegler case. It is assumed that a psychotic, militant feminist is at large.

Holly is badly shaken by the news. She calls April to be reassured that no one in The Little Sister Society could be behind the murders. She remembers Rachel's sarcastic comments about castration and how April said the woman was dangerous when she was drinking. April tells her she meant Rachel is dangerous to herself and nothing The Society has ever done was illegal. Hours later, Holly receives a call from Rachel. Her words are terribly slurred as she tells Holly she's spoken with April and heard she was worried. Rachel would never have approved bringing Holly into their group if she

Marylin Campbell/PRETTY MAIDS IN A ROW   **16**

had known she was such a coward. She threatens Holly, saying if she tells anyone about The Society or repeats anything she heard, they'll do to her what they've done to men.

David goes to see Holly only to order her to go to the police about the women she met with. They are both angry with each other, but she tells him about the threatening call form Rachel. Since she doesn't really have any proof against her, she doesn't dare go to the authorities. He informs her that, in that case, he's going to do it for her.

Seeing her again makes David realize that he's far from getting over her, but after making her secret public, he's certain she'll hate him enough to guarantee that their relationship will never stand a chance. He goes back to his contact at the FBI and makes them a deal. They get his solid lead on the two murders in exchange for first crack at a breakthrough in the cases. Also his request is granted to have an agent assigned to protect Holly until the whole matter is settled.

Another shock wave hits Holly when April calls to inform her that Rachel committed suicide after being questioned by her superior in connection with the murders. Her farewell note said she "couldn't live with the shame or guilt any longer." She never confessed to killing the two men, but Holly assumes that was the guilt she spoke of in her note. The FBI is not so sure. Agents begin questioning the other women of The Little Sister Society. They are all frightened and suspicious now. It is mentioned more than once that the murders never began until Holly Kaufman joined The Society and the two men who were killed were the ones who had raped her.

That night, the third man named on The Society's list, William O'Day, is murdered by the same method. This time, Holly has an airtight alibi– David spent the night with her, and there was an FBI agent watching her apartment. Philip shows up the next day and is shocked to find David with Holly in an obviously intimate situation. He leaves, but his hurt expression breaks Holly's heart, because she knows she should have been honest with him much sooner. They are speculating about who could be behind the murders when Philip returns and politely asks to come in. Once inside he pulls a gun on them. David tries to talk him out of doing anything foolish, since he was undoubtedly observed coming in by the agent. But Philip doesn't care what happens to him now that he knows Holly will never be completely his. All these years he had to accept the fact that she couldn't give him all of herself. All these years he believed that she belonged to him and only him, and that one day she would be his in every way, but he never understood what held her back. It all became clear the day she told him about the abusive treatment by "two college boys," and how they had gone unpunished for their crimes. As long as they were alive and free men, she didn't feel truly safe. That was when he realized what he had to do to make things right between them. He had to punish them himself. He had seen the list of names in the odd folder she had with her that day. It was easy to get the names of the two boys from her father, then check them against the list. The rest was just piecing facts together. He punished Ziegler and Frampton for her. Then when he saw that the authorities were accusing her, he killed O'Day to draw their attention away. After all, her grudge was with the first two, not the last one. Philip had ascertained that all five men on the list in her folder were fraternity brothers, so it could be assumed that O'Day was a rapist, too. Therefore, his punishment was justified. He did it all for her, to make the past go away so that she could come to him as his woman. He had believed her when she said nothing was going on between her and Wells, but he shouldn't have. She didn't have the experience to deal with the tricks of a snake like Wells. He, Philip, had paid the price, but Wells has stolen his reward.

Philip points the gun at David and fires at the same time David dives for cover behind a sofa. Before he can pull the trigger again, Holly throws herself against Philip, knocking him to the floor. She refuses to be a victim any longer. Before Philip absorbs the fact that Holly has turned against him, the FBI agent bursts in, having heard the shot. Philip shoots at the man, hitting his arm, but the agent already had his gun ready and pulls the trigger. The bullet strikes Philip between the eyes.

Marylin Campbell/PRETTY MAIDS IN A ROW   **18**

David and Holly know they have a long way to go to put their individual pasts behind them, but they both believe it will be easier if they work on a new beginning together.

REWRITING YOUR SYNOPSIS TO SPECIFICATION

Sometimes, instead of a solid yes or no, your synopsis will earn you a "maybe, if ..." If an agent or editor offers suggestions, pay attention. Any guidance you get here will be more relevant and useful than any you could receive from a critique group, book doctor or writers conference. Your willingness to rethink and rewrite a synopsis just might sell your novel.

Robert W. Walker had done one book with an editor and then had struggled for nearly five years to sell another title to "the only company in Publication Land who'd ever purchased a thing from me."

He was nearly crushed when the synopsis for a book to be called *Downfall* got rejected. So he telephoned the editor and asked why he'd been turned down (something we usually advise against doing).

"Two reasons," he remembers her replying. "We're doing long books now, not short. Our novels have to be at least 80,000 words, and that leaves *Downfall* 20,000 words short."

And Reason Number Two?

"We're full up on mysteries right now. What we really need is more horror scripts," she replied.

"All right. Give me a contract, and I'll add 20,000 words and put in a monster."

She agreed, and Walker had a sale. That's flexibility.

When David Kaufelt finished his synopsis for *The Winter Women Murders* and sent it along to his agent, Diane Cleaver, she had "incisive and important comments," he reports.

Using those comments, Kaufelt rewrote the synopsis and sent it to his editor at Pocket Books. She also had "important and incisive comments," he says, so he rewrote the synopsis yet again.

That version went to the publisher, Bill Grose, "who had very incisive and very important comments," Kaufelt says.

After one more rewrite, the synopsis was accepted by agent, editor, and publisher.

Kaufelt says he goes through the same process with each of his Wyn Lewis mysteries. The result of this creative collaboration has been a popular series—first, because Kaufelt works hard at his craft, and second because he's willing, even eager, to accept guidance from publishing professionals.

Marilyn Campbell offers an experience that emphasizes the wisdom of the rewrite even more strongly.

Fourteen editors rejected her novel *Pretty Maids in a Row* in its original state, she reports, "although it was that version that landed me my agent because she believed in its potential."

After Campbell had shopped a synopsis and 250 pages of text for a year, her editor on a previous project, *Come Into My Parlor*, suggested she come up with an entirely new slant to tell her story. Campbell went right to work, created a new synopsis, and made a sale before she even rewrote any of the actual manuscript.

"Twenty-four hours after that deal was made," Campbell adds, "Villard Books, a division of Random House, bought the hardcover rights to *Pretty Maids*, also based on the revised synopsis only."

Your synopsis is an important marketing tool, and a revised synopsis, incorporating suggestions from editors and agents, can make the critical difference between rejection and publication.

THE CHAPTER OUTLINE

Much longer than the typical synopsis, the chapter outline does just what the name implies: it outlines your novel, chapter by chapter.

When do you write a chapter outline? Some authors create the chapter outline before they write the novel, using it for themselves as a guide while they write. Others construct the outline midway through the novel or even after they finish the novel—more often than not to show their agent what their new project covers. But if an agent never asks to see a chapter outline, some authors dispense with it entirely.

Occasionally, an agent might ask a new writer to submit a chapter outline along with sample chapters. But sometimes agents use the terms synopsis and chapter outline interchangeably. If in doubt about what's being requested, ask for clarification. There's no need to write a thirty-page document when a one-page synopsis will do.

What is a chapter outline? In essence, it's an account of what happens in the form of a mini-synopsis for each chapter.

Everything we said previously about the style and tone for the synopsis applies here as well. You'll want crisp, concise prose, in present tense, to move your story forward. Now, however, you can go into more detail than in the short-form synopsis.

The chapter outline, unlike the long-form synopsis, reveals the superstructure of your novel, giving you a chance to highlight transitions, flashbacks, shifts in point of view, and other structural details.

In addition, you have room here to divulge major subplots and indicate how you've planted the seeds of later plot developments in the earlier chapters.

Remember, the longer form doesn't justify wordiness. Just as with the synopsis, you don't want one unnecessary syllable in anything you send out.

SAMPLE CHAPTER OUTLINE

We've outlined the first four chapters of Stephen King's blockbuster novel *Bag of Bones*, which, in addition to being a best-seller, is a beautifully structured novel. We learned a lot from studying the craft behind King's thriller, and we recommend that you outline novels you find compelling. The exercise will help you structure your own novels.

Chapter Outline

BAG OF BONES BY STEPHEN KING

Pitch line: *When Mike Noonan's wife dies unexpectedly, the best-selling author is plagued by nightmares and develops a severe case of writer's block.*

Chapter One

Jo Noonan, 34, wife of best-selling novelist Mike Noonan, suffers a brain aneurysm and dies, leaving her young husband devastated. On top of that, it turns out she was pregnant but hadn't told him. Jo's siblings, and in particular her brother, Frank Arlen, rally to him, seeking to form a "protective shield" around him.

Mike has a horrible nightmare in which he's certain he sees Jo's spirit underneath his bed.

Chapter Two

Afflicted with writer's block for the first time in his career, Mike becomes violently ill if he even attempts to open the "Word Six" program on his computer.

In a flashback we see that his publishing career and his marriage have developed together, beginning with publication of *Being Two*. Mike produces a steady string of romantic suspense novels, which land somewhere between eighth and fifteenth on *The New York Times* best-seller list but never higher.

Flushed with success, Mike and Jo buy a second home, a lodge called "Sara Laughs" on Dark Score Lake. They develop a ritual for the ending of each novel, breaking out the champagne while Mike dictates the last sentence for Jo to type. She then pronounces, "Well, then, that's all right, isn't it?"

When Jo dies, Mike's able to finish his current novel, *All the Way From the Top*, even performing both roles in the closing ritual himself, before writer's block closes him down.

Chapter Three

Chronically unable to ask for help, Mike hides his affliction from everyone. He can get away with this for four years, because he's managed to salt away four manuscripts in a safe deposit box, having gotten ahead of the one-book-a-year pace his publisher prescribes.

He cashes in three of the four novels, which continue to be strong sellers, but he feels empty inside, like a bag of bones.

When the publisher pushes up the deadline on his next novel, he draws out the final manuscript, *Helen's Promise*. Although he actually wrote the book a dozen years before, he finds himself being praised for his new "maturity."

He begins to be plagued by a horrible recurring nightmare, in which he is walking down the driveway toward Sara Laughs at night, aware of a threatening presence lurking behind him. His legs refuse to move as the horror comes closer. In each dream, he discovers a cut on the back of his hand, sometimes on the left, sometimes on the right, always just below the knuckles.

Chapter Four

Frank invites Mike to spend Christmas with him and the rest of Jo's family. To Mike's surprise, he accepts the invitation and enjoys himself, becoming an "honorary Arlen" for four days.

He returns to his computer on New Year's Day, certain that he is at last free of his writer's block, but this time his physical reaction is so strong, he becomes convinced that, barring a miracle, his life as a writer is over.

He drags Word Six into the computer trash.

The nightmare is as vivid and unvarying as ever. In it, he always wishes on a star, and he always hears the loons on the lake. He feels the presence behind him but is unable to run away. And he has that cut on the back of his hand, just below the knuckles.

His agent is sure he can get Mike a three-book, $7.5 million contract based on his "mature" performance in *Helen's Promise*, but Mike hangs up on him, alone with his secret.

That night a storm knocks the power out, and Mike has a culminating nightmare. He is again at Sara Laughs, but this time, he's able to keep walking down the driveway. At the bottom, he sees Jo's empty coffin. A shrieking white spirit–Jo's spirit–flies out of the lodge and races toward him.

He wakes up on the floor, in the corner, in the darkness, banging his head against the wall in terror. When the lights come on, he discovers that he has a cut on the back of his hand, just below the knuckles.

Eager to read chapter five?

And that's just an outline!

Notice how many elements King has set up for development later in the novel, beginning, of course, with Mike Noonan's inevitable return to Sara Laughs to confront his demons.

Notice, too, that he hasn't mentioned the mystery of the secret pregnancy again since the first chapter.

Want to bet that pregnancy will figure in the plot before the story is done?

King has many lessons to teach us here–about how to structure a successful suspense novel, of course, and how powerful a mere bare bones (pun intended, of course) outline can be.

Armed with your query, your synopsis, and your chapter outline, you're ready to approach any agent, giving them exactly what they want. All that remains is an effective cover letter to introduce your submission package. We take up the cover letter in the next chapter.

Chapter Eight: Crafting the Cover Letter

"Wearing down seven no. 2 pencils is a good day's work."

—ERNEST HEMINGWAY

You're ready to send your manuscript and your synopsis to an agent. And you're prepared, in case they ask for a chapter outline. First, though, you need one more item to complete your submission package: a cover letter.

Unlike the query letter, which goes out unaccompanied (except for the SASE) and often unsolicited, the cover letter is part of a solicited package and literally covers that package. Its job is to reintroduce you to the agents or editors who asked to see more and to remind them of who you are and what your project is.

Just as your query letter was designed to get your foot in the door, the cover letter and the package it covers strive to make sure you can keep it there and walk inside.

No less important than your other selling tools, this letter must be professional, typo- and error-free, and well written.

GREETINGS AND SALUTATIONS

With your query letter, you might have floundered a second or two before settling on the correct, formal salutation. But now you've been provided a clue for your cover letter's greeting. If the request for more you received came as a letter or e-mail, your clue comes in the way the agent or editor addressed you. If it's "Dear Blythe" or "Dear Marshall," you may follow in kind and address the editor or agent by first name. But if the letter came to "Dear Ms. Camenson" or "Dear Mr. Cook," you should continue to use the more formal address.

If the request for more came via telephone or at a writers conference, take your cue from the tone of the conversation: chatty and relaxed or formal and professional.

As in any professional correspondence situation, if you don't have the written name in front of you for reference, call the agent's office or the editor's publishing house to verify the spelling.

WHAT DO YOU SAY AFTER YOU SAY HELLO?

Find a balance in your cover letter between gushy chattiness ("Hiya, pal") and formalistic language ("In re: your communiqué of 1 November ..."). Clear, conversational language works best: "As you requested, I've enclosed my manuscript ..."

Whatever you say after the greeting, make it clear, concise, brief, and to the point.

Include these items as appropriate:

1. Reminder of Face-to-Face Meetings. Don't assume the editor or agent remembers that quick conversation you had in the hallway during the afternoon break at the writers conference. It may have been one of the most exciting encounters of your life, but unless you spilled coffee on his tie or wine on her blouse (and we don't recommend this), the meeting probably wasn't quite as memorable for the publishing pro.

Remind them that they "know" you: "I enjoyed chatting with you at the Kansas City Writer's Conference last week." Don't overdo the reminder, however. "I was enchanted by your amusing anecdotes" is laying it on way too thick, and in any case, only reminds them of their part of the conversation—not yours.

With the reminder of where you met, don't forget to mention that he or she requested your package. Solicited submissions, more often than not, gain attention more quickly than unsolicited ones. This point is so important that many agents and editors expect to see the words "Requested Material" stamped across the outside mailer.

We again suggest that you give 'em what they want.

2. Summary of Past Communication. Just as you need to remind the agent or editor of a past meeting, you also must refer to past written correspondence. You can't assume editors or agents remember previous letters, no matter how enthusiastic they seemed at the time. They deal with hundreds of people.

This holds true for e-mail communications as well. Always paste into the bottom of the e-mail the record of the previous communication. Type your new responses at the top of the message so it is the first thing they see when they open the e-mail. Don't make an agent or editor go hunting through paragraphs to find the current transmission.

The most important prior communication is an agent or editor's stated willingness to read your submission. Again, don't fail to jog memories that your manuscript is requested material. As agent Kathleen Anderson reminds us, "The only thing worse than going into a publisher's slush pile is going into an agent's slush pile."

3. Referral Reminder. If you have a referral, you pointed that out in your query letter or at the conference. The cover letter provides a second chance to lay this important card on the table. State the reminder sinply; something like, "As I mentioned to you previously, you just signed my good friend and critique partner, whose writing style is similar to mine."

4. Type and Length of Novel. Repeat the vital statistics you gave in your query letter or at the conference appointment you had with an agent or editor: your novel's genre and word count. Again, state it simply and straightforwardly, as in the sample cover letters on pages 196 and 197: "*Calculated Risk* is a 71,000-word mystery."

5. Pitch Line. That one-sentence summary, crafted with such sweat and care, serves you well here. Include it in your cover letter. "In *Calculated Risk*, Newport Beach, California, actuary Liz Matthews discovers counting dead people for a living can be murder when the bodies start multiplying."

6. Your Credentials. In your query letter you gave a full account of who you are and what qualifies you to be the author of this book. At a quick hallway meeting at a conference you probably didn't have enough time for that. So judge accordingly how much detail to go into in the cover letter. Certainly remind them of the most pertinent information, such as relevant professional experience, related publishing credits, and your time spent in the location in which your book is set.

When you're readty to stop ... Stop! Don't repeat yourself. Don't beg. Don't state the obvious ("Enclosed please find my manuscript, along with a self-addressed ..."). They know what to do.

COVER LETTER FORMAT

Just as with the query, the cover letter is a business letter and should be formatted as such. Use letterhead stationery, a standard typeface, and a quality printer. Make sure your letter is single-spaced with either indented paragraphs (with no line spaces between them) or the more tidy block style (with no idents and extra line spaces between paragraphs). (Review chapter four for more details on letter formatting.)

SAMPLE COVER LETTERS

Take a look at both of the following sample cover letters. The first letter does a good job of reminding the agent where she and the writer met, and that the agent had requested the material. It is a generic sample, with a formal, fill-in-the-blanks type of approach, which any writer could use. Insert your name, book title, and circumstances and there you go. But be sure to use your own writing style and let who you are shine through.

The second one, written by a real author to a real agent, does that as well, but goes on to provide a catchy synopsis of the story, a bio that shows "she's got connections" and a background perfect for writing this book.

GENERIC COVER LETTER

Cover Letter #1

Date
Agent Name
Agency
Agent Street Address
City, State, Zip

Dear ____,

It was a pleasure meeting you at the Midwest Writers' Conference two months ago. I appreciate the time you took to discuss my 90,000-word paranormal romance, *Heaven's in Love*, and its potential for a book series.

As you requested, I've enclosed the first fifty pages and a one-page synopsis, along with a brief summary of my proposed sequels. The manuscript for book number one is complete.

I look forward to your reaction.

Sincerely,

Sally Writer

Street Address • City, State, Zip • Phone number • e-mail

COVER LETTER CALCULATED RISK BY DENISE TILLER

Cover Letter #2

Date
Ms. Paige Wheeler
Creative Media Agency
240 West 35th Street, Suite 500
New York, NY 10001

Dear Ms. Wheeler:

We met last month at the Maple Woods Writers Conference in Kansas City and you invited me to submit my manuscript for your review.

In *Calculated Risk*, Newport Beach, California, actuary Liz Matthews discovers counting dead people for a living can be murder when the bodies start multiplying. Liz builds her life around things she can count on: numbers, her father, and her cop boyfriend, Jack. She tells everyone her runaway mother is dead. When Liz rescues a rape victim and gets a call from her mother pleading for help with Liz's half sister, Liz is thrown into a desperate race to find a murderer/rapist. Armed with a black belt in mathematics, she uses her intuitive and analytic skills, unearthing a trail of blackmail and betrayal to find a man who will risk everything to protect himself and his family. In the battle to save her sister and heal her own childhood scars, Liz must confront her father and her emotionally controlled existence and risks losing Jack when she betrays his trust.

One of my good friends, Kathy Klein, recently signed a contract with you. Until February, I lived in Pound Ridge, New York. Kathy and I formed a critique group and worked on our first drafts together. While our books fit in the same general mystery slot, my voice is closer to Janet Evanovich and Joan Hess. I'd call the high concept for my novel "Dharma (after thirteen years of Catholic School) and Greg meet The Thin Man."

I'm a Fellow of the Society of Actuaries and I worked in Newport Beach for several years. My textbook, *Life, Health, and Annuity Reinsurance*, is on the Society's exam syllabus and is in its second edition. I'm president of the unpublished writers' section of Sisters in Crime. I also belong to Mystery Writers of America and a professionally led critique group.

Calculated Risk is a completed mystery manuscript of 71,000 words and won the CNW/FFWA Florida State Novel Chapter and Best in Fiction awards. Thank you for this opportunity.

Sincerely,

Denise Tiller

Street Address • City, State, Zip • Phone number • e-mail

Sample cover letter #2 is much more detailed. Note that, if modified, deleting mention of where they met, this cover letter could also double as a query letter. But it functions well as a cover letter. Notice the following cover letter elements:

- reference to a previous meeting (first paragraph)
- a good opening pitch line (second paragraph)
- a second sentence that's a good story summary (second paragraph)
- the reason the author has approached this particular agent: the "I've got connections" card (third paragraph)
- A "handle" to help the agent understand how to categorize the writer's book (third paragraph)
- strong background statement showing the writer is clearly qualified to use this plot setting (fourth paragraph)
- crisp, businesslike closing: no nonsense and no begging

Here's the background information to this cover letter, supplied by the writer, Denise Tiller:

"My critique partner in New York called me to let me know she had just signed with agent Paige Wheeler. And what a lucky coincidence. This same agent was speaking at a writers conference I was planning to attend in Kansas City. Paige Wheeler had just finished conducting the 'What Agents Want' workshop but it ran late. She had to be somewhere else. I caught her in the hallway at the conference, introduced myself, and told her about my critique partner and that an editor I pitched to had just requested my manuscript. She said something like, 'That's great. Send it to me.'

"I honestly didn't know what to do with the cover letter. She probably guessed it was a mystery because she knew the editor, but she had no clue what my book was about. I decided it was better to give her too much information instead of not enough. That's why this cover letter could double for a query if need be.

"The agent read my manuscript and agreed to represent me. A month later, I went to the Greater Dallas Writers Association conference and won three major awards for my manuscript on Saturday afternoon. The publisher from Timberwolf Press caught me before I left and said to e-mail the manuscript to him as soon as I got home. Monday morning he e-mailed an offer. The book came out later that year."

THREE ITEMS NOT TO INCLUDE

You want your cover letter to look professional, but there are some surefire signs that reveal you're an amateur. Here are three bits of information you should not include in your cover letter:

1. Notification of Rights Offered. Your contract will cover all ancillary or subsidiary rights, including paperback and foreign-language editions and adaptations to another medium. (Yes, that means movie rights, among other things.) You or your agent will negotiate these matters when the publisher offers that contract. Including a rights notification in your cover letter indicates that you don't know the routine.

2. Social Security Number. Publishers need your Social Security number when they pay you money so they can report that payment to the Internal Revenue Service. Nobody's offering you any money yet.

3. Response Deadline. You probably wouldn't kick off a job interview by leaning back in the chair, plopping your feet on the interviewer's desk, and saying, "I'll need to know your decision by this afternoon. I've got plans to make." You wouldn't if you really wanted to get the job, anyway. Establishing a response deadline for the agent or editor is pretty much the same thing and every bit as well received.

Yes, it's hard to wait. And yes, some editors and agents take what seems to be an interminably long time to respond. In many cases, it seems interminable because it is. But that doesn't give you license to be rude and presumptuous, and to do so would create a horrible impression. (We help you with handling the wait in the next chapter.)

THIRTY-SEVEN WAYS TO WRITE A ROTTEN COVER LETTER

How many of the thirty-seven mistakes in this cover letter do you recognize?

BAD EXAMPLE OF A COVER LETTER

Bad Cover Letter

January 1, 2000
William Bonney, novelist ❶
1234 Backwoods Rd.
Vilanelle, LA 98765-4321

The Super Agent Go-Getter Agency
Jack Superagent
1313 Thirteenth Ave. SE
New York, NY 10011

©William Bonney, 1999, ❷ all rights reserved ❸

Dear Jack, ④

I enjoyed the three hours I spent with you at the Pennsylvania Writers Conference. ⑤ I wondered where you had disappeared to, but I decided to send you my manuscript anyway ⑥ and give you the unprecedented opportunity ⑦ to represent one of the finest fiction novels ⑧ written in the twentieth century.

The Middle of Midnight examines the life and times ⑨ of American Civil War, also known as The War Between the States, or as the Rebs called it, The War of Northern Agression. ⑩

What makes this gripping novel ⑪ completely unique ⑫ is the fact that its author, yours truly, ⑬ tells the tale from the point of view of the young soldier assigned to take care of Lee's famous horse, Traveler. ⑭ You may not get this right away, since everything takes place in the kid's head, but it comes clear after about the third chapter. ⑮ If Tom Clancy had decided to write about the Civil War, the result might have been *The Middle of Midnight*. ⑯

My writing teacher at Vilanelle Tech says the first chapter is the best thing she's seen all semester ⑰ —and she doesn't hand out the compliments at the drop of a hat, ⑱ believe you me. ⑲ Several classmates told me they literally could not put this book down. ⑳ It's that good. ㉑

I haven't had anything published yet, ㉒ but that goes to show how rotten the publishing world is today, ㉓ when a really talented writer ㉔ can't get published, and all those hacks like Tom Clancy ㉕ keep cranking out all that garbage ㉖ and selling millions of copies. ㉗

I've been a Civil War buff ever since I took an American history class last semester, ㉘ and I really know what I'm talking about. ㉙

[The letter is going on too long. ㉚ Let's skip to the closing.]

I'm not going to grovel or anything, ㉛ but I'd really really really appreciate your taking me on. ㉜ It would mean a great deal to me, and also to my mother, who wants to prove to my old man that I really can amount to something after all. ㉝

Let me know in the next couple of weeks. ㉞ If you're not smart enough to snap this surefire novel up, I'll bet somebody else will be! ㉟

See you on the best-seller list, ㊱

Billy the Kid ㊲

1. If Billy has to tell the agent he's a novelist, he's already in trouble. Plus, it sounds pretentious.

2. A copyright statement is one of the three tip-offs that a writer doesn't know what he's doing. It also indicates that he doesn't really trust the agent.

3. Yes, that's basically what "copyright" means., No need to say it once, much less twice.

4. Don't be overly familiar here. You should address the agent as Mr. with his last name.

5. But we'll bet the agent didn't. Billy has abused the agent's willingness to spend time with writers.

6. Big mistake. The agent probably doesn't even want to see a proposal from Billy. He certainly won't want the entire manuscript. Nor will he read it.

7. Oh, if only it were unprecedented. But alas, agents see this sort of thing all too often.

8. As opposed to a nonfiction novel? Fictional history? All novels are, by definition, ficiton.

9. "Life and times" is a vague, empty cliché.

10. We'll bet Mr. Superagent already knew that … and had no desire or need to know the rest of it.

11. Silly brag and boast.

12. Is that like being "totally pregnant"? "Unique" is not subject to qualification.

13. Flippant, overly familiar tone.

14. The agent might put a little more faith in Billy's expertise if he had spelled the name of the horse correctly.

15. If Billy feels the need to explain the first two chapters, he doesn't stand a chance of selling them.

16. But probably not.

17. Now there's a real celebrity endorsement! Praise from family members, friends, and even former English teachers really carries no weight in the publishing field. You're much better off not including such comments.

18. Or the drop of a cliché?

19. See 13.

20. No, they told him figuratively (unless Billy coated his manuscript with glue).

21. Inappropriate boast.

22. A fact that will be painfully obvious to the agent by now. Writers should stress the positive in the credentials statement.

23. The agent is, of course, and integral part of that "rotten" publishing world.

24. See 21.

25. Wasn't Tom Clancy a great paragon of writers a couple of paragraphs ago?

26. Like the sort of "garbage" the agent would very much love to represent.

27. Selling millions of copies is the idea!

28. Any information that speaks to your knowledge of the subject matter you deal with in your novel can be an appropriate credential to list. But here, the credential is too skimpy (one unnamed class) and too recent (only one semester) to be helpful. Delete it.

29. See 21.

30. Something a cover letter must never do! Keep it under a page.

31. Billy is groveling, of course. Not very attractive, is it?

32. You seem to be asking for a personal favor here. This is a business proposal. You must let the novel stand on its own merits.

33. A biographical detail the agent doesn't want or need to know.

34. Agents are busy people and don't appreciate having demands put on their time. They'll get back to you according to *their* schedule, not yours.

35. Don't insult the agent's intelligence, and don't bet the rent money.

36. Now that he shouldn't bet on!

37. Billy is presuming that he and the agent are good enough friends that he doesn't have to be professional, not that it matters at this point. He could have signed this, "Clueless."

Chapter Nine:
Handling the Wait ...
And the Rejection

"Never confuse a single defeat with a final defeat."
—F. SCOTT FITZGERALD

Here's our definitive word about waiting: Don't!

You've bundled up your submission and sent it out into the world. You feel that mixture of fear and anticipation all writers experience at such times. You cringe at stories of manuscripts lost in the mail. Every trip to the mailbox becomes an experiment in approach-avoidance conflict. You want the letter to be there and yet you're terrified that it will be. Ditto for your e-mail account. You've signed on so many times, your keyboard is wearing out.

How can you possibly bear the waiting?

By not waiting for one single minute. Don't stare at the mailbox or your inbox. Don't listen for the footfall of the postal carrier. Don't haunt the post office. And especially don't call the agent or editor to see if he's received your submission. First, it will bug him. Second, you can easily dispel that anxiety by enclosing a self-addressed, stamped postcard along with your material. And third, the United States

Postal Service has a remarkably good record for reliability. The odds of your package getting lost are really quite small.

Instead of wasting your time waiting, get busy on your next novel. We won't advise you not to think about your submission; that isn't possible. You wouldn't be human if you didn't care passionately. But when you catch yourself thinking about it, gently send those thoughts away, and get back to work. Waiting won't bring an answer one minute sooner, and worrying won't change that answer.

"A writer's job is writing," agent George Nicholson reminds us, "and the writer should continue to write, regardless of whether what he or she has written is currently selling."

HOW TO ANALYZE THE SILENCE

Having said that, we know you'll do some waiting and wondering anyway. We all do, especially the first few times out.

"They've had it for four weeks now," you think. "That's a good sign. They must be considering it."

Next, despair chases optimism.

"They've lost the manuscript," your inner voice wails. Or, "It was so bad, they threw it out." Or even, "They haven't stopped laughing long enough to put the rejection slip in the envelope."

What does the silence mean—if it means anything at all? Does a longer wait mean you're in the running?

Maybe.

"How I approach my submissions is in the nature of triage," agent Nancy Yost says. "The ones that are going to die, you get rid of right away. The ones that you are really excited about, you ask for right away. The ones that look as if there might be something there but don't really stand out tend to sit the longest."

"We respond fairly quickly to the ones that clearly aren't right for us," says editor Kent Brown. "It is the same with the one or two we get a year that hit us over the head. The problem lies with all the ones that are in between. We try to figure out what to say to the authors to make it right."

So, yes, the easy rejection will probably come fast. If your project is under consideration, the response might be slower. But we'll stand by our original advice: all such speculation is futile. Get on with your work and let the agents and editors do theirs.

HOW LONG SHOULD YOU WAIT?

Please don't take anything we've said so far to indicate that we think you should sit quietly for weeks, months, or forever while the editor or agent remains silent. If an agent or editor asked to see your material, you deserve an answer, and you shouldn't have to wait forever for that answer. (If, on the other hand, you disregarded our advice and sent out sample chapters or even the whole manuscript unsolicited, you might not hear back at all, especially if you also neglected to enclose an SASE. If that's the case, chalk it up to experience, start over with a new agent or editor, and do it the right way.)

So how long is long enough to wait for a reply?

"I dislike it when an author calls up two weeks or a month after she sent in her project and wants to know if I read it yet," editor Karen Taylor Richman says.

The same applies for e-mails. Editorial director John Scognamiglio says, "Don't follow up with a phone call the day after e-mailing me. I try to respond to all e-mails. If you haven't heard from me in a week, e-mail me again. If another week goes by, I probably didn't receive your e-mail, so follow up with a letter via regular mail."

Reviewing a submission can take two or three months. Many agents send manuscripts through as many as four readers to get additional opinions.

Add extra time if you've approached a publisher directly rather than going through an agent. "I will read unagented manuscripts," editor Laura Anne Gilman says, "but my response time is longer, somewhere between three and five months—longer if something's getting a second reading—simply because of the sheer volume." Agented manuscripts get a faster response, Gilman says, another good argument for seeking an agent in the first place.

"I think it's a mistake for authors to wait three to six months to find out whether or not we ever got their manuscript," Kent Brown says. "The process of writing is slowed down too much by that. And we're doing our best not to get too far behind."

There's no set rule about waiting time. It varies with the publisher and the agency. It also varies depending on the editor or agent's workload. Most professionals state estimated response times with their guidelines or in the marketing guides. We suggest you take the maximum estimated response time and add a week. If the agent promises a response in "two to six weeks," take the six weeks, add the one-week cushion, and plan on waiting seven weeks before following up. Then take out your calendar and mark the target follow-up date so you won't forget. (Believe it or not, if you get busy on new projects, you actually might forget!)

Patience is more than a virtue here. It's a necessity if you want to preserve your sanity and establish good working relationships with editors and agents.

HOW TO FOLLOW UP

Some agents and editors won't respond to your query letter. Not a phone call, not a letter, not even a form rejection slip. It's a cold, hard fact of publishing life. They are very busy people. Many are inundated with queries. They do their best to keep up, but sometimes the rejects go straight into the recycle bin–especially those that come without an SASE.

Don't worry about it. Don't analyze the silence. And don't bother following up on an unanswered query. You'll just be wasting your time and theirs. Move on. If you're marketing smartly, targeting your queries, and sending to several likely editors or agents, you'll be too busy to worry about the no-shows.

A solicited manuscript is a different matter. Once an agent or editor has asked to see all or a portion of your novel, he or she owes you a response to your work. If you don't receive one, you have three follow-up options: a short note via regular mail, a short note via e-mail, or a phone call.

There's something to be said for a written follow up. A note won't intrude on the editor's or agent's workday, and thus it's less likely to seem pushy or annoying. Also, you can work out the wording carefully, just as you did with the original query, making sure you create a good impression.

Here is an example of an effective follow-up note:

> Dear (insert agent or editor's name here),
>
> I sent you (title of your manuscript) at your request three months ago.
> Could you please let me know its status?
>
> (Sign your name here)

That's all you need. Keep it short and to the point, with a reminder that the manuscript was solicited and the date it was sent. Even though the agent or editor already received an SASE from you with your original submission, send another one.

However, a note is also easier to ignore. Although e-mail is fast, a regular mail exchange takes a lot longer than a phone call. And let's face it: The major reason to send a note instead of phoning is because it's so much easier on your nerves.

We suggest that you call, but only if you do it right. First, only call if you're following up on solicited material. Then, when you call, don't beg or badger them. Have a plan. Be businesslike. "I sent my manuscript to you on January 2. I'm wondering if there has been any decision on the project."

You might get a brush-off or an evasive nonanswer: "Ms. Agent is in conference right now. I'm sure you'll be hearing from us soon." (Translation: "Don't call us, and we probably won't call you, but we will get to your manuscript eventually.")

You might get shot right between the eyes: "If you haven't heard from us, it means we're not interested."

But you might get confirmation that they have received your material and an estimate of how much longer you'll need to wait before getting a response.

You might even get a quick telephone interview with the agent. Have your pitch line ready and be prepared to answer questions about your book. You just might be able to do you and your novel a lot of good.

HOW TO HANDLE REJECTION

When the answer does come, it might, of course, be "no." Some of the most successful novelists have suffered numerous rejections.

The novel *Auntie Mame* "circulated for five years," explains its author, Patrick Dennis. "It went through the halls of fifteen publishers, and finally ended up with Vanguard Press, which, as you can see, is rather deep into the alphabet."

Sinclair Lewis published short stories in popular magazines and produced five novels, none of which got any attention. Lewis said, "I lacked sense enough to see that, after five failures, I was foolish to continue writing." His sixth novel, *Main Street*, became a literary sensation.

Betty Smith's classic *A Tree Grows in Brooklyn* was turned down ten times. Grace Metalious's blockbuster *Peyton Place* received fourteen rejections before finding a publisher. Irving Stone's *Lust for Life* endured seventeen rejections, then went on to sell twenty-five million copies. Cult classic *Zen and the Art of Motorcycle Maintenance* by Robert M. Pirsig was rejected 121 times.

"When I hear that Louis L'Amour was rejected some 350 times before his first publication, I can only say, 'Try a thousand rejections and see me in the morning,'" says Robert W. Walker, author of the highly successful Instinct series of thrillers.

"I have been rejected by every major and minor publisher two and three times over on more than thirty novels or various speculative proposals," Walker says. "I liken it to being turned down by every girl in school for the big dance. After running out of candidates, it becomes actually quite funny."

Funny?

"Yes, I have scoffed at rejection," Walker says, "and yes, I have laughed in the face of rejection. It takes that and the patience and tolerance of Job to deal with the god of New York City, the publishing giants."

David Kaufelt once got a letter from a famous agent that said, "Dear Mr. Kaufelt, I can't do a thing with this and neither can you." Kaufelt shrugged off this "advice" and became a successful mystery writer.

One of the biggest parts of writing is getting rejected.

"Be prepared for rejection," Rob Cohen says. "As agents, we get more rejections than any author could ever imagine getting. It just becomes part of the business you're in."

Don't take those rejections personally. It does not reflect on you. It does not mean you're a bad writer. It only means that a particular agent or editor decided he couldn't sell your book right now.

Read that last sentence again, slowly. If you're like most of us, you're going to take some convincing. A rejection doesn't mean that the universe hates you. It doesn't mean you'll never make it as a writer. It doesn't reflect on your worth or talent. You'll drive yourself crazy trying to find deeper meaning in the rejection.

Fiction is extremely subjective. Nobody knows that better than the people who write it, but we forget that when we send our work out for judgment. "No" means "no." No more and no less. It doesn't mean you should quit.

T.S. Eliot said, "You will find that you survive humiliation, and that's an experience of incalculable value."

"Even if I send an encouraging rejection letter, asking to see the next project," editorial director John Scognamiglio says, "sometimes I never hear from the writer again." And that's a big mistake. Agents and editors don't offer encouragement unless they think you've got a chance. You should get another submission out to them as soon as you can. "I know that writing is tough and takes discipline," Scognamiglio says, "but if someone wants to be a writer, he should find the time for his craft. Decide how badly you want it and don't give up."

Nancy Yost cautions new writers not to worry about form rejection letters. Writers "get upset because no one gave them any feedback," she says, but "sometimes the very best thing next to a quick "yes" is a very quick "no." A lot of times, it's just that the agent or editor knows right away it's something they're never going to be interested in. It's got nothing to do with the quality of the work. If I'm not the right person to handle it, it's better they know right away."

If you want advice, editor Anne Savarese says, "It's better to seek it out in a class or writers group. When you send your work to a publisher, it should be something you are satisfied with. You shouldn't be expecting feedback."

WHEN TO REVISE AND RESUBMIT

Sometimes a "no" comes with suggestions. When that happens, allow yourself to feel very encouraged. Any personal attention is a good sign. And when an editor or agent speaks, listen. School is in session.

"Generally, if people do get a long reply, it means the editor is interested in the book and thinks it can be improved," editor Anne Savarese says. "He'll usually say so up front. But whether to revise or not is up to the writer. There are no guarantees. If the editor does give a practical, concrete tip, it's good to pay attention to that."

"If I think someone has promise," John Scognamiglio says, "I'll suggest revisions on the current work, and then I'm happy to take a second look at it."

"If it's something I can help with, I'll write back," agent Rob Cohen says, "but it will have to be very close to being finished. I'm not going to do an editor's job."

"If I really love a book but it needs work before I could sell it, I'll suggest that the author revise the work," agent Richard Henshaw says. "I won't even suggest it if I'm not convinced that I'd take the book on if the author succeeds in making the changes that I've suggested."

Should you listen when pros like Savarese, Scognamiglio, Cohen, and Henshaw talk? You bet. If you do, you'll find yourself a giant step closer to getting your novel published.

You may get conflicting criticism. One agent loves your plot but not your hero. The next really buys the hero but thinks your plot limps. A third likes both plot and hero but finds your writing uninspired. You're obviously not going to be able to please them all and shouldn't even try. But, if you get the same consistent comment, and if that comment makes sense to you, it's time to rewrite.

After that rewrite, can you send your novel back to the same agent who rejected it before? If the agent asked to see a rewrite, absolutely. You'd be a fool not to. Send it back with a cover letter reminding them of your previous correspondence and his suggestions.

What about the agent who gave you encouraging comments but didn't offer to read a rewrite? You can feel fairly safe resubmitting your manuscript. Your cover letter should thank the agent for the suggestions and point out how you followed them.

If an agent offered no hope the first time around, you're probably wasting your time and postage sending back the revised manuscript.

As we mentioned previously, you could certainly get away with submitting the same manuscript with a different title to another editor within the same publishing house you approached before. "One of my perverse pleasures in life," agent Kathleen Anderson says, "is to sell books to houses that have rejected them."

We're not suggesting that you do anything to your novel you don't feel right about. It's your story and your writing career. You have to make the final call. But we are urging you to listen carefully, with an open mind, to suggestions from publishing professionals. They may be leading you out of rejection and into publication.

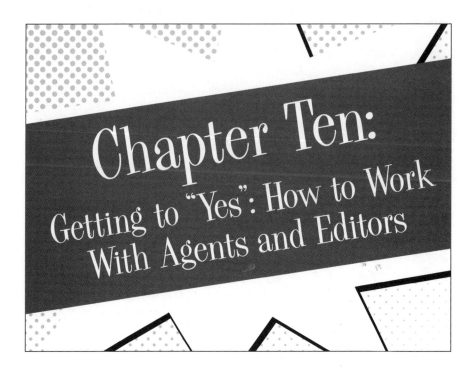

Chapter Ten:
Getting to "Yes": How to Work With Agents and Editors

"The two most beautiful words in the English language are 'check enclosed.'"—DOROTHY PARKER

So far we've looked at three possible reactions to your novel proposal sent to agents:

1. No response
2. "No"
3. "Maybe"

Now let's talk about how to handle the response you've been waiting to hear all along. Let's get to "yes."

Veteran writers have a bit of cynical sounding advice for novelists savoring their first taste of success: Don't quit the day job. Rejoice, yes. An agent's faith in your work is a wonderful affirmation, and that faith carries weight in the marketplace.

Congratulate yourself. You've beaten huge odds and taken a giant step on the journey to publication. But don't think the job's done, and don't assume that gaining representation by an agent ensures publication.

WHAT TO EXPECT WHEN AN AGENT SAYS "YES"

When an agent agrees to represent your novel, she becomes a powerful ally, a savvy marketer with contacts, credibility, and inside information. Agents are highly motivated to get you a book contract because they don't get paid until you do. The larger the advance they get for you, the larger their initial payday, too.

Most agents interested in representing you will offer you an agent/client contract right away. Many will defer creating such a contract until they actually make a sale for you. And a few agents still work on the basis of a handshake or a verbal agreement, waiting to add a clause covering their representation in any publishing contract they get for you.

If you aren't offered an agent/client contract right away, don't panic. There's a good reason for this seemingly lackadaisical way of doing business and it can work in your favor. Suppose you start off as a romance writer and your agent sells a book or two for you. But then you decide to branch out into another genre or into nonfiction. That's fine, as long as your agent also handles those categories. If he or she doesn't, then a strict agent/client contract could bind you to a relationship that suddenly has become stifling.

If the agent handles only one genre, but you've signed a contract making it difficult or even impossible for you to seek representation elsewhere on other kinds of projects, you might be in a pickle, unless, of course, your agent simply agrees to release you from the contract. But having said that, most contracts offer some sort of loose escape clause.

Without a contract, most one-genre agents would be willing to refer you and your project to another agent and continue to handle any other work of yours that falls into their specialty areas.

Not all agents work with contracts. Some will discuss their terms with you verbally or in a letter of intent, then attach an addendum to the publisher's contract for any sales they might make on your behalf. This is a perfectly legitimate and common way of operating.

However, more and more agents use a standard contract, and more and more writers insist on signing it. As with all contracts, when they're designed correctly, they protect both parties.

As with any contract, be sure to examine it carefully before signing it. If you are confused by any of the language, find someone who is familiar with literary law to help you sort through the legalese.

WHAT YOUR AGENT/ WRITER CONTRACT COVERS

Here are some terms to look for in your agent/writer contract:

1. Material to Be Represented. You might have only one book completed now, so you aren't concerned about limiting the work your agent might represent for you. But, if you're a published nonfiction writer with established relationships with publishing houses, for example, you don't want to give a percentage of your advances for those projects to an agent who had nothing to do with those book deals. The contract must specify what work(s) your agent will represent.

2. Commissions. Most agents take 15 percent for domestic sales and 20 percent for overseas and film rights. Your contract must state the agent's commission.

3. Expenses. Some agents charge for photocopying, faxes, long-distance telephone calls, messenger services, and other legitimate expenses. Make sure you know in advance how much and when you'll be charged for these expenses. You may want to seek a cap on the amount you're willing to spend.

4. Accountability. Good agents will report all submissions they make on your behalf and all responses from publishers. They will consult with you before accepting or rejecting any offer. A good contract spells out these obligations.

5. Termination. Your contract should also spell out procedures for ending your agent/client relationship. Most contracts allow for either party to do so with reasonable notice, but they also call for the agent to receive commission for any deals she initiated before the termination of the contract.

WHAT YOU NEED TO DO FOR YOUR AGENT

You should expect honest effort and open communication from your agent; he has the right to expect no less from you.

Tell your agent about any previous submissions you've made and rejections you've received on your novel. Share all correspondence. Your agent must create an effective marketing strategy for you. Withholding relevant information from the agent makes about as much sense as lying to your doctor.

This underscores another excellent reason to seek an agent for your novel before you approach publishers directly. If a publishing house has already rejected you, the agent can't approach them with the same project now. Had the agent made the proposal in the first place, the publisher might have accepted it.

After the "Yes": Important Points From Agent Anne Hawkins

DURING DEAL MAKING:

- If you have any important requests for your contract, make sure your agent knows about them before she begins negotiation.

- Make sure you thoroughly understand all of the terminology in the proposed deal.

- If you receive multiple offers, feel free to ask to speak with the editors before making a commitment.

- Discuss possible editorial changes and think about whether you are comfortable with them.

- Get a feel for your compatibility with the editor and publishing house.

- Never discuss any business details or deal points with the editor. Leave that to your agent.

- In the case of multiple offers, listen to your agent's take on the pros and cons of each. Money isn't the only issue.

- Remember, only you can accept or reject a proposed deal.

DURING CONTRACT NEGOTIATION:

- Let your agent do her job. She's the expert on contracts.

- Carefully review the contract. Be sure you understand the important issues.

- You probably don't need your own attorney except under special circumstances.

DURING THE EDITORIAL PROCESS:

- Respectfully listen to your editor's suggestions for revision.

- Don't react too quickly. Give yourself some time to digest the suggestions.

- If you strongly disagree with the suggestions, first discuss these issues with your agent and get her advice, then present your argument to the editor calmly and constructively.

- Should things come to an impasse, again call on your agent for help.

DURING THE PRODUCTION PROCESS:

- Promptly supply necessary materials such as photos or author bios.

WHAT YOU SHOULDN'T DO FOR YOUR AGENT

Don't try to do the agent's job for him. Allow your agent to represent you. You're entitled to phone him from time to time for progress reports or to discuss new projects, but if you call too often, you'll soon become a pest.

If you run across leads, such as the name of an editor who might be looking for a book like yours, pass them on to your agent. But making unreasonable demands won't fly.

You and your agent now have a working relationship you both hope will be productive and profitable. But your agent is your representative, not your therapist or your best friend. Remember to keep this new relationship in its proper perspective.

HOW AGENTS WORK

Agents often use a variety of approaches when trying to sell your work. Some make phone calls to editors and pitch your work first; some even do it in person.

Agent Anne Hawkins let us see how she operates. First she draws up a marketing plan and discusses it with the author. Then she calls the editor to make arrangements to pitch the book in person.

"I then send out the manuscript with my own letter pitching the book," she says. "The letter is quite important, especially if several editors wind up reading the book at the same house. Almost all books undergo several readings.

"That all-important letter to the editor is almost always less than one page. I very briefly summarize the book, usually in one paragraph. Then, I say what I believe is special about the book or the author's qualifications in the second paragraph. In the last paragraph I give a deadline for responses and also my thanks for the editor's time."

Hawkins takes a lot of time and care with these letters. "If a writer has sent me a good query letter," she says, "I sometimes can use parts of it for my own pitch letter, but not too often."

As with any agent, Hawkins hopes to start a bidding war among publishers. "You do need that first offer from an editor to get started. That's called the 'floor offer.' Then, if other editors express interest in the book, you spend a lot of time on the telephone convincing them to up the ante. Almost any book I put out to editors in a simultaneous submission can be a candidate for an auction."

216

But auctions, although exciting to think about, are rare occurrences and new writers shouldn't expect or demand that of their agents.

In general, a good agent will work hard for you, crafting just the right letter to describe your manuscript, or working magic on the phone or in person, pitching your book.

Although agents might have different styles when approaching editors and pitching your work, the goal of every agent is the same: sell your book to the best possible publishing house for the best possible financial deal.

WHEN YOU HAVE TO FIRE YOUR AGENT

You work so hard to get an agent! Would you really ever want to throw one away?

You should never give up on yourself, but you may have to give up on your agent. Even an excellent agent representing a great novel might fail—and not all agents are excellent. You may find that you aren't being adequately represented. A bad agent may even do you more harm than good. When that happens, you have to support your novel, not your agent. Knowing when to fire your agent is the first step. Knowing how to do so politely and painlessly is the second. We have suggestions for you on both.

Seven Reasons for Cutting Your Agent Loose

1. You Never Hear From Your Agent. Unseasoned writers sometimes have unrealistic expectations about how often their agents should call or write. There are lots of good reasons why an agent might not return your call. But if you and your work aren't important to your agent, you need a new agent.

2. Your Agent Doesn't Know Who You Are. When you finally get her on the phone, you get the distinct feeling she's desperately trying to remember if you're the historical romance set in the Civil War South or the tale of the mob set in 1920s Chicago. If she's lost track of you, you should lose her.

3. You Don't Know What Your Agent Is Doing. You should be in on your agent's marketing plans for your novel. You should know where your manuscript has gone and what responses it has gotten. You have the right to see all correspondence regarding your novel. If your agent won't tell you about these things, tell your agent goodbye.

4. Your Agent Doesn't Seem to Know What He's Doing. Your agent submitted your gothic romance to House of Westerns. Even you knew better than that! He's just hoping to make a lucky sale. Tell him his luck has run out.

5. You've Gotten Lost in the Shuffle. Your agent's office looks like a recycling center. She can never find important letters, contracts, or royalty statements, and editors aren't getting the information they need from her. Your agent needs a workshop on clutter management. You need another agent.

6. You're Anything But "Agent's Pet." Your agent gives other clients better treatment. He's pushing them for the top markets, and you're getting the leftovers. You and your work deserve better.

7. Your Agent's the Only One Who Thinks She's an Agent. Anyone can call herself an agent, print up letterhead stationery and business cards, and start submitting manuscripts to publishers. If those manuscripts end up on the slush pile along with unsolicited material from unpublished writers, the publishers have decided that she isn't really an agent at all. You should decide the same thing. Get a real agent.

You can't afford to settle for an agent who lacks the experience, the drive, the contacts, and the commitment your novel must have to stand a chance of getting published by a major house. Don't settle for less, and don't stay with a bad agent. Move on.

HOW TO FIRE YOUR AGENT

First and foremost, if you have a written contract, follow its conditions for termination to the letter. Most agreements stipulate a specific term for the relationship (a year or eighteen months is fairly typical), but most also allow for termination of the relationship by either party with proper notification. Make sure to insist on this type of clause.

If you don't have a contract, write a brief business letter to your agent, including the following points:

1. Inform the agent you wish to stop being a client because you feel the relationship is no longer beneficial to you.

2. Ask the agent to stop making submissions of your work.

3. Stipulate that the agent will continue to represent you on any submissions that are still active, and if a deal the agent put together should later come about, no matter how much time has passed, the agent will still get his or her commission.

4. Ask for a complete history of anyone who has seen your material.

5. If you choose, you can also ask for the return of any manuscripts the agent has.

6. State that for work already published, the agent will continue to receive royalties on your behalf and then forward statements and your share of the income to you within thirty days of receipt.

Don't feel guilty. Authors change agents. Agents reject authors. It's all part of the business. But burning your bridges isn't. It's not kind, and it's not good business. End on a positive note. This sample termination letter illustrates how to do that.

Sample Letter of Termination

As with any professional letter, you should format a letter of termination using letterhead stationery and addressing your soon-to-be-former agent by name.

SAMPLE LETTER FOR TERMINATING YOUR AGENT

Sample Letter

Dear ____,

In accordance with the terms of our contract, I am notifying you that I would like to terminate our agent/writer relationship. Although I appreciate your efforts on my behalf, it doesn't seem that we are producing any successes together.

Please don't make any more submissions for my novel, *Rocky Road*. I understand that two publishing houses are still considering it, and if a positive response should come back from one of them within sixty days, you, of course, would continue to represent that project.

It is not necessary to return any copies of my manuscript to me.

Above all else, I want to thank you for your encouragement. You helped validate my fiction writing ability, and me. Without that, I doubt I would have had the confidence to start my second novel. I wish you the best, and I do hope we stay in touch.

Sincerely,

Name

STARTING THE HUNT AGAIN

You probably think you should have another agent lined up before you move on. Being on your own again, not represented, is a scary thought. But the hunt for a new agent shouldn't begin until after you've terminated your relationship with your current agent.

If you plan to go it solo, without an agent, you shouldn't begin submitting your work directly to publishers until your agent/writer relationship has been officially terminated.

HOW TO GET AN OFFER

It's not all about rejection. Getting an offer for your novel can and should be a part of the business, too.

Here's how it happens when all goes well:

1. You write a wonderful novel.

2. You study your markets and select a slate of likely agents to represent your novel.

3. You write queries to those agents.

4. An agent likes your query and asks to see more (a synopsis and the first three chapters, let's suppose), which you, of course, send in.

5. An agent loves your synopsis and sample chapters and asks to read the entire manuscript, which you load into a cannon and fire back immediately.

6. An agent offers to represent your novel and you sign a client/agent contract.

7. Your agent creates your marketing strategy and mails out copies of your novel with a cover letter to selected editors. Some agents make telephone contact with likely editors before submitting your manuscript through the mail.

8. An editor decides (often after sending your manuscript around to several other readers for their opinion) that your novel has merit and might make a good addition to their list.

9. Unless she works for a very small house, the editor must now sell your book to her editorial board.

10. The editorial board has to convince the P&L (that's profit and loss) folks that the project makes economic sense.

11. If all that adds up, the book contract comes next.

WHAT TO DO WHEN THE CONTRACT COMES

Of course no writers ever forget their first acceptance. Truman Capote once said: "One fine day when I was seventeen, I had my first, second, and third, all in the same morning's mail. Oh, I'm here to tell you, dizzy with excitement is no mere phrase!"

If your agent gets your book contract for you, he will also negotiate its terms on your behalf. If you sent your proposal directly to a publisher and got a contract for it, you might decide to negotiate the contract yourself.

Wherever that contract comes from, don't just sign it and send it back. Make sure you understand what you're signing.

Oh, you'll want to sign immediately before they change their minds. Don't do it. Believe it or not, a bad contract can be a lot worse than no contract at all.

Read your contract carefully and then get some help. Call your agent or publisher for clarification of any points that aren't clear to you. Seek advice from published writers.

If you don't have an agent, you might want to pay an attorney to evaluate the contract, but only an attorney who knows literary property law. You might even want to seek representation by an agent at this point, even though you've successfully sold your book yourself. An agent can negotiate your contract for you and also guide future submissions. They're usually well worth their 15 percent.

Certain provisions of your contract may look horrible but turn out to be standard and no reason for alarm. The "hold blameless" clause, wherein the publisher disavows all knowledge of you if you get sued for libel, is especially scary.

Other inclusions may look harmless to you but may in fact cost you lots of money and limit your ability to market your work later. Phrases like "all rights" and "work for hire" are especially noxious.

Whether you receive a simple two-page contract or a twenty-two-page single-spaced cloud of legal vapor, be sure you understand it fully before you sign it. Don't be afraid to ask for changes. If an agent got you your contract, she'll continue to earn her commission now by negotiating on your behalf.

Glossary of Terms
for Negotiating the Contract

Agent Anne Hawkins has provided information on contract negotiations, as well as definitions of some terms you should know.

"An author may imagine a deal negotiation as a pitched battle between agent and editor, but most of the time it's a pretty civilized process," Hawkins says. "Of course, the agent is trying to grab the most money and the most favorable terms for her client, and the editor wants to hoard money and rights for her company. But the experienced agent and experienced editor come to the negotiating table with a pretty shrewd notion of what a good, fair deal should be, and both of them know that they'll eventually have to make some concessions. After all, if one party refuses to budge an inch, the other can walk.

"Every author is different, and so is every deal. Something that may be vitally important to one author will be inconsequential to another. As we've said before, a smart agent will talk with her author before the deal negotiation to explain the process and determine whether or not the author has any priority issues. Manuscript delivery dates, requests for special, one-time-only provisions, and payout schedules are examples of the kinds of points that need the author's input in advance so the agent can represent him effectively.

"Certain issues must be agreed upon when the deal is struck, while others can wait until the contract gets negotiated."

Let's look at some terms common to almost all deal negotiations:

Accounting: This only applies to multi-book contracts. If the books are singly accounted, the publisher pays royalties and revenues as soon as the advance for each book is earned out. In joint accounting, the advance for all books in the contract must be earned out before royalties and revenues are paid. Obviously, single accounting is far preferable.

Advance: The amount of money the publisher agrees to pay the author up front as an advance against royalties.

Author's right of consultation: An agent tries to get consultation rights for the author over such things as cover art, cover copy, flap copy, and catalog copy. Very prominent authors can often get right of approval.

Bonuses: Sometimes, publishers will add money to the advance under certain conditions. An example would be a best-seller bonus if the book reaches the top ten on *The New York Times* best-seller list one or more times. Bonuses always require negotiation.

Delivery date(s): The date when the author will deliver the finished manuscript. In a multi-book contract, delivery dates for proposal materials and finished manuscripts for all other books are specified.

Format: The type of initial publication—hardcover, trade paperback, or mass-market paperback.

Length: The length of the completed book(s) in either word count or number of pages.

Option: Publishers usually insist on a first look at the author's next book after the current contract is fulfilled. The agent must negotiate exact terms of this option at the time the deal is struck, since a bad option clause can hog-tie an author later on.

Payout: The schedule for paying the advance, for example, one third on signing, one third on delivery, and one third on publication.

Projected publication date: The agent always wants to discuss this with the editor. She rarely gets it cast in stone as a deal point, but it's good to broach the subject at the outset.

Royalties: The schedule of royalties for hardcover, trade paperback, or mass-market paperback editions. These are fairly standard for major presses but need close examination with smaller publishers. Make sure to ask for a percentage of the retail price, not the net price.

Subsidiary rights: Authors sometimes think that the advance is the big payout in the deal. Wrong. Subsidiary rights can be enormously lucrative, often earning many times the amount of the advance. Some of the rights that aren't major moneymakers can help drive the visibility and sales of the book itself. The trick is to understand their potential and handle them effectively. Examples include first serial, commercial, multimedia, reprint (in some cases), audio, and electronic. These days, almost all major publishers insist on retaining electronic rights. Normally, authors retain all performance rights.

Territories: The publisher purchases the right to publish the book or license another press to do so through these specific territories: North American rights (basically in the United States and Canada); World English rights (English language publication throughout the world); and World rights (publication in all languages throughout the world). If the publisher keeps World English or translation rights, the author's percentage share of the proceeds must be negotiated. With major houses, these percentage shares are fairly standard, but with mid-sized or smaller presses this can be an important negotiating point.

HOW YOU GET PAID

As the author, you get a royalty: a percentage of the price of every book sold. Publishers usually pay royalties on the full retail price of the book, but some pay on the net price, which could be half or less of the cover price.

Many publishers use a three-tiered royalty scale based on the number of books sold. For a first press run of fifteen thousand hardcover copies of your novel, for example, your royalty schedule might look like this:

Copies 1 to 5,000: 10 percent

Copies 5,001 to 10,000: 12.5 percent

Copies 10,001 and up: 15 percent

The contract may also call for lower royalty percentages for books sold through book clubs or other special cases.

The publisher monitors sales and issues a royalty statement and a check for royalties due you, usually quarterly but in some cases twice a year or just annually. These royalty statements may be quite tricky to read (unless your day job involves spreadsheets and double entry bookkeeping). If you have an agent, ask him or her to explain the data for you. The agent may have to call the publisher for clarification. If you don't have an agent, call the publisher directly with your questions.

What about that $17 million Stephen King got just for signing his contract? That's an advance. Although many small publishers will not offer you an advance, all large publishers and most midsize ones will. But your advance will have considerably fewer zeros to the left of the decimal point than Stephen King's.

Whatever the size of the advance, you need to know it by its full name: advance against royalties.

If you fulfill the terms of your contract and submit an acceptable manuscript, the advance is yours to keep, even if your book goes directly to remainder-table oblivion. But you don't get another penny until your book earns back its advance.

Let's do the math, using the royalty schedule above. Suppose you received a $20,000 advance, and your book sells for $20. For the first 5,000 sales, you earn $2 per book, or $10,000. But instead of a check in the mail, you get a royalty statement indicating your balance as "($10,000)," or negative $10,000, meaning you still have to pile up another $10,000 to equal your advance before you begin earning more money.

How many more books do you have to sell before you that happens? (We'll wait while you get a pencil.)

The next 5,000 sales earn you 12.5 percent, or $2.50 per book. So the next 4,000 sales will earn back the second $10,000.

When copy number 9,001 sells (the first 5,000 at 10 percent, the second 4,001 at 12.5 percent), you break into positive royalty territory.

What about the paperback?

Generally, permission to issue your novel as a paperback constitutes a separate right with a separate advance and a separate royalty schedule. The same goes for the right to make a screenplay from your novel, the right to translate it into another language, and the right to print up T-shirts with your protagonist's face on them. Agents earn their keep negotiating these ancillary rights for you.

OH YES, YOU WILL NEED EDITING

Once the contract is signed, you can sit back, put your feet up, and wait for the royalties to pour in, right? Not even close.

Now your manuscript undergoes editing. The bigger the house, the more editors it will go through. You should be an active partner in the editing process. As a writer, you have to have stamina and perseverance, even after your book has been accepted. You need to be willing to work with an editor through the editorial process. If you feel that every word you wrote was etched in stone and you're not willing to budge, then you'll most likely end up having problems in this industry.

"I cannot think of anybody who doesn't need an editor," says Pulitzer Prize-winning novelist Toni Morrison, "even though some people claim they don't." The editor doesn't really want to slice and dice your manuscript to the point where you barely recognize it. It just seems that way sometimes. Most editors subscribe to the same motto that guides doctors: "First, do no harm." They want to preserve your voice in the novel while doing the necessary cleanup and clarification.

Your job will be to work with your editor, listening carefully to criticism and recognizing the value of her experience, perspective and insight. Pick your fights and defend your positions with reason, not emotion.

You may end up experiencing "irreconcilable differences" with your editor. It doesn't happen often, but it does happen. If you can't agree on revisions, the publisher may exercise its option of not publishing your book and may even ask you to return all or part of your advance. Now you really need an agent/advocate to fight for you so that you don't have to return the advance until and unless you sell your book to another publisher. If you don't have an agent, seek help from one of the writers groups listed in the appendix.

But such horrors are the rare exception. A willing author and a capable editor usually form a powerful team. Together, you can produce a better novel than you thought possible.

AFTER YOUR NOVEL IS PUBLISHED: A NEW JOB BEGINS

"The real work begins once you've sold a book and begin promoting it," agent Julie Castiglia says. As a first-time author, you may be disappointed that you aren't immediately booked on *The Oprah Winfrey Show*. Publishers spend most of their promotional dollars on established authors (thus making them even more established).

"But you can do a lot to help promote your book yourself," editor Kent Carroll says, "and the more attention a book gets, the better it sells."

The smaller the publisher, the more of the promotional load you'll have to shoulder. But even if Simon & Schuster or Bantam Books publishes your novel, you should do everything you can to get that book noticed. Along with your publishing contract, your publisher will send you a questionnaire asking, among other things, who should get review copies and where the publisher should seek personal appearances for you.

Give these questions time, effort, and creative thought. Guide the marketing department to local talk shows. Give them names of specific book reviewers and editors of relevant specialty magazines and newsletters. Suggest stores where your novel might be the only book on the counter. Then be willing to put your body where your books are. To promote *The Year of the Buffalo*, Marshall has signed books in bookstores, of course, and has also sat behind a card table on Main Street, downwind from the hot dog stand, while a parade rolled by. Because the book has a minor league baseball motif, Marshall has shown up at ballparks with books in hand and a smile on his face. He also keeps a box of books in the trunk of his car. You just never know when you might run into somebody who wants to buy your book. It's all part of being an active promotional partner.

But bugging your publisher every day isn't!

"I think some writers read in a magazine somewhere that if you pester your publisher enough, they will do all of these things for you," Carroll says. "Not true. If you pester your publisher enough, they may stop doing anything for you."

Don't bug them, but help them every way you can. You both want the same thing, after all–to sell as many copies of your book as possible.

HOW NOT TO BE A ONE-BOOK WONDER

Getting your first novel published will provide a sense of satisfaction like no other in the writer's world. But you don't want your career as a novelist to end there and neither does your agent.

The sad truth is, most first novels don't sell well. Agents and editors know this better than anybody. They're more likely to be interested in you if they believe you have more than one good book in you, possibly even a series based on the protagonist of your first novel.

When your second and third novels gain a growing and devoted audience, a publisher may even reissue that neglected first novel in a fancy new cover to a brand new readership.

The basic question is whether your book sold at least as well as your publisher anticipated (as evidenced by the size of your advance and the initial pressrun). But other factors may testify in favor of giving you a second outing, including strong reviews in important places.

What is your job in all of this? Get into it for the long haul. Work on developing story ideas. Pitch the best of them to your agent or publisher, and follow their advice. Be willing to modify your stories to the marketplace, if necessary.

WHEN YOU AREN'T GETTING TO "YES"

All of this is well and good for when you get that initial "yes". But what should you do if you are only getting rejection after rejection? Should you give up? In a word: "no."

"If you have a book you really believe in, and you really worked hard on it and think it's something good, you shouldn't give up," urges editor Anne Savarese. "There is a market for first novels out there, and though it is competitive, it's not impossible to get published. If writing is something you are committed to, you should keep trying and do everything you can to hone your craft."

"Rejection is something you have to get used to if you are going to be a writer," editor Jennifer Brehl says. "Only if you continue to write will you become a better writer. As a new writer, realize that it takes time to develop your work."

Send your work to other agents. Get started on a new project. Rewrite your book, taking helpful advice, while letting unhelpful criticism go.

"I admire people who continue to send me things, but only if their work has improved and only if they listen to advice and only if they are appreciative and pleasant," agent Julie Castiglia says.

There's only one certainty in the publishing world: Your novel will never sell while it's sitting in your desk drawer.

"This manuscript of yours that has just come back from another editor, don't consider it rejected," best-selling novelist Barbara Kingsolver says. "Consider that you've addressed it 'To the Editor Who Can Appreciate My Work' and it has simply come back stamped 'Not at this address.' Just keep looking for the right address."

Apply the techniques you've studied in this book. Be patient and persistent. Believe in yourself and your work, and you will find the right address.

Appendix: Resources for Writers

"I cannot live without books." —THOMAS JEFFERSON

Writing can be a difficult and lonely job, but you've got lots of great resources available to help you. Here's information on valuable reference books, newsletters and other publications, writers associations, and online resources. Take advantage of them.

MARKET GUIDES

Market guides are one of the main ways new writers find editors and agents. Most are annuals that list editors and agents alphabetically or by subject published or represented. The market books provide submission instructions, as well as contact information, including e-mail and Web site addresses. Although market guides can be outdated almost as soon as they see print—editors and publishers tend to move around a lot—Web sites seem to get updated more frequently, so don't forget those as a viable resource.

Guide to Literary Agents, annual, F+W Publications, Inc.

Guide to Literary Agents lists more than six hundred literary and script agents, as well as contact information for production companies, independent publicists, script contests, and more. All of the agents listed in this annual directory do not charge any fees and abide by the code of ethics and standards set forth by both the Association of Authors' Representatives and the Writers Guild of America. The book also contains essential advice from recognizing a scam to mastering fees to understanding your rights when working with an agent. You'll also find tips on contacting agents, as well as sample book proposals and other advice on preparing your submission.

The International Directory of Little Magazines & Small Presses, annual, Dustbooks

This is the definitive guide to small, regional, and specialty publishers. You'll even find a complete listing of small and alternative magazines, including lots of markets for fiction. This reference is more than useful; it's an education in publishing.

Literary Market Place, annual, RR Bowker, LLC

In this thick annual directory, you'll find, among other things, the most comprehensive listing of publishers and agents, but the summaries provided for each are sketchy. The *Literary Market Place* is very expensive, but you don't need to buy it. You can find it in the reference section of your public library.

Novel & Short Story Writer's Market, annual, F+W Publications, Inc.

This market guide is devoted solely to book publishers and magazines that publish fiction, including over two thousand paying markets and many prestigious, but nonpaying, markets not listed in *Writer's Market*. It also contains articles on writing techniques and getting published.

Jeff Herman's Guide to Book Editors, Publishers, and Literary Agents, Writer, Inc.

This popular guide gives brief histories on editors and book publishers and also indicates which editors handle which genres for each house. It also lists dozens of agents.

230

Writer's Market, annual, F+W Publications, Inc.

Writer's Market lists over eight thousand magazine editors and book publishers. In addition to editors' names, addresses, and phone numbers, *Writer's Market* provides e-mail addresses and Web sites.

Writer's Market Deluxe Edition, updated daily, F+W Publications, Inc.

This guide provides all the benefits of the standard *Writer's Market,* but also includes a one-year subscription to the *Writer's Market* Web site www.writers-mar ket.com, which regularly updates all entries.

Genre Market Books

Writer's Digest Books publishes several other genre-specific guides, including *Children's Writer's & Illustrator's Market* and *Poet's Market.* In addition to offering places to send your work, these books also function as how-to guides.

ADDITIONAL BOOKS TO HELP YOU PUBLISH YOUR NOVEL

Agents, Editors, and You: The Insider's Guide to Getting Your Book Published, edited by Michelle Howry, F+W Publications, Inc.

Dozens of industry pros give you tips on everything from preparing your manuscript to exploring e-publishing.

Writer's Market FAQs by Peter Rubie, F+W Publications, Inc.

Fast answers in a handy Q&A format on working with agents and editors and much more.

How to Write & Sell Your First Novel by Oscar Collier with Frances Spatz Leighton, F+W Publications, Inc.

For over twenty years, this book has given definitive writing and publishing advice for new writers.

AND FOR THOSE WHO ALSO WRITE NONFICTION ...

How to Sell, Then Write Your Nonfiction Book by Blythe Camenson, McGraw-Hill

From idea to contract to execution, this guide helps you sell your ideas and yourself before you invest time and effort in writing your book. You'll find tips for pitching and writing proposals for various nonfiction categories. Blythe provides multiple suggestions from agents, editors, and published authors.

PRINT PERIODICALS

ByLine Magazine

This excellent monthly magazine, established in 1981, offers market updates and instruction through feature articles and columns. (Marshall J. Cook is one of their columnists.) They also publish fiction and run numerous contests. Editor Marcia Preston publishes one of the most positive and helpful writer resources around. Contact: *ByLine Magazine*, P.O. Box 5240, Edmond, OK 73083-5240; phone: (405) 348-5591; Web site: www.bylinemag.com.

Creativity Connection

Marshall J. Cook edits this quarterly, twenty-page newsletter, subtitled "The Writer's Quarterly Encouragement." You'll find how-to articles, profiles, columns, reviews of newsletters, magazines and books, and Marshall's infamous "marginal humor." A sample issue is free on request. Contact: *Creativity Connection*, 610 Langdon Street, #622, Madison, WI 53703; phone: (608) 262-4911; e-mail: mcook@dcs.wisc.edu. (You can contact Marshall for any other reason at these addresses, too.)

Poets & Writers Magazine

Excellent writer interviews and tons of information on writing contests, grants, awards, and conferences make this thick, meaty bimonthly magazine a fine resource. Contact: *Poets & Writers Magazine*, 72 Spring Street, New York, NY 10012; phone: (212) 226-3586; fax: (212) 226-3963; Web site: www.pw.org/mag.

Small Press/Small Magazine Review

Len Fulton's fine monthly two-in-one newsletter supplements *The International Directory of Little Magazines & Small Presses*. You'll find reviews and updates on small and independent publishers. Contact: Dustbooks, P.O. Box 100, Paradise, CA 95967; phone: (916) 877-6110; fax: (916) 877-0222; e-mail: dustbooks@telis.org; Web site: www.dustbooks.com.

Writer's Digest

The biggest and best known of all writers' magazines, *Writer's Digest* offers market updates, how-to articles, and profiles of successful writers. The magazine is part of F+W Publications, Inc., which also publishes Writer's Digest Books and runs its own book club for writers. Contact: *Writer's Digest*, 4700 East Galbraith Road, Cincinnati, OH 45236; phone: (513) 531-2222; Web site: www.writersdigest.com.

ONLINE PERIODICALS

Tidbits

> The e-mail newsletter for Blythe's Fiction Writer's Connection (FWC), *Tidbits* provides tons of useful publishing tips, including markets, contests, and conferences. Contact: via e-mail at bcamenson@aol.com; Web site www.fiction writers.com.

Publishers Lunch

> This great e-newsletter comes highly recommended by agent Nancy Yost. The editors summarize all the publishing news and lists sales of new projects. It's part of Publishers Marketplace, which we've listed under "Web Sites for Writers." Contact: e-mail: publishersmarketplace@yahoo.com; Web site: www.pu blishersmarketplace.com/ lunch/free.

WRITERS ASSOCIATIONS AND ORGANIZATIONS

American Society of Journalists and Authors (ASJA) 1501 Broadway, Suite 302, New York, NY 10036; phone: (212) 997-0947; fax: (212) 937-2315; e-mail: asja@compuserve.com; Web site: www.asja.org.

> The ASJA is leading the fight to protect writers' rights online. They supply updated information via e-mail and on their Web site, conduct an annual conference, and sell audio tapes and other resources.

Fiction Writer's Connection (FWC) E-mail: bcamenson@aol.com; Web site: www.fictionwriters.com.

> Blythe's organization for new and seasoned writers offers help with novel writing, information on finding agents and editors, and other tips on getting published, including a one-on-one mentoring program. Member benefits include the e-mail newsletter *Tidbits*, free critiquing and consultation, mentoring programs, and discounts on e-mail courses—see those under "Online and E-mail Writing Courses" below.

Horror Writers Association (HWA) P.O. Box 50577, Palo Alto, CA 94303; e-mail: hwa@horror.org; Web site: www.horror.org.

> In its own words, HWA "was formed to bring writers and others with a professional interest in horror together, and to foster a greater appreciation of dark fiction in general."

Mystery Writers of America (MWA) 17 East 47th Street., 6th floor, New York, NY 10017; phone: (212) 888-8171; fax: (212) 888-8107; e-mail: mwa@mystery writers.org; Web site: www.mysterywriters.org.

The premier organization for mystery writers, MWA sponsors symposia and conferences, presents the prestigious Edgar Awards, and provides information. Membership is open to authors, editors, screenwriters, and other professionals in the field.

Romance Writers of America (RWA) 16000 Stuebner Airline Road, Suite 140, Spring, TX 77379; phone: (832) 717-5200; fax: (832) 717-5201; e-mail: info@rwa national.org; Web site: www.rwanational.org.

The group for romance writers, RWA is organizational home for nine thousand published and aspiring romance writers. RWA hosts conferences, provides information and resources, and sponsors the RITA and Golden Heart awards.

Science Fiction and Fantasy Writers of America, Inc. (SFWA) P.O. Box 877, Chestertown, MD 21620; Web site: www.sfwa.org.

Another fine organization for genre writers, SFWA provides plenty of information under headings like "Writer Beware," "Writing: The Business," and "Writing: The Craft." They also sponsor the Nebula Awards.

Small Publishers Association of North America (SPAN) P.O. Box 1306, Buena Vista, CO 81211-1306; phone: (719) 395-5761; fax: (719) 395-8374; e-mail: SPAN@spannet.org; Web site: www.spannet.org.

A home for authors, self-publishers, and independent presses, SPAN offers book publishing and marketing know-how and a yearly conference.

WEB SITES FOR WRITERS

The Internet is the fastest and most varied source of information, and it provides great ways to communicate with agents, editors, and other writers. You'll find online courses, writers' associations, booksellers, news of conferences and contests, and research sites.

Use one of the major search engines to begin your online quest. We like Google (www.google.com). Type the subject you're pursuing into the search engine and watch the screen fill with potential sources.

Be aware that Web addresses can change. If you have trouble finding a site, you can always go to a search engine like Google and type in the organization's name.

The Internet Sleuth www.isleuth.com

This is another great place to begin your search. This site offers specialized search engines on a variety of topics, including government and news. If you don't find what you need with one search engine, try another.

234

MediaFinder www.mediafinder.com

This site provides a searchable database of newsletters, magazines, catalogs, and journals, along with search engines for online services and CD-ROMs.

The Association of Authors' Representatives (AAR) www.aar-online.org

The AAR is a not-for-profit organization of independent literary and dramatic agents. It gives you an inside look at the qualifications an agent must possess to become a member, as well as lists member agents. At the site, you can read the AAR's Canon of Ethics, access helpful articles, and find links to related Web sites.

Fiction Writer's Connection (FWC) www.fictionwriters.com

In addition to membership benefits, this site offers free tip sheets on the writing and publishing process, and reports of scams writers need to be aware of.

The WritersNet Directory of Literary Agents www.writers.net/agents.html

This useful site lists only agents who don't charge fees. You can search for specific agents or browse through listings by agency, state, or specialization.

The Market List www.marketlist.com

This fine site caters to writers of science fiction, fantasy, and horror. They offer a well-organized list of markets, information on anthologies and contests, and other resources.

Poets & Writers, Inc. www.pw.org

Poets & Writers provides many useful links with information about conferences and grants, small presses, organizations, and other resources for writers.

Publishers Marketplace www.publishersmarketplace.com

These are the folks who produce the free Publishers Lunch daily online newsletter. You can get the deluxe version of the newsletter plus a lot more information and resources, including job listings, by subscribing for a monthly fee.

WritersDigest.com www.writersdigest.com

This site features market updates, a weekly e-newsletter, "Market of the Day," and much more, all from the same people who bring you *Writer's Digest*, *Writer's Market*, and this book.

Writing Corner www.writingcorner.com

This site offers links for fiction writers, agents, interviews, markets and jobs, research links, and much more. It even includes home pages for readers and young writers and the *JumpStart* newsletter. This is one of the best reader and writer resources in cyberspace.

PUBLISHERS AND AGENTS WEB SITES

Most major publishers and many small presses and many literary agencies now have Web sites where you can order books, view online catalogs, and read writers' guidelines and submission requirements. You can also get an idea of the type of books each publisher publishes.

Online browsing provides an easy way to target potential markets for your projects. Fire up your Web browser and enter keywords such as "book publishers," or specific publishing companies such as Random House or Contemporary Books.

Some sites have obvious Web addresses, such as www.harpercollins.com; others you'll have to search for.

ONLINE AND E-MAIL WRITING COURSES

Taking a class online or through e-mail offers tremendous benefits. Fees are usually very reasonable, you don't have to fight traffic or hunt for a parking space, and you can come to class in your pj's. You can take asynchronous (one-on-one) classes at your convenience and at your own pace. Synchronous classes have a specific meeting time online. Many programs offer e-mail consultations and critiques, and some even have chat rooms, bulletin boards, and archives for students.

Check out these online courses to see if any might be perfect for you.

Fiction Writer's Connection www.fictionwriters.com/courses-query.html; www.fictionwriters.com/courses-synopsis.html

> In these two e-mail courses, "How to Write Winning Query Letters" and "How to Write a Novel Synopsis," students learn the dos and don'ts for query letters and synopses. Students get up to four drafts of a one-page query letter or a one-page synopsis critiqued by this book's co-author, Blythe Camenson. She also offers an online novel writing course and a mentoring program. Visit the Web site or e-mail Blythe directly at bcamenson@aol.com.

The University of Wisconsin-Madison, Division of Continuing Studies www.dcs.wisc.edu/lsa/writing

> This book's other co-author, Marshall Cook, and his colleagues at the University of Wisconsin offer a variety of writing and publishing classes, including Marshall's classes on writing and publishing fiction. He also offers thorough writing critiques. All classes are one-on-one; you go at your own pace; and you may

e-mail the instructor any time with questions and comments. Visit the Web site or e-mail Marshall directly at mcook@dcs.wisc.edu.

Writers.com/Writers on the Net www.writers.com/classes.html

This site offers a large variety of synchronous classes throughout the year. Teachers are published authors as well as experienced instructors. Writers in almost any genre will find a class here.

Writers Online Workshops.com www.writersonlineworkshops.com

Presented by *Writer's Digest*, you'll find professional instruction on fiction, the business of writing, grammar and composition, poetry, life stories, and non-fiction.

SITES FOR WRITING CONFERENCES

The Guide to Writers Conferences & Workshops by ShawGuides, Inc. http://writing.shawguides.com

This site lists more than four hundred conferences, workshops, seminars, and festivals. The site is free and frequently updated.

Romance Writers of America www.rwanational.org/conference/conference.htm

These folks host one of the largest annual writers conferences in the United States. Their site includes information on state RWA chapters, which often organize their own conferences.

The University of Wisconsin-Madison, Division of Continuing Studies www.dcs.wisc.edu/lsa/writing

Go to this site and follow the links to three of the premier writers conferences in the country, the Writers' Institute, Write-by-the–Lake Writer's Workshop and Retreat, and the School of the Arts at Rhinelander. Marshall teaches in all of these programs.

Writers Write www.writerswrite.com/conf.htm

You'll find a list of lots of conferences along with enough information to decide if the conference is right for you. The site includes addresses, phone numbers, and e-mail addresses for requesting additional information.

The Zuzu's Petals Literary Resource www.zuzu.com/worklink.htm

This great site offers an alphabetical listing of conferences and workshops with links to each site.

RESEARCH SITES

Encyberpedia www.encyberpedia.com/ency.htm

Encyberpedia lists such subjects as medicine, sports, biographies, fact books, legal, and government.

HighBeam Library Research www.highbeam.com/library/index.asp?

This site replaces the old eLibrary. The service offers basic (free) and full membership levels.

iTools www.itools.com

You can search for just about anything on this site, including language translations, Bible references, maps, facts, and much more.

John McDonnell's Really Useful Sites www.reallyusefulsites.org

This site contains different categories to help narrow your search, then offers the best links for that particular subject. There's also an "expert" category that lists Web sites where you can find experts to answer your questions.

NewsLink http://newslink.org/news.html

This site helps you find current events information on specific towns and cities. Thousands of dailies, weeklies, and specialty papers are online and available to you through American Journal Review's NewsLink.

Experts.com www.experts.com

These directories give you access to thousands of listings of experts, spokespersons, and consultants in all fields.

Writers Free Reference Desk www.writers-free-reference.com

On this site, you'll find hundreds of useful links, all free, that are of interest to writers, including copyright information, quotations, links to newspapers, maps, ancient literature, and Internet libraries.

About the Authors

BLYTHE CAMENSON

Blythe Camenson is a full-time writer with four dozen books and numerous articles to her credit. As director of Fiction Writer's Connection (FWC), a membership organization for new writers, she edits and writes for *Tidbits*, the FWC newsletter, provides a free critiquing service to members, free consultation, and also teaches e-mail courses on query letter and synopsis writing. In addition, she offers a mentoring program to help students get their novels started on the right track. Through these programs and FWC she has helped to answer the questions of hundreds of new writers.

Some of Blythe Camenson's titles include *How to Sell, Then Write Your Nonfiction Book; Careers in Writing; Career Portraits: Writing; Great Jobs for Communications Majors; Careers for History Buffs*; and many others, all published by Contemporary Books and McGraw-Hill.

She currently lives in Albuquerque, New Mexico, where she designs the renovations for old houses and co-exists peacefully with her two cats, Cory and Shelby. Visit her website at www.fictionwriters.com or e-mail her at Bcamenson@aol.com.

MARSHALL J. COOK

Marshall J. Cook teaches workshops, seminars, and online courses on writing and editing, creativity, stress management, and media relations for the University of Wisconsin-Madison, Division of Continuing Studies, where he is a professor in the arts. He's a frequent speaker at conferences nationwide and edits *Creativity Connection*, a national newsletter for writers and independent publishers.

His novel, *The Year of the Buffalo*, was published by Savage Press in 1997. The sequel, *Off Season*, followed from Savage Press in 2002. Bleak House Books published his first mystery, *Murder Over Easy: a Monona Quinn Mystery*, in 2003. The second in the series, *Murder at Midnight*, came out in 2005.

He is also the author of nineteen nonfiction books, including: *Freeing Your Creativity: a writer's guide, How to Write with the Skill of a Master and the Genius of a Child*, and *Leads and Conclusions*, all published by Writer's Digest Books. His book *Slow Down and Get More Done* (Betterway Books) landed him an appearance on Oprah as a guest expert on the subject.

He's also a regular columnist for *ByLine Magazine*. Marshall's currently at work on a novel set in Madison, Wisconsin in 1944. He lives in Madison, more or less in the present, with wife Ellen, a Schnauzer named Sprecher, and two Persian cats named Ralph and Norton.

Index

A

Accounting, definition, 222

Adult education programs, 9–10

Advance, definition, 222

Agents
appointment
arrangement, 107
approach, 44
approval
expectation, 213
protocol, 215
characteristics, 45–46
contract, coverage, 214
discovery, 41
enemy status, 49–50
etiquette, 131–136
firing/termination
letter, sample, 219
process, 218–220
reasons, 217–218
follow-up response,
process, 207–208
helping, 214
ideal, 46–47
impact. *See* Writers

conferences
inexperience, 218
interaction
process, 212
protocol, 216
interviewing, 109
noncommunication, 217
nonrecognition, 217
nonresponsibilities, 57–58
query letter requirements,
66–67
recognition, 56–59
referral scams, 53–54
responsibilities, 54–56
search, 220
location, 58
organization, 41–42
scams, 53
selection
checklist, 47–48
reasons, 81
silence, analysis, 205
truth, 48–49
web sites, resources, 236
working process, 216–217

Authors, consultation right
(definition), 222

B

Background details,
problems, 20

Black Heron Press, 31

Bleak House Press, 31

Bonuses, definition, 222

Books
packagers, path, 35
prices, 28
producers, path, 34
selling, top categories,
27–28

C

Chapters
outlines, 188–189
sample, 189–191
submission, 119
sample, submission,
116–117

Characters
problems, 15–16
sketches. *See* Synopsis

Conservatory of
American Letters, 38

241

Content, problems, 18

Contract
arrival, procedure, 221
negotiation, 215
terms, glossary,
222-223

Cooperative publishers,
path, 34

Copyright information,
121-122

Core conflict. *See* Synopsis

Cover letter
contents, 193-195
creation, 192
credentials, 195
face-to-face meetings,
reminder, 193-194
format, 195
greetings/salutations, 193
items, noninclusion,
198-199
novel type/length,
description, 194
past communication, sum-
mary, 194
pitch line, 195
referral reminder, 194
response deadline, 199
rights (offering),
notification, 199
sample, 195-198
Social Security Number,
inclusion, 199
submission, 118-119
writing style, sample/
examination, 199-202

Cross+Roads Press, 31

D

Deal making, protocol, 215

Delivery date(s), 223

Dialogue
problems, 16-17
usage. *See* Synopsis

Direct referral
approach, 44

Dustbooks, 32

E

Editing process, 225-226

Editorial process,
protocol, 215

Editors
appointment
arrangement, 107
approach, 44
discovery, 41
etiquette, 131-136
follow-up response,
process, 207-208
ideal, 46-47
interaction process, 212
query letter requirements,
66-67
search
location, 58
organization, 41-42
selection, reasons, 81
silence, analysis, 205

Electronic publishers,
path, 38-40

Electronic publishing
(E-publishing),
advantages, 40

E-mail
query checklist, 105
subject lines, 103-104
usage, 102-103
writing courses,
resources, 236-237

F

First novels, problems, 13

Format, definition, 223

Francis, Dick
(synopsis writing), 139-140

G

Grammar, problems, 21

H

**Hard-sell book-doctoring
scams,** 52

Hidden costs scams, 51

Hook. *See* Query letter;

Synopsis
problems, 14

How-to books, learning
(avenues), 8-9

I

In-person pitch, 106

Internet, usage, 64-65

L

Length, definition, 223

Longer synopsis, 163-187
sample, 164-187

M

Magazines/newsletters,
learning (avenues), 9

Manuscript
cleanliness, 133
formatting, 120-121
problems, 134
packaging, problems, 134
submission, 117
rules, 120

Market
guides, 63
writing, tailoring, 6-7

Market guides, 229-231

N

Narrative tension, problems,
14-15

**National/international
publishers,** path, 29

**Nonfiction writing
resources,** 231

Nouns, selection.
See Synopsis

Novels
crafting, 22-23
offer, procedure, 220-221
one-book wonder, 227
post-publication process,
226
problems. *See* First novels
publication, resources,
231

synopsis writing, contrast,
140–141
type/length, description.
See Cover letter

O

Olmsted, Robert, 38
One-page synopsis
building, 155–163
sample, 156–163
Online periodicals,
resources, 233
Online writing courses,
resources, 236–237
Opening hook. *See* Synopsis
Option, definition, 223
Organizational/sponsored
presses, path, 33
Over the transom
approach, 43–44
Overwriting, problems,
20–21

P

Pacing, problems, 14
Payment procedure,
224–225
Payout, definition, 223
Periodicals, resources.
See Print periodicals
Phone calls
gimmicks, 133
inappropriateness,
131–132
manuscript arrival
question, 133
rejection explanation, 132
Pitch
anatomy, 110–112
giver, identification,
107–108
line. *See* Cover letter
uses, 112
preparation, 109
Plot highlights. *See* Synopsis
Plotting, problems, 13

Presentation, importance,
119–120
Print periodicals, resources,
232
Product, polishing, 12
Production process, protocol, 215
Projected publication date,
definition, 223
Publication
paths, 29–41
process. *See* Novels
Publishers
approach paths, 43–44
characteristics, 45–46
web sites, resources, 236
Publishers, ownership, 28,
35–36
Publishing
contract scams, 52
options, 26
Pushcart Press, 31

Q

Query checklist. *See* E-mail
Query fax/e-mail
submissions, 134–135
Query letter, 66
approaches, 82–87
decision, 99–100
checklist, 98–99
closings, 71–72, 80–81
connections opening
approach, 86–87
credentials, inclusion,
75–76
credits, 76–78
definition, 67–68
elements, 72–82
endorsements, inclusion, 82
formal start approach,
83–84
formatting, 70–72
greeting, 70–71
handle, 73–74
hook, 73
hook start approach,
84–86
full sample, 87–89

mini-synopsis, 75
offerings, 78–80
paragraph style, 71
plotting, 99
quality, building, 89–98
recipient, identification,
68–69
requirements, 101–102.
See also Agents; Editors
samples, 82–87
sending, timing, 69–70
simultaneous/multiple
submissions, 100–101
summary statement
approach, 84

R

Reading fee scams, 51
Referrals
approach. *See* Direct
referral approach
necessity, 82
reminder. *See* Cover letter
scams. *See* Agents
Regional presses,
path, 29–32
Rejection
handling, 204
process, 208–210
repetition, 227–228
Research sites, 238
Resubmission, timing,
210–211
Revision, 24
timing, 210–211
Royalties, definition, 223

S

Salable product
creation, 4
steps, 4–12
Savage Press, 31–32
Scams. *See* Agents; Hard-sell
book-doctoring scams; Hidden costs scams; Publishing;
Soft-sell book-doctoring
scams; Reading fee scams
identification, 50–54

Self-addressed stamp envelope (SASE)
submission, 118
usage, 72

Self-publishers, path, 36–38

Self-writing, 7–8

Seminars, approach, 62–63

Silence, analysis. *See* Agents;
Editors

Simultaneous submissions,
136–137

Small presses
list, 31–32
paths, 29–32
publisher, portrait, 38

Snail mail, usage, 102–103

Soft-sell book-doctoring scams, 52

**Spirit That Moves Us Press,
The,** 32

Steerforth Press, 32

Stories, beat (identification),
109–110

Storytelling, problems, 15

Submissions. *See* Query
letter; Simultaneous
submissions
checklist, 137
fax/e-mail usage, 134–135
identification, 115
package, 116–119
protocol, 135–136
timing. *See* Resubmission

Subsidiary rights,
definition, 223

Subsidy publishers, path,
33–34

Success, becoming
(struggle), 42–43

Synopsis
building. *See* One-page
synopsis
character sketches,
145–146
checklist, 155
conclusion, 148–149
core conflict, 147–148

dialogue, usage, 150
elements, 142–149
format, 142
length. *See* Longer synopsis
decision, 151
nouns/verbs, selection,
150
omissions, 141
opening hook, 143–145
plot highlights, 146–147
quality, 138
rewriting, 187–188
samples, 151–155
speak, avoidance, 150
structuring, process,
149–150
submission, 119
tense/person, selection,
150

Synopsis writing.
See Francis
contrast. *See* Novels
difficulty, explanation,
140–141
style, selection, 150
timing, 141–142

T

Territories, definition, 223

**Trade journals/
newsletters,** 63–64

Treatment, sample, 123–130

U

University presses, path,
32–33

**University writing
programs,** taking, 9

V

Verbs, selection. *See* Synopsis

Viewpoint, problems, 19

Voice, problems, 19

W

Waiting
handling, 204
timing, 206–207

Word count,
problems, 21–22

Writer
associations/
organizations,
resources, 233–234
books, 64
contract, coverage, 214
resources, 229
Web sites, resources,
234–236

Writer conferences,
10, 58–62
agent impact, 113
attending, 62–63
model attendee, 61
networking, 61
price, 60
services/needs, 59–60

Writing
conferences, sites
(resources), 237
courses, resources.
See E-mail; Online
writing courses
critiques, 11–12
learning, 8–12
preparation, 23–24
problems, 17–18
resources. *See* Nonfiction
writing resources
study, 4–6
style, usage. *See* Synopsis
writing
support groups, 10–11